Independent Operators Derbyshire

Neville Mercer

© 2016 Neville Mercer and Venture Publications Ltd
ISBN 9781905304783

Contents

Front Cover
In the summer of 1961 word got around that the very last AEC Q in PSV use in the UK, Silver Service's 1934 vintage ARA 475, was about to retire. A veritable swarm of enthusiasts then descended onto Darley Dale to sample the beast while they still could. This shot of the vehicle was taken during a private-hire organised by Manchester area bus fanciers. *(John Holmes)*

Inside Front Cover
In Part Two of this book there is a black and white shot of Naylor's VO 8566, a pre-war AEC Regent with a post-war Burlingham body, taken by Roy Marshall. To commemorate the 35th anniversary of Naylor's selling out to Trent, local transport artist Keith Hudson (sadly no longer with us) produced this 'colourised' version of Roy's photograph in 1991 as a limited edition print. *(Dennis Johnson Collection)*

Back Cover
A line-up of eight of Blue Bus Services' Daimler double-deckers at Willington garage. From left to right they are Willowbrook-bodied Daimler CD650s PRA 388, SRB 425, SRB 424, and PRA 387, and Northern Counties-bodied Fleetlines ARA 762B, 324 YNU, 325 YNU, and JRB 481D. A ninth Blue Bus double-decker (one of their two Daimler CVG6s) is parked nose-on at the far left. *(DW Marshall via David Stanier)*

Title Page
Here is the rarest vehicle mentioned in this book, the one and only Leyland Panda, WG 9519. Built as a prototype for a model abandoned due to the outbreak of the Second World War, it had an underfloor engine and was fitted with an Alexander B45C body. It entered service with W Alexander in September 1941 and was sold to Truman of Shirebrook (see Part Two) in June 1946. *(Robert F Mack)*

AUTHOR'S NOTES

The main intention of this series of books on independent bus operators is to provide concise histories of companies still active in stage carriage work in the post-war period up until deregulation. As regular readers will already know, the amount of space available dictates the precise 'survival date' which will ensure an operator's inclusion in the main sections of the book. For this volume covering Derbyshire the period under study begins in January 1950 and ends with the first deregulation Act in 1980. It should be stressed, however, that operators thus chosen for inclusion are covered from their foundation to their ultimate demise, although post-deregulation developments are presented in brief. A few fairly insignificant minibus operations, most of them aimed at the seasonal tourist market, have been deliberately ignored and, as usual, the focus is on stage carriage services available to the general public rather than schools and works contracts which required a stage carriage licence.

A roll call of the dozens of independent operators which ceased to trade before the Second World War, largely as a result of their acquisition by monopolistic 'area agreement companies', can be found in the Introduction. Some of them were tiny, but others were major players. When Midland General (a Balfour Beatty subsidiary) acquired locally owned Williamson's Garages of Heanor in 1928 the deal more than doubled the size of the Midland General fleet, and gave the company a fighting chance against intrusion from neighbouring operators controlled by a much larger conglomerate – British Electric Traction.

I use my own definition of an independent bus operator, as the commonly accepted definitions are seriously flawed. Many, for example, will argue that LUT and West Riding were independents, but this categorisation does not withstand closer scrutiny. Both were controlled by alliances of London based investors, and in LUT's case the two most powerful shareholders were British Electric Traction and Balfour Beatty. They were also both founded as statutory tramway operators, giving their subsequent histories an entirely different flavour to that of a locally owned independent. Their disqualification leaves Barton as the country's largest independent operator, and Barton's name is mentioned many times in this volume as its territory included a small but densely populated part of Derbyshire. It was, however, based in Nottinghamshire and will be covered in a later volume in this series.

For ease of reference the county has been divided into three geographical regions. Part One (North-Western Derbyshire) covers the area once claimed by the North Western Road Car Co, while Part Two (North-Eastern Derbyshire) covers the erstwhile territories of East Midland and Midland General/Notts & Derby. Part Three (Southern Derbyshire) deals with independents in the areas where Trent and Midland Red were the predominant 'Combine' companies.

Descriptions of individual vehicles in this book incorporate the widely accepted bodywork codes allocated by the PSV Circle. The initial letter indicates the type of vehicle, with B meaning a single-deck bus, C a single-deck coach, DP a dual-purpose single-decker (usable as either a bus or a coach), H a highbridge double-decker (with a central gangway on the top deck), and L a lowbridge double-decker (with bench seating and a sunken offside gangway upstairs). The figures that follow represent the seating capacity and for double-deckers this is divided between the upper deck (before the slash) and the lower deck (after the slash). The final letter indicates the passenger door layout with C meaning central, D indicating two doors (usually front and centre), F meaning front or forward (the latter defined as being as close to the front as the chassis design will allow), and R signifying the rear. An additional letter D after the doorway code R reveals that platform doors are fitted – an optional extra on rear-entrance models.

The first book in this series, way back in 2009, covered the independents of Staffordshire and since then my Venture Publications colleague Eric Wain has produced excellent full-length histories of two of the companies I covered, Berresfords and Stevensons. I live in hope that this present volume may have similar worthy successors, for although there are already definitive histories of Blue Bus, Hulley and Victoria Motorways, there are no equivalent volumes available for Silver Service or Booth & Fisher. Are there any volunteers?

Neville Mercer
October 2016

ACKNOWLEDGEMENTS

Much of the research for this book was compiled in the Archive of the Greater Manchester Transport Society at the Museum of Transport in Boyle Street, Manchester. As usual my thanks go to GMTS archivist George Turnbull, who was unerringly helpful and patient during my many visits. Moral support has been donated by many GMTS members, but special mention must be made of John Holmes for allowing me access to his vast collection of Hulley and Silver Service photographs, and of John Dixon who contributed much information about the independents in the North Western Road Car Company's territory.

My spiritual home on line is the Old Bus Photo's website, and many of the friends I have met there have contributed both information and photographs. They include Chris Barker, Les Dickinson, and John Stringer. Photographic contributors are credited individually in the photo' captions, but special mention must be made of Tony Moyes for contributing some wonderfully evocative images of Bedford OBs and their contemporaries in their natural rural environment.

Assistance in covering the fleets of north eastern Derbyshire came from John Hellewell, Dennis Johnson, Chris Rischer, and Michael Elliott, while in southern Derbyshire I was able to draw on the collective wisdom of David Stanier, Tim Jeffcoat, and Eric Wain. David Stanier is the undisputed master of all things to do with Blue Bus, and he was also kind enough to supply an extensive selection of photographs, most of which are included in this book.

For any bus industry author, historian, or researcher, the records of the PSV Circle are an essential resource beyond compare and their publications a joy to behold (and very reasonably priced). I would not hesitate to recommend their entire publishing list, but those with particular relevance to the subject of Derbyshire independents are those which cover East Midland, Trent, Midland General, Chesterfield Corporation (which includes Hulley and Silver Service), and South Yorkshire PTE (covering Booth & Fisher). Access to older (unpublished) PSV Circle records was provided by John Kaye who also assisted with various obscure queries about vehicles long since vanished. His help is always invaluable, as is that of John Bennett who read the manuscript and made many helpful suggestions.

Despite the unwarranted disdain of some amateur historians, village websites are an excellent place to find information about small locally owned bus companies and also to make contact with members of their founding families. Occasional failures of memory are easily offset by the wealth of accurate recollections to be found, providing a human background for a story which can otherwise become rather dry. On this occasion I am particularly grateful to the websites in Parwich (Parwich.org) and Tideswell (Villagevoice. org) who put me in touch with surviving family members from Steeples and Bull respectively.

Other on line resources which were employed during the writing of the book included Peter Gould's Transport History pages (which provide a slightly different fleet history for Booth & Fisher), and the irreplaceable 'Bus Lists on the Web', which just keeps going from strength to strength both in presentation and content. There is of course a natural affinity between bus enthusiasts and the information age – the PSV Circle was already using Wikipedia's methods for crowd-sourcing its data back in the days when computers were as rare as Sentinel buses and still contained valves and gremlins. It was all, admittedly, hand-written and often obscured by ink smudges, but the principle was the same.

The printed word is still the most important medium for most bus enthusiasts, and among the various periodicals it is hard to find one more worth its cover price than 'Bus & Coach Preservation'. I speak not only as an avid reader, but as a regular advertiser in their free classifieds section, and would like to thank everyone at B&CP for enabling me to make contact with dozens of knowledgeable contributors. Several of the rarest photographs in this book have come from such sources.

My technical ineptitude is legendary (a computer is basically just a word-processor in my hands) so my thanks go to my talented daughter Helena for enhancing some of the more challenging images received, and to my good friends Philip Cryer and Samantha Hardy for acting as my unpaid IT department. Thanks are also due to Mark Senior. Ian Stubbs. and all at Venture Publications for their work on this book, and to David and Mary Shaw for proof-reading the finished manuscript. As always any mistakes which remain are my own.

INTRODUCTION

Derbyshire is an extremely attractive county. I first discovered its charms from afar, gazing eastwards across the flatlands of the Cheshire Plain from my childhood home near Northwich. Beyond the menacing death-ray dish of the Jodrell Bank radio telescope, only eight miles away, the horizon was dominated by the magnificent back-drop of the Derbyshire Peak District. It was the English equivalent of living in Kansas and staring wistfully at the Rocky Mountains. My grandfather would point out individual peaks from Kinder Scout to Axe Edge (the field of vision between wooded areas) and regale me with tales of trips he'd taken in his younger years. These reminiscences soon led to my grandmother organising a coach trip to Buxton, followed a year later by another to Bakewell and Matlock.

By then my unnatural affection for buses had already become manifest. Buxton Market Place gave me my first experience of East Midland, PMT, Sheffield JOC, and Trent, as well as a completely different set of North Western vehicles to those found in Northwich. Bakewell had Sheffield buses from both the Corporation and the JOC and introduced me to the vehicles of two quite splendid independents, Henry Hulley and Silver Service. More Silver Service machines were found in Matlock along with more East Midland and Trent and my very first encounter with Midland General. I was thoroughly hooked, and when I began to travel on my own a few years later Derbyshire became a high priority alongside Staffordshire and the West Riding.

The Peak District is, of course, only part of the story. As my income from my part-time job (delivering pools coupons) increased, I began to sample the more distant parts of the county. The X1 from Manchester would take me to Ashbourne where a quick glance at the vehicles of no less than five local independents would be followed by a trip through the far east of Staffordshire to Burton-upon-Trent, courtesy of Stevenson of Spath. Burton offered some Corporation antiques, some 'home-built' Midland Red vehicles, and two further Derbyshire independents, Victoria Motorways of Woodville and Blue Bus of Willington. A Blue Bus Loline or Fleetline would then carry me to Derby in style, in time

to record numerous Barton vehicles and a pair of representatives from yet another Derbyshire independent, Felix of Stanley (they nearly always came in pairs) before clambering back on to an X1 for the trip back to Manchester. A good day out was always guaranteed by adopting this 'multiple venue' approach.

While the X1 was my gateway to southern Derbyshire, the X2 provided the basis for another grand tour. This involved leaving Manchester for Bakewell at 0815 and then transferring to Hulleys for a ride to their base in Baslow and then on to Chesterfield. After checking out the corporation there a 35 minute ride on East Midland's Rotherham service would take me into the territory of that most northerly of Derbyshire independents, Booth & Fisher, and allow a quick visit to their garage at Halfway. The return element of my ticket would then take me back to Chesterfield in time for a connection by East Midland to Matlock and a hurried visit to Silver Service's base at Darley Dale before the X2 came along bound for Manchester. It was a rather frantic but intensely enjoyable itinerary, and one which I still partially relive every year when High Peak's 'TP' service (the modern equivalent of the X2 as far as Ambergate) carries me to the Peak Park Gathering at Rowsley.

Because of my age I'd already missed some of the best. The fleet of Truman of Shirebrook had been sold to East Midland when I was a toddler, and the more I found out about this operator (Derbyshire's answer to Berresford of Cheddleton) the more I felt cheated by having been born just a few years too late to experience it in person. By the time I started travelling the few Truman vehicles which still survived had been scattered far and wide – I even missed the unique Leyland Panda which lingered on for some time with Aston of Marton before its tragic destruction.

Truman had operated into Mansfield where its vehicles found themselves in proximity to those of several prominent Nottinghamshire independents along with representatives from the fleet of another fine Derbyshire operator, Naylor of South Normanton. This firm had also vanished during my toddling years, but a couple of its Seagull coaches remained in the Trent inventory for long enough to be seen by me (and quickly noted down) as they passed through Knutsford on their way to Blackpool one Saturday afternoon in 1960.

Despite these relatively recent losses, the independents were still thriving in 1960s Derbyshire and continuing to serve small local communities with reliable and relatively frequent operations. In fact they were so efficient at their work that no BET or THC affiliate could have provided equivalent services without making a massive loss. The independents had lower overheads, a good selection of older vehicles which were already fully depreciated when they arrived but kept roadworthy by dedicated and capable artisan engineers, and excellent relationships with their passengers who relied upon them for far more than just a seat on a bus. Many of the independents' drivers and conductors would willingly do shopping for a small consideration, collecting lists and money from customers' front gates and then returning with the specified merchandise and any change after their two or three hour market town layovers. Newspapers were carried from town to village shops, and postmen often used the services to reach their rural delivery areas. In earlier days the carriage of livestock ranging from chickens to lambs and small pigs had also been a feature of independent operation, but the new Traffic Commissioners had frowned on this and the practice had largely ceased by the start of the Second World War.

THE MONOPOLY PLAYERS

Derbyshire is not a particularly large county and yet the 20-plus operators covered in this volume would once have been the tip of the iceberg. For every firm which survived into the post-war era another four had vanished during the 1930s alone, swallowed up by affiliates of the would-be bus monopoly known as 'The Combine'. This leviathan had its roots in the Tilling & British Automobile Traction Co (T&BAT), the joint instrument of the Thomas Tilling and British Electric Traction (BET) groups. Its principal architect, the secretive financier John Soame Austen, was the chairman of BET along with many other companies in the orbit of a group of investment trusts variously known as 'The St Davids Group' (in honour of its aristocratic founder, the Earl of St Davids) or the '117 Old Broad Street Group' (after the address of its main offices). It was well-known that this group invested on behalf of the Royal family,

senior members of the peerage, and the Church of England. The group had taken effective control of BET during the First World War when it suffered a financial crisis, and although the founding Garcke family kept a shareholding, its positions on the company's Executive, and a hereditary directorship, Austen was very much the man in control from 1920 onwards when he replaced Emile Garcke as BET chairman.

BET's rapid change from a near bankrupt tramway operator with an ever-diminishing portfolio of systems to a leading owner of regional bus companies was financed partly by Austen's 'Establishment' investors and partly by an alliance with the Tilling group. Thomas Tilling had its origins in the London horse-bus trade and had needed to convert to motor-buses in a hurry in order to survive. As a result it had little capital to invest in provincial bus companies, and an alliance with BET meant that the two groups could share the start-up costs of new regional subsidiaries. Austen arranged a large bond issue for Thomas Tilling to fund their participation in this partnership and Tilling used the money to buy shares in BET's BAT operation and in many of its existing regional affiliates.

By 1928 the Austen-brokered alliance was already the most powerful bus grouping in England, and in May of that year the partnership was formalised when BAT changed its name to Tilling & British Automobile Traction (T&BAT). The consolidation of interests came about because Austen was disturbed (as were many in the industry at that time) by a new Act of Parliament which gave the 'Big Four' mainline railway companies carte blanche to diversify into bus operation. The railways showed their intent by acquiring some of the larger companies which had so far escaped the T&BAT net such as the Bristol Tramway & Carriage Co (which became a subsidiary of the GWR), the Taylor family's Crosville Motor Co (which was bought by the LMS), and EB Hutchinson's far-flung United Automobile Services empire (which passed to the LNER). Austen concluded that the best solution would be for BET and Tilling to make a further alliance with the railways, resulting in an almost complete monopoly of the bus industry.

Thus 'The Combine' was born in 1929-1930, as the geographically appropriate member(s) of the four mainline railways acquired an interest in

TELEPHONE: 57 MATLOCK. TELEGRAMS: MOTORS.

E. Williams & Co., Ltd.
South Parade,
MATLOCK BATH,
DERBYSHIRE.
Automobile Engineers.
Established 1906.

Up-to-Date
REPAIR SHOPS.

Capable of
ALL REPAIRS.

Batteries charged.

S.K.F. Ball Bearings.
Large Stocks.

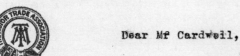

- 7 OCT 1929

Oct. 05. 1929

Dear Mr Cardwell,

Thanks for your letter of 4th inst
and the enclosed particulars may be of some guide to you.
I had no t anticipated the vehicles being of much use to
you, as I have had all this over with another concern, only
2 weeks ago. However, on the Ashbourne route there is, save
during a few weeks in the summer, no demand for a vehicle of
really good class. The users are all of the farming community and all sorts of articles are carried, such as calves
in sacks and forls in crates, Rabbits, Eggs and farm imple-
ments, besides produce.

The present vehicles are good enough for this service, if
reliable, and any oldish vehicles could work out a prosper-
ous old age on this service.

The question is really not so much as to what are the vehicles worth but what are ultimate prospects for the future.
Enclosed are timetables of the 2 routes to Ashbourne, dealing with Last Winter, and the present summer. As all the
tables were out of print for one route I have just put in
essentials in ink on an old sheet.

sincerely yours

G Williams Ltd

A letter from the proprietor of E Williams & Co of Matlock Bath (operating as Spa Motor Services) to George
Cardwell of the North Western Road Car Co. The interesting thing is the date – October 1929. Spa would not
actually sell out to North Western until March 1932. Mr Williams' typewriter was apparently no better than his
vehicles! *(GMTS Archive via John Dixon)*

This Spa Motor Services letterhead includes a line drawing of a dual doorway 'forward control' vehicle with a seating capacity of 26 or thereabouts. The only similar vehicle operated by Spa was a 1927 Vulcan VWBL, TE 1578, bought from Ribble (which had inherited it from Lancashire & Westmorland) in 1931. That machine, however, had 32 seats so the vehicle shown might well be a generic image. *(John Dixon Collection)*

T Slack & Sons of Darley Dale sold out to North Western in October 1934. This letterhead includes an artistic representation of two of the vehicles which passed to North Western, Gilford AS6/Willowbrook B24F bus RB 5733 (new to Slack in 1932) and Gilford 168OT/Willowbrook 32-seater UT 8540 (a 1931 machine acquired by Slack in 1933). They became North Western fleet numbers 184/182 respectively. *(John Dixon Collection)*

regional bus companies equivalent to that of the existing T&BAT shareholdings, while T&BAT was given a similar shareholding in companies previously controlled by the railways alone. Directorships were also allocated in proportion to the new shareholdings, with railway nominees joining the boards of most regional bus operators. A similar deal was done between the railway companies and four Yorkshire municipalities, creating 'Joint Omnibus Committees' in Halifax, Huddersfield, Sheffield, and Todmorden.

In Derbyshire the principal affiliates of 'The Combine' were East Midland (based in Chesterfield), Midland Red (the Birmingham based giant whose services could be found in the extreme southern tip of the county), North Western (based in Cheshire but with services into Derbyshire from its earliest days), and Trent Motor

Traction of Derby. Other parts of the county were served by subsidiaries of the Balfour Beatty group such as Midland General, or by the country's largest (genuine!) independent bus operator, Barton Transport. Although Barton's vehicles could be seen in profusion in the Derby, Ilkeston, and Long Eaton areas, the company's base was just across the border in Nottinghamshire and so it will be dealt with at a later date except for mention of the Derbyshire independents which it acquired.

Derby Corporation buses operated almost entirely within the borough's limits, and as a result no independents were acquired as none had been at liberty to start up inside their territory. The other municipal operator in Derbyshire, Chesterfield Corporation, had a longer reach and its services crossed the boundaries to reach nearby mining communities such as Bolsover and

Clay Cross. Several small operators (the largest brought three vehicles with it) were acquired to achieve dominance in these areas. Chesterfield also operated a service to Sheffield, jointly with Sheffield Corporation.

Sheffield Corporation was notoriously imperialistic and their transport department's senior managers decided to expand their territory deep into north-west Derbyshire. A service to Bakewell was acquired from McKay of that town in 1925, and services to Ashopton, Bakewell, and Buxton were bought from AF Hancock of Bamford. Aaron Frost Hancock had made his first fortune in the grocery business, opening a string of village shops in the same communities which were soon being served by his bus routes. He also had a substantial char-a-banc business based inside the Sheffield city limits and was persuaded to sell his stage carriage routes (which started in 1921) to the corporation during 1927. The 'Tilling & British' owned North Western Road Car Co immediately lodged a protest about this municipal invasion of its territory and a year later Sheffield repented by allowing North Western a half-share of the former Hancock routes for just over £4,000.

North Western

North Western had been founded in 1913 as the Macclesfield Branch of the BET subsidiary BAT (the British Automobile Traction Co) and one of its first services took its vehicles across the Cat and Fiddle Pass to Buxton in Derbyshire. The route was suspended for the duration of the First World War but recommenced in 1919 and the company's managers were quick to notice the lack of a local motor-bus operator in Buxton. This led to the company's second base being established in the Derbyshire spa town in the Spring of 1920 and by 1924 North Western (as the company had become in 1923) was offering inter-urban connections from Buxton to Ashbourne, Glossop, Leek, Macclesfield, Matlock Bath (via Bakewell and Matlock), and Stockport, as well as local services to Burbage, Ladmanlow, and Peak Dale.

Glossop, in the far north-west of Derbyshire, had services to Marple Bridge (via Charlesworth and Chisworth) and to Mottram (via Charlesworth and Broadbottom) by 1924, as well as the Buxton route listed above. Further opportunities in the town came in December 1927 when the Urban

Electric Supply Co decided to abandon its street tramway after Glossop council refused to buy the operation. The four and a half mile line ran westwards from the town centre to Woolley Bridge on the Cheshire/Derbyshire border and North Western provided a replacement bus service within two days of its closure. This caused some controversy locally as the Glossop Carriage Co had already ordered a trio of Karrier CLs with Northern Counties bodywork with which to operate the route when the tramway closed. The council ended up on North Western's side and the Karriers (at least one of which received GCC livery) were sold elsewhere.

It was North Western's second experience of tramway closure in that year. In September 1927 Matlock UDC had decided to close its short cable tramway which ran from Crown Square to the top of the precipitous Matlock Bank. The council held discussions with the four main operators of local bus services in the town (Alfreton Motor Transport, Hands Garage, North Western, and Spa Motor Services) and between them they arranged a seamless transition in a far more dignified manner than that occasioned by UES's abrupt withdrawal from Glossop three months later. One side-effect of the Matlock agreement was that North Western began to out-station a couple of Buxton garage vehicles at the Matlock premises of AMT.

North Western's Buxton to Matlock Bath service had been timed from the outset to offer connections via Trent Motor Traction to Derby, and in 1928 a 'through' joint service began. Apart from this minimal change North Western observed its peace treaty with local independents until after the award of Road Service Licences by the new Traffic Commissioners. These licences, ironically, made the independents more tempting targets for acquisition as they removed the possibility of new entrants popping up to replace them. The free market had been exiled from the bus industry.

Spa Motor Services of Matlock Bath was the first to succumb, passing into North Western's hands on the 1st of March 1932 along with four vehicles, a frequent service from Matlock to Wirksworth, and two rather less frequent services from Matlock to Ashbourne. The sale price was £4,150. On the same day North Western bought Alfreton Motor Transport's Matlock-Bakewell service for £300, removing a competitor from their Buxton-Derby trunk route. On the 7th of April 1932 it was the turn of Watts Bros of Wirksworth, who received £1,900 for one vehicle and their services from Matlock to Wirksworth and Bonsall Cross to Derby.

A less ambitious move saw a Mr Farrow of Peak Dale receive £150 in May 1932 to cease his service to Buxton which had been running a few minutes ahead of North Western's own vehicle on the route. By comparison SH Slack of Wirksworth received £2,000 in July for two vehicles and routes to Matlock and Middleton-by-Wirksworth. This eliminated the last competition on the Matlock-Wirksworth corridor. The acquisition of Hands Garage of Matlock a year later for £9,187 brought new stage services to Ashover, Elton, Hackney, Oaker, Starkholmes, Tansley and Winster, along with 17 vehicles and the garage next door to AMT's Matlock premises. Hands operated as a subsidiary until July 1934.

In September 1933 North Western bought the business of Murdock McKay of Bakewell for £1,350. Two vehicles were included but the main attraction was McKay's stage route from Bakewell to Ashford, Great Longstone, Wardlow, Litton, and Tideswell, with some journeys extending to Cressbrook. Eight years previously McKay had sold his most profitable route, from Bakewell to Sheffield via Calver, to Sheffield Corporation. October saw North Western take another bite out of Alfreton Motor Transport when it paid the company £5,000 for its Matlock Bath-Matlock-Bonsall route, Matlock area excursion licences, and its Matlock garage – conveniently next door to the premises acquired with the Hands business three months earlier. AMT retained their main Alfreton area operations (along with two routes from Alfreton to Matlock) until April 1936 when the controlling Kenning family sold the company to Midland General.

With the two leading independents left in the area (Hulley of Baslow and Silver Service of Darley Dale) having announced repeatedly and loudly that they were not for sale, North Western went for the next most important operator. T Slack & Son of Matlock was acquired in October 1934, and although the deal involved five vehicles and a fairly frequent service from Matlock to Baslow (with some journeys continuing to Calver Sough) the purchase price of £5,000 seemed to be markedly over-generous. By comparison the assets of North Western's final acquisition in

Derbyshire seemed to have been subject to a rather miserly valuation. Jennie Payne of Castleton sold out to North Western in March 1935 and received a paltry £628 for three vehicles (one a four year old Bedford), a garage in Castleton and a frequent stage service from Castleton village to Hope Station which was a very good earner during the tourist season. Small wonder that the remaining 'station bus' operators in the North Western area at that time (The George Hotel of Tideswell, Pashley of Bradwell, and White of Calver) decided to retain their independence well into the post-war era.

East Midland

The company which became East Midland Motor Services started operations in September 1920 at Clowne in Derbyshire, trading as WT Underwood & Co. Those suspicious of the new company's rapid expansion would have been justified. By the end of 1920 the Underwood company had no fewer than 16 AEC buses in use, all of them supplied by EB Hutchinson's United Automobile Services. UAS was already a major power in the bus industry, having branches all along the east coast from Suffolk to Northumberland, and – for reasons which are still not entirely clear – had decided to enter the East Midland region under a pseudonym. The WT Underwood of the title was one of Hutchinson's top lieutenants, sent to Derbyshire to create another outpost of the empire.

The company's only acquisition in Derbyshire during the Underwood era was that of East Derbyshire Motor Services, Doe Lea, in May 1922. EDMS operated in the Chesterfield area and four of its vehicles passed into the Underwood fleet. WT Underwood (the man) left WT Underwood (the company) in March 1927 after a major disagreement with Hutchinson. The Underwood company was re-named as East Midland Motor Services within weeks while Mr Underwood went on to found Underwood Express during 1928, a pioneering long-distance coach service operator based in Sheffield which survived for a few years before being swallowed up by the Yorkshire Services pool.

In July 1929 Hutchinson sold his majority shareholding in UAS to the London and North-Eastern Railway Co. The sale did not include EMMS which (although owned by Hutchinson)

THE ALFRETON MOTOR
TRANSPORT
COMPANY, LIMITED.
ALSO AT BAKEWELL ROAD, MATLOCK.

SALOON BUSES FOR PRIVATE PARTIES MAY BE BOOKED.
PETROL, OIL, AND TYRES IN STOCK.

Registered Office :

Angel Square, Alfreton,

Mr Womar.,
General Manager
North Western Road Car Co.,Ltd.,   July 26th   193 3.
120 Charles Street
Stockport

Dear Sir.,

     Enclosed please find the following licences.,
to which we have also attached their applications.,

E.07543., Primary Licence., Stage , Matlock Bank-Bonsall.,
E.05473., Primary Licence   Ex & Tours from Matlock.,
B.01003., Backing Yorkshire   -do-
D.01520.,   "   West Midland   -do-
Backing, North Western, as granted but not yet received
(paid for.) Ref. ECS.22/2.

     Yours faithfully.,
THE ALFRETON MOTOR TRANSPORT COMPANY LIMITED

     A.C.Stewart
     Managing-Director

This letter of July 1933, from Alfreton Motor Transport to North Western, indicates that the takeover of AMT's Matlock assets was a done deal long before the official date of October 1933. The remainder of the AMT business remained independent until April 1936 when the Kenning empire sold it to Midland General. *(GMTS Archive via John Dixon)*

Alfreton Motor Transport was controlled by motor trade mogul George (later Sir George) Kenning until he decided to sell off his stage carriage assets. The company's Matlock area operations went to North Western and the remainder to Midland General. This is Alfreton's RA 1735, a 1927 Leyland PLSC1 Lion with a Leyland B31F body. *(A Cuthbertson)*

Commercial Car Hirers, with a registered office at Cambridge Circus in London W1, was a subsidiary of the company which made Commer vehicles. Their Derbyshire operation took delivery of this Commer WP with 25-seat Scammell & Nephew bodywork, LE 9601, in 1911. The bus is route-branded for a Clay Cross-Tupton-Chesterfield service, although the back of the postcard describes it as 'A Trent Motor Traction omnibus in Derby'. *(Margaret Jones Collection)*

had never been legally connected to the rest of the organisation, but the writing was obviously on the wall. Two months later Hutchinson sold EMMS to a consortium of the LNER and LMS railways, and under the 'Combine' agreement they offered a share equal to their own joint participation to T&BAT. This was taken up in March 1930.

Under its new ownership the company became noticeably more acquisitive. Mather Bros of Tupton was the first target in Derbyshire, being acquired (jointly with Chesterfield Corporation) in December 1933 along with a route from Chesterfield to Barrow Hill, a 32-seat Guy FC bus, and a Morris Viceroy coach. April 1934 saw the acquisition of a Clowne-Oxcroft route from Briggs & Greaves of Stanfree, and in June 1934 EMMS bought the Palterton to Bolsover route of WH Booth. No vehicles were involved in either purchase. In September 1934 the more substantial business of W Stoppard & Sons of Clay Cross was acquired, bringing new services from Clay Cross to Clay Cross Station (some distance from the village!), Ashover, and Matlock. Three Stoppard vehicles entered the EMMS fleet, a 19-seat Dennis bus, a 32-seat LT5 Lion bus and a brand-new Bedford WTL coach. The company's expansion into this area to the south of Chesterfield continued in November 1934 with the purchase of the business of W White of Ashover. White ran from Ashover to Chesterfield by two different routes and contributed a 14-seat Chevrolet bus and a 20-seat Citroen coach to EMMS stock. The final pre-war acquisition of stage carriage assets (in Derbyshire at least) came in February 1936 when EMMS bought the Chesterfield to Uppertown service of Naylor of Brampton. No vehicles were involved.

Trent

Of the four T&BAT affiliates operating in Derbyshire, Trent Motor Traction was by far the most acquisitive. It also had the strangest history of the four. In the summer of 1910 Sir Peter Carlow Walker, proprietor of breweries in Warrington, Lancashire, and owner of Osmaston Manor near Ashbourne in Derbyshire, went on a grouse-hunting expedition to Scotland. While there he was impressed by his host's 'Commercial Cars' shooting-brake and resolved to have one for himself. This was arranged by an early form of

vehicle leasing and the small (14-seat) bus chosen, registered to Commercial Car Hirers Ltd, arrived in Derbyshire in the summer of 1911. As the baronet Walker only required limited use of the vehicle it was soon put to work on regular runs between Ashbourne and Derby available to the general public and advertised under the 'CCH' banner.

By 1913 CCH had six vehicles at its Derbyshire base and was operating services from Derby to Alfreton, Ashbourne, Melbourne, and Uttoxeter, and from Alfreton to Chesterfield. The directors of Commercial Cars (later known as 'Commer') decided that the sideline would fare better as a stand-alone business and offered shares in a new Trent Motor Traction Co in November of that year. The main purchaser was BET subsidiary BAT which acquired a controlling interest in the company. CCH remained as a minority shareholder until 1923, while Sir Peter died in 1915. His son and heir produced no offspring and Osmaston Manor fell into disrepair before being demolished after the Second World War.

Trent fared better than either of its birth-parents (Commer went broke in 1925 and became a subsidiary of Humber), and under BAT control it was soon on the look-out for potential take-over targets. The first acquisition in Derbyshire took place in February 1916 when Trent bought the business of Dawkins & Ballard of Alfreton, including a stage service to Derby via Ripley and a Thornycroft bus, for £1,150. This move was in the nature of removing a competitor, as was the purchase in February 1917 of the joint service operated by J Harrison and Derby Motor Service (both of Ashbourne) between Ashbourne and Derby via Brailsford. They had to share £750, suggesting that the single vehicle included was less impressive than the Thornycroft mentioned above.

After 12 years in which not a single Derbyshire operator was acquired by Trent, the company began a major buying spree in 1929. First to be acquired (on the 21st of January) was the District Omnibus Service of Horsley Woodhouse, operating routes from Derby to Alfreton, Heanor, and Ilkeston in direct competition with Trent. The purchase price of £12,500 reflected the inclusion of 14 vehicles and a garage. Another major operator, George Chapman & Sons of Belper, sold out to Trent on the 4th of March. The price was just over £8,000 and included 11 vehicles, a garage, and services between Belper and Derby and from Belper to

Ripley by three routes. In May it was the turn of Wright Bros of South Normanton, who operated between Alfreton and Mansfield. No vehicles or property were involved and so the price for the bus service was a modest £750. October saw the purchase of the Derby-Mickleover route of Eagle Motor Services for a more generous £2,175. Eagle continued in business and Trent would come back for more as the enterprise slowly disintegrated. The year's buying activity ended in November when Trent paid an almost derisory £45 for the Ripley-Belper route of Daley's 'Guy Service'

The 1930 shopping list began with routes from Derby to Belper and Spondon, acquired from TPS Omnibus Services of Derby in May for £2,000. TPS continued to operate a service to Spondon via a different route until March 1935 when Trent came back for a second (£2,500) bite which also included TPS's coaching licences. In August 1930 the company acquired the amusingly named Wagg's Super Service of Derby with services to Melbourne and Swadlincote. Only three vehicles were included, so the purchase price of £4,500 reveals the value assigned to eliminating competition on these key inter-urban routes. The final purchase of 1930 removed another substantial competitor. HD Bayliss & Sons of Ashbourne had been competing with Trent on its original Ashbourne-Derby route for more than a decade. The deal was concluded in November and the Bayliss family received £14,000 for their two services to Derby and 11 vehicles. With the implementation of the 1930 Road Traffic Act just around the corner Trent could be reasonably certain that no new entrant would have time to replace Bayliss.

There were no new purchases in Derbyshire in 1931, and only two in Nottinghamshire. It would seem that Trent was far too busy filing its own applications for licences or challenging those of others to get its wallet out. The company more than made up for this during 1932. On the 20th of January Trent bought the Belper-Ripley route of Poundall, Belper, along with two vehicles for a total of £1,350. Poundall continued to operate another service from Belper to Shottle which later passed to HS North of Derby (see below and also Part Three). On the 9th of March a service from Derby to Tutbury was acquired from Mason's Bus Service of Derby for £3,150, despite no vehicles being included. On the 22nd of April Trent

swallowed up three independents in a single day. Barlow of Belper operated from his home town to Derby and received £2,900 for his route and one vehicle. The other two operators operated jointly between Derby and Spondon where both were based. The larger of the two, known as 'Spondon Ex-Servicemen's' received £1,500 while Liewsley's Omnibus Service was valued at £875. On the 13th of May three operators on the Derby-Borrowash-Ockbrook route sold out. Trading as 'Orange Coaches', 'Vincent's Devonian', and 'Vincent's Reliance' the proprietors received £1,525 between them. As no-one called 'Vincent' was involved in the last two firms the names remain a mystery. The 2nd of August produced the last purchase of the year in the form of the Alfreton-Ripley route operated jointly by four members of the Alfreton Bus Association co-operative. The price was £2,000 for the service alone. Members of the ABA continued to operate on the Alfreton-Heanor route but later sold out to Midland General.

The major acquisition of 1933 was that of Rhodeland Motor Services of Derby on the 21st of March. The operator's name came from its founders (Messrs Rhodes and Holland) and its prize asset was the busy route from Derby to Wirksworth. For its £6,000 Trent also got five vehicles and a garage. In June Henshaw's White Lion Service of Jacksdale contributed an Alfreton-Spondon route which Trent valued at £275. This might be compared to the £900 paid to Maroon Services of Whatstandwell in December for their service from that village to Ripley.

In Part Three of this book we will remember an independent operator which ran in to Derby trading as 'Blue Bus', but there was another company using that name until 1934. Whitehall & Brannan of Derby operated as Blue Bus Services on routes to Heanor, Horsley, and Ilkeston, selling out to Trent on the 8th of May 1934 for the princely sum of £9,000. As no vehicles were acquired the high price was obviously paid to eliminate competition. There were no vehicles from Wood of Riddings either (acquired in August), but he was forced to accept a lowly £275 for his Alfreton-Ripley operation. A very quiet 1934 ended on New Year's Eve with the purchase of routes connecting Derby with Sunnyhill and Stenson from Eagle Services of Little Eaton for £2,150. This was the same Eagle Services previously encountered in 1929, but in the meantime the firm had changed ownership and location. The original owner, a Mr J Turner, had floundered and his remaining operations had been transferred to Mr SO Stevenson. Stevenson was a lieutenant of motor-trade mogul Sir George Kenning, who had sold small buses to a legion of independents on hire-purchase terms. As the worldwide financial depression continued many of these entrepreneurs found it hard to make payments, and rather than repossess the vehicles involved (which would be hard to place elsewhere) Sir George allowed the operators to continue under the stern supervision of Stevenson. In many cases the only way to raise the cash to clear the debts was by selling the licences to Trent or Midland General.

Eagle Services under Stevenson's direction was used, in effect, as a holding cell for bankrupt operators. Few escaped. Sir George and his minion had also become involved in the affairs of Kingfisher Services and its subsidiary HS North, both of Derby, which came close to liquidation in early 1935. Kingfisher, which had routes from Derby to Allestree, Darley Abbey, and Quarndon, passed into Trent ownership on the 23rd of March for £7,750. By then HS North had been disentangled from Kingfisher and separately received £9,750 for its services from Heanor to Derby and Belper. One suspects a certain amount of financial sleight of hand here, but however it was done the North family ended up with a viable business again and continued for many years. Their story will be found in Part Three.

In April 1935 Stevenson's version of Eagle Services sold two further ex-Turner routes to Trent, both of them works services running from Derby to Littleover. The price of £60 hardly seemed worth the trouble. October brought a more substantial transfer when all the remaining licences held by Eagle Services were sold to Trent for £4,850. These included Derby to Sutton-on-the-Hill and Trusley (the last of the Turner era routes), Derby to Hollington and Longford (acquired by Stevenson from Yeomans of Rodsley), Derby to Spondon (ex-Cox of Derby), Heage to Spondon (from Eaton of Heage), and Belper-Ripley (from Bell of Bargate).

The largest of all of Trent's purchases in Derbyshire also took place in October 1935 when the company paid a staggering £20,000 (roughly £400,000 in today's money) for the 'Pippin

Services' network operated by AJ Daley & Sons of Ripley. For its money Trent received services from Ripley to Alfreton, Ambergate, and Belper and from Belper to Alfreton and Crich, plus excursion licences from Ripley, eight vehicles, and a garage. There was one more purchase before the end of the year, that of Partlow & Tarlton of Heanor on the 30th of December. The sale price of £2,850 included a stage service from Heanor to Kilburn and three vehicles.

The supply of available independents was beginning to run dry, but in January 1936 Trent paid £8,350 for the business of Red Star Service, Duffield, including a daily service from Derby to Belper via Duffield, a local (Sunday only) circular in the Duffield area for churchgoers, and three vehicles. In July 1936 the Heanor & District Omnibus Co sold its Heanor-Ilkeston route to Trent for £300. The Heanor company then struggled on until May 1938 when it was jointly acquired by Midland General, Trent, and Barton. Trent paid £2,583 for its quarter-share and in exchange received a daily Ripley to Ilkeston service, a works service from Horsley Woodhouse to Mapperley Colliery, and a quarter share of the proceeds from selling the Heanor fleet, none of which were operated by the purchasing companies.

The only other acquisition in Derbyshire during 1937-39 came in March 1938 when Trent bought a works service from Vallance of Stanley Common (also to Mapperley Colliery) for £325. After the outbreak of the Second World War expansion was limited to a single purchase. In November 1940 the company bought Wells' Service of Aston-on-Trent, paying £3,000 for a daily service from Derby to Weston-on-Trent. It was agreed that Mr Wells would receive a further payment if earnings from the service exceeded £3,000 in the first twelve months of Trent ownership, but no record of such a payment has been found.

Midland Red

The Birmingham & Midland Motor Omnibus Co, commonly known as 'Midland Red', covered a vast swathe of central England from Shropshire to Leicestershire and from Staffordshire to Oxfordshire. In many counties it was the dominant operator but in Derbyshire its presence was limited to the peninsula-shaped area to the south of the River Trent, bounded by Staffordshire to the west and south and by Leicestershire to the east. Midland Red services first reached this part of the county from its garage across the border in Tamworth, but a local base was soon established in Swadlincote. This was the half-way point of the company's trunk service from Burton in Staffordshire to Ashby-de-la-Zouch in Leicestershire and the company soon became concerned by the level of independent competition on the Swadlincote-Burton section of the route.

In June 1928 BMMO bought the Gresley-Swadlincote-Burton route of Regent Motor Services, Church Gresley, the most important of the independents in the area. One of Regent's founders, William Lloyd, had already left the company by then to start a new operation (Viking Motors) in Burton. The remaining Regent directors kept their vehicles after selling the stage service, and one of them (Victor Dennis) went on to found Robin Hood Coaches in Nottingham.

Another of the leading independents, Victoria Motorways, came to an unusual agreement with Midland Red to ensure its survival, the details of which will be found in Part Three. Victoria was later involved in Midland Red's acquisition of Brooks Bros stage service from Swadlincote to Linton in May 1945. The proprietors of Brooks (based at Castle Gresley) had developed a deep personal aversion to dealing with Midland Red after years of sniping and disparaging in front of the Traffic Commissioners, and so sold the goodwill of the service to Victoria Motorways instead. Victoria immediately resold the service to BMMO at a slight loss, but in exchange for their help the Birmingham company agreed to withdraw their route from Donisthorpe and Overseal to Burton which competed with Victoria's main service for much of its mileage.

The Demise of T&BAT

The notorious 'Combine' had been the brain-child of one man, John Soame Austen, and the different parties to the agreements (BET, Tilling, and the four main-line railway companies) were very much kept in line by knowledge of his relationship to the 'Establishment' and his enormous financial reach. Many commentators have found it unusual that T&BAT disintegrated during wartime, when BET and Tilling might have been expected to bury any disagreements in the interest of the nation.

Few have noticed that T&BAT fell apart within weeks of Austen's death in the spring of 1942.

The truth seems to be that the directors of BET and those of Thomas Tilling had been falling out for years over both strategies and tactics, but had been kept in the same room by Austen's substantial financial authority. The final straw came a fortnight after Austen's death when Tilling supremo Frederick Heaton circulated a document suggesting that the entire bus industry should be placed into government ownership, and that 'The Combine' should lobby to hasten this outcome, in exchange for reasonable compensation. This proposal was anathema to Sidney Garcke and his lieutenants in the BET Executive. Following Austen's death there was a period of interregnum at the St Davids/Broad Street group (many of the other senior partners were at war) and during that brief hiatus the members of the BET Executive seized the opportunity to elect one of their own, Richard J Howley – a Garcke family loyalist since tramway days – to succeed Austen as BET chairman. The new regime immediately gave notice to Frederick Heaton of Tilling that they wished to dissolve T&BAT at the earliest opportunity. It seems that Tilling were also glad to see the end of the marriage as they co-operated fully in a scheme to divide the T&BAT affiliates equally between two new companies, BET Omnibus Services Ltd and Tilling Motor Services Ltd.

For some reason Tilling received most of the former railway owned companies such as Bristol, Crosville, Eastern/Southern/Western National, Southern Vectis, and United Auto, while BET took back most of its own from the BAT days including Midland Red, North Western, and Trent. An exception to this rule was East Midland Motor Services, which had been owned by the railways immediately before the advent of the 'Combine' but now found itself in the BET camp.

By all accounts the railway companies' directors were not well pleased by the divorce of BET and Tilling, but there was little that they could do and much else to occupy their attentions. Their decision to invest a king's ransom in the bus industry suddenly seemed rather ill-advised as the time-worn infrastructure of the railways themselves became apparent under the strain of the war effort.

E & J Bramley of Cotmanhay (trading as Prince of Wales Services) operated between Ilkeston and Nottingham until bought out by a consortium of Midland General and two of its existing subsidiaries (Dawson's Enterprise and Williamson's Garage) in March 1930. NU 7973 was a Guy BB with Guy B26F bodywork, new in 1925, and is seen at the Nottingham end of the Bramleys' stage route. *(Martin Walton Collection)*

This Thornycroft A1 with Challands & Ross bodywork (either NU 6704 or NU 7953, both new in 1925) is in the livery of Dawson's Enterprise Omnibus Co, of Cotmanhay. Dawson's ran on the Ilkeston-Nottingham route and sold out to Midland General in July 1929. It was retained as a group subsidiary until July 1931. *(Martin Walton Collection)*

JG Severn & Co of Alfreton traded as Severn's Motor Auctions and used the fleet name 'SMA' for their bus fleet. Their services from Alfreton to Nottingham and Ripley passed to Midland General in March 1931 along with a solitary double-decker (an AEC Regent), four AEC Regals, and three ADCs. This is RA 6969, an ADC 416 with Hall Lewis B32F bodywork, new to SMA in 1928. *(Martin Walton Collection)*

J Williamson & Son of Heanor (later known as Williamson's Garage Ltd) ran stage services from both Heanor and Ilkeston into Nottingham. NU 3356 was a 1924 Reo Speedwagon with a 14-seat Hartshorn body. *(Martin Walton Collection)*

Midland General and Barton

Balfour Beatty, formed in 1909 to construct and administer electrical power stations and their associated local tramways, was one of several groups which competed with BET for the ever dwindling amount of tramway mileage left under private control. The firm entered the East Midlands region in 1913 when its Tramways, Power, & Light subsidiary acquired the Notts & Derby and Mansfield & District systems. Notts & Derby boasted one of the longest tram lines in the country, covering more than 15 miles between Nottingham and Ripley. The Mansfield company's network was more localised, but remained as one of the more profitable systems not yet 'municipalised' by the local corporation.

A third company was added to the Balfour Beatty portfolio in the area in 1920 with the creation of the Midland General Omnibus Co (MGOC) as the motor-bus arm of Notts & Derby. Two years elapsed before the arrival of the first buses, two Vulcans, and steady progress followed as the new company developed a route network connecting the Ripley-Nottingham tramway to adjacent communities on either side of the line. Trent Motor Traction was already active in the area and Midland General soon began to acquire independent bus operators in order to achieve enough critical mass to compete with the BAT affiliate.

The company's first of 26 acquisitions in Derbyshire came in July 1925 with the purchase of the South Normanton Bus Co and its South Normanton-Nottingham service. Four vehicles were included in the deal, three Leyland G7s and a Vulcan VSC. The next acquisition, in January 1928, was of far greater significance. Williamson's Garage of Heanor operated major inter-urban services from both Heanor and Ilkeston to Nottingham. No fewer than 41 vehicles (35 Reos, 2 Thornycrofts, and 4 brand-new 32-seater Bristols) were operated at the time of the take-over, more than doubling the size of the MGOC fleet. Williamson's was kept as a subsidiary until 1931 when its operations were merged into those of Midland General. Between 1928 and 1931 the subsidiary acquired several other independents on behalf of its parent company. These included Tarlton & Brown of Codnor (acquired in September 1928 along with a Heanor-Ripley service and three Reos), the Reliance Omnibus Co of Ilkeston (bought in May 1929 and

contributing an Ilkeston-Eastwood service and five vehicles), J Saxton & Sons of Heanor (taken over on 25th September 1929 for its Heanor-Ilkeston service), Hamilton's 'Teddy Bear' service of Heanor (acquired on the same day as Saxton and offering a Ripley-Heanor-Nottingham route), and J Argyle of Codnor (operating between Ripley and Heanor until acquired by Williamson's in January 1930).

There were also other deals in which Williamson's played a part. On the 1st of January 1929 Midland General had acquired the important Cotmanhay-based operator known as Dawson's Enterprise Omnibus Co along with 11 vehicles and a service from Cotmanhay to Nottingham. In July 1929 ownership of Dawson's was transferred from MGOC to the Williamson's subsidiary. A more complicated manoeuvre took place in March 1930 when the Bramley family's 'Prince of Wales Service' was acquired by a concert party of Midland General, its subsidiary Williamson's, its subsidiary's subsidiary Dawson's, and Trent Motor Traction! The 'Prince of Wales' main-line ran from the company's base in Cotmanhay to Ilkeston and Nottingham and nine vehicles were operated at the time of the take-over. Trent's participation in the purchase was notable as it paid half of the purchase price but ended up with only a third of the service, suggesting that its interest was more in establishing a 'common road' between Ilkeston and Nottingham which would act as a boundary between its own territory and that of MGOC. The significant thing about this is that a 'Combine' affiliate (Trent) had acknowledged the rights to an operating territory of a 'non-Combine' bus company (Midland General).

Midland General itself made the next group acquisition in Derbyshire when the company bought WJ Wright's service from South Normanton to Nottingham in April 1930. The parent concern followed this purchase, on 26th March 1931, with the acquisition of JT Boam of Heanor (trading as 'The Ray Service') along with a Heanor-Ilkeston route and six modern Leylands. Five days later MGOC bought out another key independent, JG Severn & Co of Alfreton which traded as 'SMA Service'. The 'SMA' stood for Severn's Motor Auctions, the family's main business interest. SMA's main routes ran from Alfreton to Nottingham and Ripley and the take-over included an AEC Regent double-decker (a former demonstrator), four AEC Regals, and three ADCs.

On the 16th of July 1931 Midland General absorbed Williamson's and Dawson's operations. No further acquisitions in Derbyshire took place until the 11th of April 1933 when MGOC bought an Ilkeston-Kimberley service from FU Charlton of Ilkeston. Charlton's other scheduled operation, a works run from Cotmanhay and Ilkeston to Shipley Colliery, continued until February 1935 when it too was sold to Midland General. These deals were chicken-feed when compared to the events of July 1933. The company's target was the town of Alfreton. On the 4th of July MGOC acquired the businesses of F Porter & Son of Stonebroom and E Wharton of Morton. Porter operated services from Chesterfield to Alfreton (via two routes), Mansfield, and Sutton-in-Ashfield plus a variety of colliery journeys, and the deal included five Leylands and six Guys. Wharton (trading as Morton Bus Service) ran from Alfreton to Clay Cross with two vehicles. Three more operators were acquired on the 17th of July. Viggars of Alfreton also operated on the Alfreton to Clay Cross service and passed two Leyland Lions to MGOC. The other two targets on that summer's day were Fearn of Alfreton and Severn Bros of Swanwick, who ran a joint service between Alfreton and Heanor. Both operators used Morris Viceroys, three of which were transferred into MGOC ownership.

By this time the Notts & Derby trams had gone, replaced by brand-new trolleybuses which also reached Ilkeston for the first time. The Ilkeston tramway had been of a non-standard gauge and thus forced to operate separately, but conversion to trolleybus equipment eliminated this consideration. Balfour Beatty's resources were far from infinite, and the investment in rail-less traction at Notts & Derby (and new motor-buses at Mansfield to replace the trams there) caused a brief pause in Midland General's crusade to eliminate the independent bus operators in its area. The campaign resumed on the 27th of March 1934 with the acquisition of two operators on the same day. JH Booth of Westhouses (near Alfreton) operated from Alfreton to Chesterfield via Tibshelf (competing with one of MGOC's ex-Porter services) and contributed a Lion, a Tiger, and a Morris Dictator to the Midland General fleet. WE Topham of Leabrooks had a Ripley to Pinxton service and came with two Guys and an Albion. Another business operating between

Ripley and Pinxton, George Shaw & Sons of Ironville, was bought one month later and the sale included two Dennis Gs.

By early 1935 Ilkeston had become the focus of Midland General's attentions. Trent (and T&BAT behind it) had already conceded that the area to the north and north-east of Ilkeston was MGOC territory. Developments in other directions had been more confused as Trent had been slow to develop services in the triangular area bounded by Derby, Ilkeston, and Long Eaton. While it was true that Trent had created (largely by acquisition) a thriving Ilkeston-Derby route, an attempt to operate a service from Ilkeston to Long Eaton had ended in 1926 after less than a year. This withdrawal had been prompted by competition from a swarm of small independents, most of whom became members of the 'United Bus Service' owners' co-operative in 1928. A further (non-UBS) independent had joined the fray in March 1927 when Barton opened a service from Old Sawley and Long Eaton to Ilkeston.

If the UBS members were minnows of the independent bus world, then Barton was a whale. From its base just across the border in Nottinghamshire it had already developed high-frequency bus services between Nottingham and Derby via Beeston and Long Eaton, successfully challenging Trent on some of the T&BAT company's premier routes. Now it was looking northwards from Long Eaton and seeing Ilkeston as a very attractive target for expansion. The whale began to swallow up some of the UBS minnows. At the same time Midland General was contemplating expansion southwards into the void left by Trent's inactivity and also began to acquire UBS members with Long Eaton licences. Prices paid to willing sellers became ridiculously out of proportion to the assets on offer, and Barton and Midland General were soon forced to sue for peace. The treaty between the two was complicated, but the essence of it was that Barton would receive any stage services from acquired operators which ran south from Ilkeston towards Long Eaton while Midland General would end up with acquired services which ran to the north or east of Ilkeston. Excursion licences would be similarly divided, with excursion licences from Ilkeston itself going to Midland General. From MGOC's viewpoint in 1935 this must have seemed like the best deal it was likely to get from the ever-combative Barton, but with the help of a crystal ball it might have negotiated for a lot longer. The area ceded to Barton included the small village of Kirk Hallam, later the site of a major housing estate and a new source of revenue as substantial as Ilkeston itself. Outside of the Ilkeston triangle Midland General's only acquisitions in Derbyshire during 1935 were the works service from FU Charlton already mentioned and the business of Brewin & Hudson of Heanor, acquired in August with a Heanor to Hucknall route and four small Fords.

By 1936 Sir George Kenning had decided to get out of the bus operating business. Most of the small companies he had acquired inadvertently as a result of their failure to make hire-purchase payments had already gone by then, either placed into liquidation or brought back to health by SO Stevenson and then sold to Trent to clear their former owners' debts. After the successful re-launch of the HS North business (see Part Three) all that remained was the jewel in Kenning's bus operating crown, Alfreton Motor Transport. As already mentioned, the company's Matlock-based operations had been sold off to North Western. On the 1st of April 1936 Midland General bought the rest of the business, including two routes from Alfreton to Matlock and others from Alfreton to Brackenfield , Lea Mills, and Wheatcroft and from Lea Mills to Wessington and Whatstandwell. Vehicles transferred to MGOC included six Leyland Lions, two Gilfords, two Karriers, and a Commer. The Alfreton company was retained as a (non-operational) MGOC subsidiary until 1946. Sir George continued to be a minority shareholder in Trent Motor Traction, an interest he had acquired from Commercial Car Hirers after the end of the First World War, and was well-known as a leading light in the motor dealership sector both in the East Midlands area and well beyond.

In May 1938 the Heanor & District Omnibus Co fell into financial difficulties and its assets were acquired by a coalition of Midland General (55.74%), Trent (24.6%) and Barton (19.66%). Trent took the Ripley to Ilkeston service and a works journey to Mapperley Colliery, Barton got two works services from Smalley and Stanley Common to the Celanese plant at Spondon, and Midland General took the rest including services from Ripley and Brinsley to Spondon, both operating via Heanor. The Heanor company had 18 vehicles in use before the take-over, but few were deemed roadworthy enough to serve in the purchasers' fleets.

Meanwhile, the 'Ilkeston Triangle' operators of the UBS had been selling out to the Midland General/Barton coalition in slow motion. The final survivors, the Grainger Bros of Ilkeston who traded as 'Blue Service', eventually gave up the fight in September 1941. As with the rest, Barton took the services (which ran southwards from Ilkeston) and Midland General acquired the Ilkeston-based excursion licences.

Unlike the T&BAT affiliates (and indeed Midland General) Barton was not a particularly acquisitive firm by nature, preferring to grow by innovation while taking no nonsense from its competitors. The Barton brothers did, however, make an occasional purchase when the seller was willing, the assets attractive, and the price within reason. Apart from the UBS carve-up mentioned above such purchases were few and far between on the Derbyshire side of the border. In October 1929 Barton bought a Derby to Nottingham service from Mr J Turner's 'Eagle Services' (see *Trent* entry above for details of Eagle's other services). Turner had acquired three Gilfords for the Nottingham service and then become unable to make the payments after Trent reacted ferociously and 'chased' his new route into the ground. Barton got the service (and the three Gilfords) for a knock-down price and Turner struggled on for a little longer with his other routes. Trent's managers were not pleased as Barton was already competing with them between the two county towns, albeit via Long Eaton rather than the slightly more direct route used by Trent (and, briefly, Turner). The Barton brothers were warned that this could mean all-out war, with Trent threatening to start a cut-price service between Derby and Long Eaton to demonstrate the company's displeasure. Barton took the only sensible option and sold the Turner service to Trent within days.

Barton's only other Derbyshire purchases were at the southern end of the 'Ilkeston Triangle'. W Upton of Long Eaton (operating as 'Cosy Services') and JW Kirkland of Sawley operated between their two locations without venturing northwards into the 'Triangle' itself. Both were acquired in 1933 with Upton contributing an ADC, a Maudslay, and a Star to the Barton fleet.

Aftermath

So this is the 'roll-call of the dead' in the period up to the mid-1940s. At the end of the Second World War the British electorate surprised everyone (especially Churchill) by choosing a Labour government hell-bent on nationalisation. Oddly, the 'non-Combine' Balfour Beatty companies were the first to be transferred into state ownership. This came about as they were officially subsidiaries of the Midland Counties Electric Supply Co, the Balfour Beatty holding company for its power generating facilities in the area. When the electrical supply industry was nationalised in 1947 the British Electricity Authority found itself in possession of several bus companies. They were quickly transferred to the new British Transport Commission (BTC).

The Tilling Group took the view that nationalisation was inevitable and sold out voluntarily to the BTC in 1948. In exchange the group continued to be responsible for the management of their assorted bus companies and also assumed that function for the former Balfour Beatty companies in the East Midlands area recently transferred into BTC ownership. In 1946 the chairmanship of BET had passed from RJ Howley to Harold Charles 'Harley' Drayton, the new head of the 'St Davids Group' of investment trusts. Drayton was a very different man to his predecessor and mentor, John Soame Austen, who had preferred to remain in the shadows. He was a regular visitor to the night-clubs and entertainment houses of the West End of London and became a favourite of several newspaper gossip columnists who described him as an influential tycoon and 'head of the Drayton Group'. The new BET chairman was also known as a fierce champion of private enterprise and vehicles belonging to

BET affiliates were soon festooned with slogans opposing the nationalisation of the bus industry. This tactic was pursued despite the fact that most of BET's bus-operating ventures had substantial railway shareholdings and the railway companies had already been taken into state ownership. As far as Drayton was concerned the railway appointed directors could take their dividends and put up with it.

The other prominent figure in the post-war history of BET was John Spencer Wills who became the company's Managing Director. Wills (despite suggestions elsewhere) was nothing to do with the Wills tobacco fortune. His grandfather had been transported to Australia after a conviction for highway robbery, but after his return to Britain the family's circumstances had gradually improved and JS Wills received a good education. He secured a job as Emile Garcke's personal secretary before marrying the BET founder's grand-daughter. His way to the top was further assured by a spell in the senior management of Midland Red. He too vigorously opposed nationalisation and the BET campaign was partially responsible for the Attlee government's decision to delay a compulsory purchase of the company's assets. Labour hesitated long enough to lose an election and BET survived as a bus operator for another two decades before finally selling its interests to the state.

Trent Motor Traction went through the horrors of the National Bus Company years and then re-emerged into private ownership after deregulation and the dismemberment of NBC. A few years later it bought the bus operations of Barton Transport and the combined Wellglade group has gone from strength to strength, winning numerous awards for excellence. The company has come a long way from its origins at Osmaston Manor.

Williamson's liked Reos and in 1925 stepped up to the Reo Pullman which was larger than the Speedwagon. This one is NU 7283 which carried an Eaton B20F body. When Midland General acquired the Williamson business in January 1928 no fewer than 35 of the 41 vehicles involved were of Reo manufacture. *(Martin Walton Collection)*

Williamson's also had two Thornycrofts and four brand-new Bristol Bs with Roe B32F bodywork. In this Charles H Roe pre-delivery shot Bristol RA 4519 is seen outside the body manufacturer's Crossgates works. Midland General kept Williamson's as a (vehicle owning) subsidiary until the late 1940s, but after 1931 its buses were operated in full Midland General livery. *(Martin Walton Collection)*

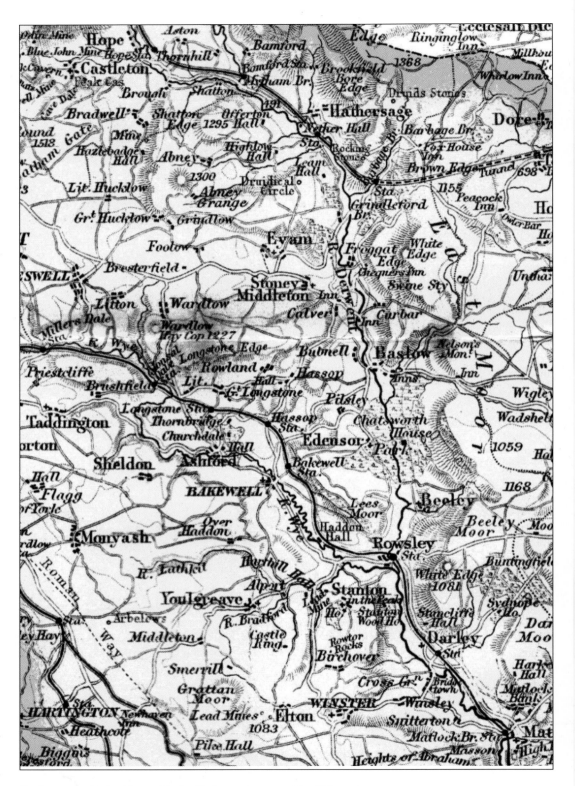

North-western Derbyshire as it looked in the early years of the 20th century.

PART ONE
NORTH-WESTERN
DERBYSHIRE

The scenery of the Derbyshire Peak District is little less than sensational, and rugged enough to tolerate the scars left upon it by millennia of stone quarrying and mining. Upper-class Victorian tourists 'discovered' the area at the end of the 19th century, spurred on by a desire to see its great stately homes or experience its mineral spas and then becoming captivated by its natural beauty. Agriculture is also a major contributor to the local economy (especially sheep farming, but cattle are important in the valleys), and in the early 1800s the swift running waters of the local rivers attracted a large number of textile mills to the area, many of which are still standing although long since 're-purposed'.

According to the 2001 census the largest town in the area was Glossop with 33,000 residents, but many of these were newcomers from the previous four decades when the electrification of the rail service to Manchester attracted upwardly mobile commuters to the new housing estates attached to the fringes of the traditional community. Glossop is a fascinating place for many reasons (not least as the home town of Venture Publications!), but has no significant history of independent bus operations before deregulation. The North Western Road Car Co became the dominant force in local bus services, and the same is true of the other communities along the old Cheshire frontier such as Buxton (population 20, 836), New Mills (9,521), and Chapel-en-le-Frith (8,635). In addition to the traditional local industries the latter has a major factory complex belonging to Ferodo, one of the world's largest manufacturers of automotive brake linings.

Further to the east the road from Chapel-en-le-Frith to Chesterfield passes a mile to the north of Tideswell (1,820), traditionally a lead mining village but popular with Victorian tourists on account of its disproportionately large parish church, known as the 'Cathedral of the Peak'. This road continues through Baslow (1,100) where a right turn leads southwards past the grounds of Chatsworth House to Matlock (9,543). Matlock and Buxton have both grown as a result

of the tourist and hydropathic therapy trades while Bakewell (3,949), halfway between the two and once the most populous town along the Wye valley, has actually become smaller over the last two centuries despite its apparently healthy number of visitors. In the south of this part of Derbyshire is the small town of Ashbourne (7,112) which has a fair amount of local industry but is probably better known for its no-holds-barred Shrove Tuesday football match which involves hundreds of players on each side and uses the town's streets as an out-sized pitch. The town is also a convenient tourist gateway to the glories of Dove Dale.

North-Western Derbyshire has more than its share of historical sites. Stone circles and other megalithic monuments can be found throughout the area and many villages still have annual 'well-dressing' ceremonies which are a Christianised version of ancient pagan rituals. More recent history can be found in the village of Eyam (pronounced 'Eem'), just to the north of the Chapel to Chesterfield road, where the Plague arrived in 1665. The local residents voluntarily quarantined themselves to prevent the infection spreading to the rest of the region, and more than half of Eyam's 800 inhabitants died before the self-imposed siege was finally lifted.

The difficult terrain failed to deter railway entrepreneurs in the second half of the 19th century and the Peak District found itself well-served by the ingenuity of Victorian engineers. Unfortunately, only a fraction of this railway mileage remains in place, the worse losses being the lines from Buxton to Ashbourne and Matlock. Both are now reduced to pathways for hikers and cyclists except for a section of track from Rowsley South to Matlock which is kept shiny by the preserved locomotives of the Peak Rail enthusiasts' group. In June of every year the organisation's premises at Rowsley South provide the venue for the Peak Park Preserved Bus Gathering, an event which attracts vehicles from all of the former 'Combine' companies in Derbyshire although those of the local independents are a distinct rarity given the number of survivors of the Silver Service fleet in particular. This is not, of course, a criticism of the organisers who do an excellent job of providing a good day out. One thing that can (usually) be seen at the event is a modern(ish!) vehicle of the 'new' version of Hulleys of Baslow. Their buses are now painted blue rather than the traditional red, but their presence is a very welcome reminder of the local pioneers who brought regular bus services to tiny villages for the very first time. Many of those villages retain those services to the present day.

Bull of Tideswell

Tideswell never had a railway station of its own, the closest stopping point being at Millers Dale some two and a half miles to the south. This opened in 1863 and was on the Midland Railway's main-line from Manchester (Central) to Bakewell, Matlock, Derby, and London. There was a frequent shuttle-service between Millers Dale and Buxton along a spur which was also used by some of the long-distance trains. From the earliest days the George Hotel in Tideswell offered a connection by horse and trap to the station, originally just for its guests but soon made available to local residents as well. A 1905 guide-book reveals that full board at the George then cost 10 shillings (50p) per day or three pounds, seven shillings and sixpence (£3.38 in post-decimal currency) for a week. This was more than twice as much as the next most expensive option and compared with the rates of all but the very best hotels in Buxton. The fare from The George to Millers Dale was four pence (less than two new pence) and the service then operated 'between four and six times daily'.

The horse-drawn conveyances became larger as time progressed; rail fares became more affordable, and people's horizons wider. After the end of the First World War the service made use of motor-buses although no record has been found of the earliest examples – one correspondent mentioned a 14-seat Chevrolet but this has not been traced. When Road Service Licences were introduced in the wake of the 1930 Road Traffic Act it was realised (somewhat belatedly) that the hotel would need to apply for one. The new Traffic Commissioners were unwilling to accept an application from 'The George Hotel' and so the application was made by the (then current) licensee of the premises, Mr J Buckley. Predictable objections were mounted by North Western and Sheffield JOC on the grounds that their jointly operated Buxton-Sheffield service covered almost the entire mileage of the 'station bus' route, but

these were quickly dismissed on the grounds of 'grandfather rights' (The George Hotel's service pre-dated theirs by nearly six decades) and public utility (the local service was timed to connect with actual train departures rather than just happening to pass the station at two-hourly intervals). Another consideration was that the last departure from Buxton on the Sheffield service departed at 8.30pm while Tideswell locals intent on more extended entertainment could leave Buxton at 11pm on the shuttle train and find the station bus waiting to take them home.

The first Buckley vehicle to appear in the PSV Circle's records was FNU 920, a Bedford WTB with Duple C26F bodywork bought new in July 1938 and possibly replacing the unidentified Chevrolet. The stage carriage service was suspended in 1941 for the duration of the war and the WTB found alternative employment on a new contract service for the American film-maker Columbia Studios. The film company's central distribution depot in London had been evacuated to the rural idyll of Cressbrook Hall and a small fleet of lorries were based there to take new releases to cinemas all over the country. Columbia's staff members were lodged in private homes in Tideswell, Ashford, and Longstone and Buckley ran a Monday to Saturday journey through those villages to and from Cressbrook.

Up to this point the George Hotel licensees had shown little interest in the private-hire market as their solitary vehicle had been engaged upon the Millers Dale service (before 1941) or the Cressbrook contract thereafter. Capitalism abhors a vacuum, so a new operator emerged in Tideswell in the mid-1930s to cater for the village's coaching needs. This was HD Andrew of Fountain Square Garage, who built up a fleet of four Dodge coaches in the pre-war years. Andrew's business prospered on weekdays by operating works services to Litton Mill and to the enormous quarries at Tunstead, while on summer Saturdays the firm provided a non-stop contract service from Millers Dale station to the 'Holiday Homes' at Great Hucklow – a collection of wooden chalets popular with frugally minded visitors. None of these services was available to the general public.

For undiscovered reasons two additional vehicles were licensed to Mr Buckley during 1944. The more interesting of the two was ARA 889, a

Vehicles of Hulley and White were often to be found together at Grindleford Station. This image shows Hulley's Bedford OB/Duple coach BRN 61 awaiting departure for Baslow alongside White's OB/Duple coach KWB 334, bound for Eyam. *(Omnibus Society - Roy Marshall)*

Photographs of any (pre-1967) vehicles belonging to Bull of Tideswell were also as rare as hens' teeth, and this is the only usable image which could be found. Bedford SB5/Plaxton Embassy II coach 3633 R was new to Bull in April 1963 and gave more than 13 years of service before passing to an operator in Middlesbrough. *(Trevor Weckert Collection)*

Leyland KP2 Cub with a Weymann B20F body new to Chesterfield Corporation in October 1934. In 1939 the vehicle was requisitioned for use as a canteen by ARP (Air Raid Precautions) personnel but by 1944 the Luftwaffe was beaten and the Cub was allocated to Buckley. The other addition in that year was JU 3903, a Bedford WLB with Duple C20F bodywork new to Robinson of Burbage in Leicestershire in March 1934. It came to Buckley from its second owner, Bell of Chapel-en-le-Frith.

Meanwhile, Mr George William Bull (born in 1902) had started his driving career by delivering lorry loads of milk churns to Manchester for a farmer in Peak Forest. During the great depression of the 1930s he bought the lorry from the hard-pressed farmer and moved it to a new base in the old stables area of the George Hotel in Tideswell, now a garage for motor vehicles including the pub bus. When Mr Buckley decided to retire in June 1945 the brewery offered the bus service and the associated vehicles to Mr Bull. The second-hand WLB had already been sold (in January 1945), leaving the new proprietor with the WTB and the Cub. These survivors were quickly joined by JNU 619, a Bedford OWB/Duple utility bus new in July 1945 (and presumably ordered by Mr Buckley), and two ageing Gilford 168OT buses, FW 1160, with Wycombe bodywork and FW 2066 with Strachan bodywork. The Gilfords had started life with Cleethorpes Corporation in 1930/31 and both had gone by the end of 1946.

The two dilapidated Gilfords were replaced by a single vehicle, 1932 Dennis Lancet JA 2234, which had been new to North Western and carried an ECOC B31R body. The burgeoning fleet remained at four vehicles until July 1948 when a new Bedford OB with SMT C27F bodywork, MRA 315, was delivered to Tideswell. The next arrival was also new but was an Austin CXB with Mann Egerton Norfolk C31F bodywork, NRB 737, delivered in October 1949. It replaced the pre-war Cub which had finally expired seven months earlier. The following two years saw the purchase of a pair of Bedford OBs with Duple Vista C29F bodywork, ORB 767 in January 1950 and PNU 406 in March 1951. The latter was one of the last OBs to be built.

The Dennis Lancet had gone by the end of 1951, resulting in a fleet of five Bedfords (a WTB, an OWB, and three OBs) plus the Austin CXB. This expanding collection could no longer be housed at The George Hotel and in 1953 Mr Bull bought the Anchor Inn, a pub on the main Chapel-en-le-Frith to Chesterfield road just to the north of the village. The Anchor came with several outbuildings and some farmland and George's two sons, George Jr and Ron, made the revival of the farm their priority while George Sr ran the pub and the coaches.

Across the road from the Anchor Inn was a filling station known as the Anchor Garage, and when HD Andrew's coach fleet out-grew his original premises on Fountain Square he moved there to (literally) face the competition head on. According to Mrs Joyce Bull (the widow of Ron) her father-in-law was not pleased by this development. Andrew added insult to injury for a while by using the fleet-name 'Anchor Coaches' for his red and cream vehicles. Despite the antagonism between the two proprietors, Ron Bull later drove for Andrew's on a part-time basis.

Tideswell is a relatively small village, and the hamlets around it are even smaller, so competition for local private-hire work must have been intense. Nevertheless both firms continued to trade and to order brand-new coaches. Bull's first Bedford SB with Duple Vega C33F bodywork, SNU 84, arrived in September 1952 and replaced both of the 1950/51 OBs. Andrew's first SB, a second-hand example with Plaxton bodywork, arrived in the following year to restore the competitive equilibrium. The next acquisition by Bull was a Bedford OB with Yeates C29F bodywork, LRB 284, which arrived from neighbouring White of Calver (qv) in March 1952 but was re-sold to a Shropshire operator only three months later. The two Tideswell firms were also competing for contract work and buying older vehicles specifically for this purpose. Andrew bought a pair of 1933/34 vintage TS6 Tiger buses, new to Chesterfield, while Bull invested in a 1937 TS7 Tiger with a Roe B32F body, BTF 574, new to LUT but acquired from an operator in Newcastle-upon-Tyne in May 1954, and a 1938 TS8 Tiger with post-war Trans-United C33F bodywork, DHN 810, acquired from a dealer in March 1955. The pre-war WTB had been withdrawn from use in November 1953 and the 1948 OB sold in March 1955, so the fleet at the end of 1955 was made up of two Bedfords (the OWB and the SB), the Austin CXB, and the two pre-war Tigers.

In early 1956 the Tiger coach was sold to Elliot

of Sheffield. The Tiger bus went in December. Other departures during the year included the 1945 OWB (which went for use as a mobile shop in March), the 1952 SB (part-exchanged for two newer models in June of that year) and the 1949 Austin (sold for further use in *Ghana* in December). The two brand-new vehicles delivered in June 1956 were Bedford SBGs with Duple Super Vega C41F bodywork registered 725/773 BRB. The Austin was replaced by JRA 580, a 1946 Bedford OB/Duple Vista coach acquired from Pashley of Bradwell (qv) and this became the rostered vehicle on the Millers Dale run. The fleet was further reinforced by the acquisition of 1955 Bedford SBG/Burlingham C36F RVM 35 from a Scottish operator in June 1958, but numbers soon began to dwindle again when the OB's engine seized in June 1959. As a stop-gap measure RVM 35 became the regular vehicle on the Millers Dale service until it was sold in March 1960, traded in along with Duple-bodied sister 725 BRB as part payment for two new SB3s with the newer style of Super Vega bodywork and registered 969 MRB and 634 NRA. The remaining 1956 SBG, 773 BRB, then became the rostered vehicle for Millers Dale.

In March 1963 it was time for 773 BRB to move on, replaced by a brand-new (diesel powered) Bedford SB5 with Plaxton Embassy II bodywork, with the unusual registration of 3633 R. Few counties issued 'reversed' registration marks incorporating a single letter. The next three arrivals were even more exciting. First came two 1961 AEC Reliances with Duple Britannia C41F bodywork, 417/420 BLW, acquired from Global of London W1 in April 1964. They were the first 'heavyweight' vehicles in the fleet for eight years and 1960 SB3/Super Vega 634 NRA was given in part exchange. The next arrival was an even bigger surprise. NCD 98 was a Leyland-Beadle with Beadle coach bodywork, its running units recycled from pre-war vehicles to the order of Southdown Motor services in 1954. It turned up in Tideswell in July 1964 and remained in service for two years, usually on what was left of the Millers Dale service.

By September 1964 the stage service had withered away to one journey in each direction, Monday to Friday only, leaving Tideswell at 7.55am and returning from Millers Dale at 6pm. These details are taken from the last known timetable (a single typed sheet) which carries the curious assertion that 'this is not an official timetable'! By that date the Anchor Inn had been sold on to others and the firm's address is given as 'Anchor Farm', while its activities are advertised as including general haulage and vehicle maintenance as well as coach hire.

Another interesting vehicle arrived in February 1966. AEC Reliance/Weymann Fanfare coach KDB 627 had been new to North Western ten years previously and spent two years in Tideswell before migrating to Butter of Childs Ercall. The other arrival in 1966 was a brand-new Bedford VAM5 with Duple Bella Venture bodywork, KRB 40D, delivered in April.

The Beeching Report proposed the closure of hundreds of rural railway stations, Millers Dale among them. The axe fell on the 6th of March 1967. It is believed that Bull's service had finished some time before that date but details have proven impossible to find. Two months later the firm became a limited company as GW Bull (Transport) Ltd and in the following year the registered address moved from Anchor Farm to Craven House, Manchester Road, Tideswell. Coaching activities continued for another 20 years from the new address, using a mixture of brand-new Bedfords and second-hand Ford R1014s. There was also a second-hand Bristol LHL6L/Plaxton coach, OXB 399H, acquired in 1971. The firm briefly returned to stage carriage work in the 1980s, providing a (subsidised) minibus service alongside the Derwent Valley reservoirs in conjunction with Halliday-Hartle of Buxton.

George Bull Sr died in 1988 and the family then sold their coaching operations to White of Calver (qv). White's retained the business as a subsidiary until 1993 when it was merged into the parent company. The Bull name survived in GW Bull Ltd, formed in May 1991 to administer the family's farming interests. George Jr and his wife Mavis remained as directors of this company until July 2002 when Anchor Farm was sold and GW Bull Ltd ceased to trade. GW Bull's old rivals at Andrew's Coaches are still doing well and their vehicles can be found on a variety of work ranging from European tours to schools services and rail replacement contracts.

Hulley of Baslow

At the time of the 1901 census Henry Hulley of Baslow, age 27, was employed as a member of the landscape gardening staff on the Chatsworth Estate which occupied an enormous acreage immediately to the south of the village. Chatsworth House, at the centre of the estate, was the palatial seat of the Duke of Devonshire but was also open for tours by the general public on a daily basis. This was quite unusual in the first decade of the 20th century – most of the large country houses were first opened to the public between the two world wars. Some of the richer (and more daring) visitors arrived by motor-car and for Henry Hulley it was love at first sight. He resolved to find a job which would enable him to drive for a living.

The 1911 census reflects this decision. Hulley is listed as a 'motor car driver' and was working for the Baslow Grand Hotel & Hydro. This structure had been built on a hilltop to the north of the village in the 1880s and had accommodation for 150 guests. For an additional charge the hotel offered to collect its guests from railway stations as far away as Chesterfield, but this service was only available to its clients and not to the people of Baslow. Hulley sensed an opportunity and in 1914 he left the Hydro, bought a five-seat Ford Model T taxi, and set himself up in business in a yard at the back of the Peacock Hotel. Things went well and two French-built Darracq taxis soon arrived, helping to provide an income for Henry's large family. His wife Mary produced a total of nine children, in order of their birth James (1895), Gladys (1897), Thomas (1899), Phyllis (1900), Lillian (1904), Lancelot (1905), Nina (1907), John – known as Jack (1910), and Benjamin (1912). All but one became involved in the business at some stage in their lives. Their father added another source of income to the family's coffers in 1917 when he became the licensee of the Rutland Hotel in Baslow and the taxis were then housed in the yard of this establishment.

Many of Hulley's taxi hires involved trips to Chesterfield and back, and on the 29th of April 1921 he started a regularly timetabled service to the town to increase the potential number of passengers. This initially operated on Mondays, Thursdays, and Saturdays only and for the first two weeks was operated by the taxi fleet while Hulley awaited the arrival of his first real bus, a 14-seat Ford Model T registered R 6716. Demand was high, but the traffic flow tended to be 'tidal' with morning journeys to Chesterfield and late afternoon journeys from Chesterfield by far the busiest. To overcome this Hulley extended the route at the western end to Bakewell which made the service even more popular. Additional vehicles were needed quickly and the firm improvised by converting one of the Darracq taxis (R 633) into a 14-seat bus, and fitting a make-shift 14-seat charabanc body to an unidentified chassis which had previously been used as a goods vehicle.

It was soon clear that something more suitable was needed and in October 1922 the firm acquired a 20-seat Daimler CB bus, XM 1680, from a London dealer. The Daimler was named 'The Derwent' after the river which ran through Baslow. It was soon discovered that the vehicle was too large to manoeuvre into the yard of the Rutland Hotel, and Henry Hulley decided that the time had come to move both house and business. He acquired a tract of land on Calver Road and built a new residence for his large family ('Derwent House') and a corrugated iron shelter for his vehicles. When the fleet expanded still further another plot of land on the opposite side of the road was bought to provide petrol pumps ('Derwent Garage') and additional space for the bus fleet. Nobody could deny that the Hulleys were doing very well for themselves.

The next vehicle acquisition came in June 1923 when Hulley bought a Maudslay 'Subsidy' lorry chassis registered U 9108 from a government surplus auction and had it fitted with a 20-seat bus body. It is believed that most of Hulley's earliest buses (including the Maudslay) were bodied by Woodiwiss, a local carpenter. Another 'structurally amended' vehicle followed in the shape of Daimler CC type W 3500. The chassis of this machine had been new to Sheffield Corporation in 1913 and originally equipped with an open top double-deck body built by Dodson. In 1921 that body was removed and replaced by a single-deck B20F body bought from Northern General, the revised version passing to Hulley in May 1924. In early 1925 the Bakewell-Baslow-Chesterfield service was further extended at the Bakewell end to serve the villages of Youlgreave and Middleton-by-Youlgreave. The opportunity arose as the previous operator, Edward Machin, had abandoned his service from Bakewell to Youlgreave.

CX 3637, a Daimler CJK, with a rather brutal 22-seat char-a-banc body, was first registered in Huddersfield in 1919. No trace of its early career has been found, but by July 1926 it was in service with Hulley of Baslow. The vehicle lasted until the end of 1929. *(Henry Hulley & Sons)*

AEC Regal/Duple C32F coach FNU 190 was new to Hulley in June 1938 as fleet number 11. Originally fitted with a petrol engine, it received a 7.7 litre AEC diesel in 1950 and was 'up-seated' to 35. Sold to a dealer in November 1957, it found no further use. *(Robin Hannay)*

A newer version of the AEC Regal/Duple coach combination was delivered to Hulley in May 1947 as KRA 939, fleet number 25. Fitted with a diesel engine from new, it was withdrawn in December 1960 and ended its days in a scrapyard at Wombwell. *(Robin Hannay)*

Leyland TS7 Tiger EEH 132 was new to PMT in 1937 and carried a Weymann B32F body. In 1949 it received a new Burlingham B35F body and in June 1957 passed to Hulley of Baslow as fleet number 20. Withdrawn in November 1962, it was later scrapped. *(John Holmes)*

A new marque entered the fleet in November 1925 when a 20-seat 1922 vintage Thornycroft BT bus, EH 3767, was acquired from Jenks of Smallthorne in Staffordshire. This effectively replaced the original Ford 14-seater, although that vehicle remained available for use until July 1926. That month saw the arrival of CX 3637, a 1919 Daimler CK which had been fitted with a 22-seat char-a-banc body. Compared to most of Hulley's vehicles it had a brief stay in Baslow, being sold for scrap in December 1929.

Tragedy and Triumph

During the winter of 1926/7 Henry Hulley's wife Mary became seriously ill. She died in May 1927 at the age of 56. The sad loss seemed to increase Henry's already considerable determination to succeed in business. In January 1927 the first brand-new bus since the original Ford Model T had arrived in Baslow. RA 1386 was an AEC model 202 with United B25F bodywork. More new vehicles followed. The 1928 delivery was RA 5551, an ADC 407 with a United B29F body, which arrived in April. In March 1929 the choice was RA 8058, a Maudslay ML3B with a United B32R body, while March 1930 saw the arrival of a similar Maudslay, RB 962, but on this occasion with Northern Counties B32F bodywork.

In December 1930 Henry Hulley acquired the business of Stanley Eades, Baslow. Eades, who was related to the Hulleys by marriage, had been operating an Eyam-Baslow-Chesterfield service since at least 1928 using a 14-seat Ford. By 1929 the service was operating on a daily basis and becoming a nuisance to Mr Eades' in-laws. Hulleys had no need for the vehicle, which was disposed of privately, but the stage service was retained and extended westwards to Tideswell. Stanley Eades took employment with Hulleys as a driver, continuing as such until 1941. Twenty years later his grandson would become a driver with the firm, but that story will be told later in the narrative.

With Hulleys first appearance before the new Traffic Commissioners imminent, the company ordered two more brand-new vehicles for 1931 delivery. A Leyland LT2 Lion with Northern Counties B32F bodywork, RB 3592, arrived in February and Leyland KP2 Cub/Willowbrook B20F RB 5302 in November. The Traffic Commissioners were suitably impressed and

Hulleys received licences for the Middleton-Bakewell-Baslow-Chesterfield service, the Tideswell-Eyam-Baslow-Chesterfield route, and for a third (Saturday only) service from the village of Freebirch to Chesterfield.

Meanwhile, the Baslow Grand Hotel & Hydro, Henry Hulley's old employer, had closed in 1930. It was demolished in 1936. The closure of the Hydro had little impact on Hulley's business as the dozens of staff thrown out of work tended to find new jobs in Chesterfield or Bakewell. Those passengers who had previously commuted into Baslow were easily replaced by those now forced to commute out of the village.

Second-hand vehicles were favoured in 1933 and 1934. A two year old Commer Invader with Willowbrook B20F bodywork, RB 4463, was acquired in 1933, while the 1927 AEC was replaced in April 1934 by a third Maudslay ML3B. The Maudslay, UT 8075, was a 1930 example with Willowbrook B32F bodywork and came from Victory of Ibstock. Shortly after its arrival Hulley's vehicles received fleet numbers for the first time. RA 5551/RA 8058/RB 962 became Nos 1-3, UT 8075 was No 4, RB 4463 No 5, and RB 3592/RB 5302 Nos 6/7. A new Commer B3 with a stylish Waveney FC25F coach body, BRR 41, was acquired from a dealer in July 1935 and became fleet number 8.

In March 1936 RA 5551 was replaced by a new No 1 in the shape of a second-hand 1933 Bedford WLB with Willowbrook B20F bodywork, RB 8005. A month later the first use of fleet number 9 came with the arrival of a brand-new AEC Regal with Park Royal B32F bodywork, CRA 162. The third acquisition of 1936 was UA 8548, a 1929 Maudslay ML3B with Barnaby bodywork, bought from Lancashire & Yorkshire of Shafton for spares use only. Its arrival helped to keep the two Hulley's Maudslays running well into the war years. A pair of second-hand machines were added to the fleet during 1937. One was another Bedford WLB bus, but on this occasion with a Duple 20-seat body. ATC 56, a 1935 example, came from Fairclough of Lostock and replaced RB 4463 as fleet number 5. It was later given fleet number 2 to place it next to the other WLB. The other arrival was XJ 5942, a 1932 Tiger TS4 coach with a Harrington body, acquired from Osborne of Manchester and allocated fleet number 10.

On the 25th of January 1938 the business was formally incorporated as Henry Hulley & Sons Ltd. Previously a sole proprietorship, the directors now included Henry's two oldest sons, James and Thomas. The summer of that year saw two more arrivals. These were both brand-new AEC Regal coaches with Duple bodywork and had originally been ordered by Hills of West Bromwich. At the last minute Hills decided it no longer needed them and sold them to Hulleys. The first, FNU 190, arrived in June and became fleet number 11. The other arrived two months later having already been registered in West Bromwich as EA 9676 and was given fleet number 12.

The Second World War

In February 1939 the company bought a 1937 Bedford WTB/Duple coach from Walker of Oldham. CTC 38 inherited fleet number 8 from Commer BRR 41 which was then sold to Bere Regis & District. A far more important acquisition took place in May 1939 when Hulleys bought the business of Maurice Kenyon of Grindleford. Kenyon held licences for a daily service from Grindleford railway station to Baslow and for a market-day (Monday) route from Grindleford to Bakewell via Eyam and Calver. The purchase also brought two more vehicles into the Hulley fleet, 1932 Commer Centaur/Willowbrook bus TL 2241 (which became the new fleet number 3) and 1938 Bedford WTB/Duple C26F ERB 288. The latter was operated without a fleet number for a few months, but became No 9 after the Regal bus which had previously borne this number was requisitioned by the government for use at the Royal Ordnance Depot in Chilwell. It never returned.

Regal CRA 162 was not the only vehicle to be 'called up' for war service. In December 1940 Regal No 12 (EA 9676) left Baslow for the duration to serve with the War Department as an ambulance. The 'duration' in this case was rather extended as the vehicle finally came back in August 1949! It was also in poor condition and needed work (and was given a diesel engine) before re-entering service in April 1950 as fleet number 29.

The first arrival after the start of hostilities was CHX 834, a 1935 Regal II with Harrington DP36R bodywork, acquired in April 1940 as Hulleys new No 12. The vehicle had originally been an AEC demonstrator but came to Baslow from Gorseinon & District in Wales. A machine with more local origins followed in December. TV 8971 (Hulleys No 14) was a Brush-bodied AEC Regal 4 bus which had been new to Dutton's Unity of Nottingham in 1933. It then passed to Trent before being allocated to Hulleys.

May 1941 brought two more additions in the shape of Tiger TS6/Burlingham coaches TJ 8656/8657 (Hulleys Nos 19/20). These had been new in 1935 to Ashworth Heys of Accrington. As might be noted Hulleys fleet numbering had become less sequential than previously, perhaps to confuse German spies. The first arrival in 1942, a third Bedford WTB/Duple coach, took the more logical fleet number 7 to position it next to the other two already in the fleet. The unfortunately registered BAD 545 (new in 1936) came from Edwards of Lydbrook in July. A month later an ex-Ribble TS2 Tiger/Leyland C30F coach of 1929 vintage, CK 4101, arrived at Baslow and became fleet number 17.

All three acquisitions during 1943 were AEC Regals, and all three arrived in March. Two were coaches. JD 1382 (Hulleys No 15) had been new to the London Co-op in 1930 and had originally carried a Beadle C32F body. This had been replaced by a Harrington C32F body from an unknown source before it entered service at Baslow. GF 572 (Hulleys No 24!) was also a 1930 machine but had been new to Green Line Coaches in London. Its original Shorts C27R body was in an advanced state of decay and Hulleys equipped it with a 1937 Burlingham C32F body before placing it into service. The third Regal, which carried the registration plate TX 7838, was even more interesting. The vehicle was a 1931 example with a Park Royal B32F body and from the registration had seemingly been new to an operator in South Wales. War Department records were vague on this point, and we will return to this subject later in the narrative. The mystery Regal became Hulleys fleet number 13.

The final arrival during the war years was an AEC Regal 4, WX 5613, which had been new to Severn of Stainforth in 1930 and originally equipped with a Burlingham bus body. It received a Brush B35F body lifted from a Trent Daimler COG5/40, before entering service at Baslow as No 16. Henry Hulley seemed to have a knack for acquiring replacement bodies despite the shortage of such items during the war years.

This Guy Arab III with a Burlingham B35F body, LHN 574, was new to Darlington Triumph Services in February 1949. It passed with that business into the ownership of Durham District Services, and then to Hulley of Baslow in May 1959 as fleet number 27. Hulley kept it until August 1965. *(John Holmes)*

Sentinel STC4/40, NDE 555, was only two years younger than the Arab above but a world away in appearance and perceived modernity. New to Morrison of Tenby in August 1951, it came to Hulley of Baslow in July 1959 as fleet number 16 and was the company's first underfloor-engined bus. It stayed for exactly five years before departing to a scrapyard. *(John Holmes)*

Bedford OB/Duple Vista coach JNN 174 was new to Barton of Chilwell in 1947. They fitted it with a Perkins P6 diesel engine in 1951 and then sold it to Thomas of North Muskham in April 1957. The vehicle passed to Hulley in March 1960 as fleet number 6, and remained in service until August 1969. It was then scrapped. *(Chris Rischer Collection)*

RC 9673 was one of a large batch of AEC Regal I buses with Willowbrook B35F bodies delivered to Trent in 1947. In November 1960 Hulley bought the vehicle, gave it fleet number 14, and kept it for eight years before selling it for scrap. *(Chris Rischer Collection)*

The Late 1940s

By the start of 1946 Hulleys (like every other operator in the country) was desperate for vehicles. Many of the machines in the fleet were well beyond their best and in need of replacement, while the post-war travel boom offered substantial profits to any operator with the equipment available. Hulleys first purchase after the end of the war came in January 1946 when Regal VO 5457 was acquired from Wetton & Sons of Brimington. This vehicle had been new to Retford Coachways in 1931, originally as a Taylor-bodied bus. It passed with the business to East Midland in 1935 and in 1939 they replaced the body with a Leyland B35R unit removed from another vehicle. In 1945 the Regal received its third body, a Brush C30F unit transferred to it from yet another East Midland machine, and was then sold to Wetton. It gave four years to Hulley as fleet number 5.

The next arrival, a month later, had a more straightforward pedigree. HL 7510 was a Tiger TS7 with Roe B32F bodywork, new to West Riding in 1936. Originally fitted with a torque converter (making it a TS7c), this feature was removed by Hulleys before the vehicle was placed into service as fleet number 21. In May 1946 another vehicle arrived from Ribble in the form of 1933 Tiger TS6/Leyland C30R coach CK 4722. It became fleet number 18.

Henry Hulley was also looking to expand outside of the firm's traditional area. In June 1946 Hulleys bought the business of Sellars & Kent (trading as Green Bus Service), based at Ilam in Dovedale and thus just inside Staffordshire. The acquisition gave Hulleys licences from Ilam to Ashbourne via Dovedale (daily), Ilam to Ashbourne via Blore (Thursday/Saturday), Iam to Leek via Waterhouses (Wednesday), and brought a 1936 all-Dennis Arrow Minor coach (CRA 72) into the fleet as No 4. The Dennis failed to impress and was sold in March 1947.

The final additions in 1946 were a pair of 1929 vintage TS2 Tigers acquired in July. DB 5299 and DB 5305 (Hulleys fleet numbers 22/23) had been new to North Western and originally carried 26-seat Leyland bodies. In 1931 they were prematurely sold and ended up with Midland Bus Service of Airdrie. Midland was absorbed into Western SMT in the following year and in 1943 that company fitted the two Tigers with Alexander C32F bodies which is how they were equipped

when Hulleys bought them from a dealer. No 22 never ran in service but the other lasted until 1953.

In early 1947 two of the pre-war Regals (TV 8971 and TX 7838) had their existing bodies removed and replaced by a pair of 1943 Burlingham B34F units The 'new' bodies came from Tiger TS11s delivered to Yelloway of Rochdale just before they sold their Manchester stage service to the local corporations – the TS11s received brand-new coach bodies in their place. The first complete vehicle acquired during 1947 was also the first Albion to be operated by Hulleys. Albion PW67/Brush B32F bus JX 1400 had been new to Hebble of Halifax in 1934, later passing to Walton & Helliwell of Mytholmroyd before moving on to Hulleys in February 1947. Its reign as fleet number 3 was relatively brief as it was sold in December 1948.

The next arrival was Hulley's first brand-new vehicle of the post-war era. KRA 939 (fleet number 25) was a Regal I with a Duple C35F body and was delivered in May 1947. The only purchase during 1948 was VO 5603, a 1931 Regal with Brush B32F bodywork. New to East Midland, it moved to Wetton & Sons of Brimington in 1945 and thence to Hulleys in October 1948 as fleet number 4. A far more significant event in 1948 was the introduction of route numbers for the first time. The Youlgreave-Bakewell-Baslow-Chesterfield service took the number 1, and the Tideswell-Eyam-Baslow-Chesterfield run became the number 2. The Saturday only service from Freebirch to Chesterfield was the number 3, while the former Kenyon services from Grindleford to Baslow and Bakewell became the 4 and 5 respectively. The routes acquired from Sellars & Kent became the 6 (Ashbourne via Dovedale), 7 (Leek via Waterhouses), and 8 (Ashbourne via Blore).

There were four purchases during 1949. The first two were a pair of 1947 Bedford OB/ Duple coaches acquired from Scout of Preston in February. BCK 800 and BRN 61 became Hulley's fleet numbers 27 and 28 until renumbered as 7 and 8 in 1959. They remained in the fleet until 1963/64. The third arrival was a brand-new Guy Arab III equipped with a powerful Meadows 6DC engine and stylish Windover Huntingdon C33F bodywork. Its registration, NEH 155, revealed that it had originally been ordered from a Stoke-on-Trent dealership by Butter of Childs Ercall.

Their loss became Hulleys gain, with fleet number 26 becoming the pride of the company's coaching fleet for many years. It was finally withdrawn in November 1962. The last arrival of 1949 (in December) was another refugee from West Riding. Tiger TS8/Roe B32F bus HL 9088 had been new to that company in 1939 and became Hulley's No 22. Like the earlier TS7 it had its torque converter removed before going into service at Baslow, and remained in use until 1965.

Into the 1950s

Surprisingly, there were no fleet additions whatsoever in 1950 and 1951. As already mentioned, AEC Regal EA 9676 returned to service in April 1950, carrying new fleet number 29. It survived until April 1959, two years longer than its twin FNU 190. One of the reasons for the lull in vehicle purchases was the poor performance of the former Sellars & Kent services. Ilam was a tiny village, and although very popular with tourists in fine summer weather the buses were often devoid of passengers (even local people) on rainy winter days. To make things worse Ilam had two local operators with Warrington's competing for every passenger although by a different route. Henry Hulley and his children could see the problem – much of the money being made in Baslow was being thrown down the drain in Dovedale – but decided to persevere for a little while longer.

The company's first purchase of the new decade came in February 1952 when a nine year old Bedford OWB arrived at Baslow. New to Bullock of Featherstone, HL 9973 passed with that business to West Riding in 1950. By then the interior of its 'utility' Roe body had received 28 padded seats in place of the 32 wooden ones. Hulleys gave it fleet number 6 and it spent most of its time at Ilam depot, being suitable for one-man-operation. The rest of the year was uneventful except for some small changes to the route network. Service 3 was revised to run from Baslow, offering villagers in Freebirch and other communities along the route an opportunity to shop in Bakewell (by changing to service 1 at Baslow) rather than just in Chesterfield. At the same time certain journeys on service 4 which ran through Stoney Middleton and Eyam rather than via the direct route became service 9.

In July 1953 it became apparent that one of the pre-war Regals had been operating with the wrong registration marks for more than ten years! The vehicle thought to be TX 7838 (Hulley's fleet number 13) was actually FB 9221 and had been new to Bath Tramways rather than some Welsh operator. This long-standing error was not in any way Hulleys fault – the vehicle had carried the wrong paperwork when it arrived at Baslow – but new registration plates were rapidly fitted to show its true identity.

July also saw the arrival of another pre-war Regal. JX 6582 had been new to Halifax JOC in 1938 and carried a Roe B33R body. The vehicle passed to Corvedale of Ludlow in 1950 and from them to Hulleys. It became the new No 12 and lasted until May 1956. In September 1953 a third Bedford OB joined the fleet, on this occasion a Mulliner-bodied bus. CCT 954 had been new to Sharpe of Heckington in September 1947 and served with Hulleys as fleet number 1 until November 1957.

In January 1954 the loss-making operations based on Ilam were sold to Warrington's of that village along with the Bedford OWB fleet number 6. There were no new vehicles for the operational fleet during 1954 but in April the company bought a former London Transport STL class double-decker, BXD 587, as a source of spares for the remaining pre-war Regals. By the beginning of 1955 everything of any use had been removed and the rest was sent for scrap.

The End of an Era

Henry Hulley died on the 20th of June 1955 at the age of 82, more than 28 years after the death of his beloved wife Mary. The sons and daughter Nina (who never married) were all still active in the business so there was never any doubt that the firm would continue to trade. Two vehicles joined the fleet later in the year. Commer Commando/Plaxton coach EJU 268 arrived in July. It had been new to Howlett of Quorn in 1947, passing to Central Garage of Rutland in 1954 and from them to Hulleys. It became fleet number 4 and lasted until March 1959. The other acquisition was FA 9100, a 1948 Guy Arab III with a Meadows 6DC engine and Guy B35R bodywork. New to Burton-on-Trent Corporation, it had served with two small coach operators in the Birmingham area before arriving at Baslow in October as fleet number 24. It was retired in April 1961.

GAW 672, a Daimler CVD6 with Burlingham Sunsaloon FC33F bodywork, was new to Whittle of Highley in 1950. After spending time with Scarlet Band of West Cornforth, Noble of Sheffield, and Chesher of York, it passed to Hulley in March 1961 as fleet number 17. Withdrawn in November 1965, no further use has been recorded. *(John Holmes Collection)*

BMMO S9 type LHA 358 was fitted with a Brush B40F body when new to Midland Red in 1949. Three years later the body was lengthened by Roe to accommodate 44. Hulleys bought the machine in January 1963 and gave it fleet number 26. In 1965 it became number 20, but two years later received the accident damage shown here. It lingered on in the yard for two more years before being scrapped. Note Bedford tow-truck 149 MRA. *(John Holmes Collection)*

This Bedford SBO with Duple Super Vega C41F bodywork, ODL 48, was delivered to Southern Vectis in 1957. In 1967 it passed to United Counties, and at the end of the following year they sold it to Smaller of Barton-on-Humber. Hulley recovered it from a scrapyard in July 1971, intending to use it as a source of spares, but ended up placing it into service (as fleet number 9) in the summer of 1973. After withdrawal in July 1979 it was sold for preservation but had been scrapped by 1984. *(John Holmes)*

Sheffield's fleet of 30ft Leopards with Weymann bodywork were frequent visitors to the Bakewell/Baslow area and apparently made a favourable impression. Hulley bought many of them as they became available. 6171 WJ, a 1960 Leopard L1 with Weymann Fanfare C41F bodywork passed from Sheffield to Midland Red in April 1970, meaning that it was the right colour when sold on to Hulley as fleet number 18 in August 1971. *(Geoff Lumb)*

Hulley's service numbers 6-8 had vanished with the sale of the Ilam operation to Warrington's, so when a route from Bakewell to Hartington opened in April 1956 it became the 'new' number 6. The service operated on summer Sundays only and followed the number 1 route to Youlgreave but then continued to Friden and Hartington. Through ticketing was offered from Baslow and Chesterfield and the service quickly became popular with hikers and other tourists. The mood of optimism found its physical expression in the purchase of a brand-new Bedford SBG/Duple coach, 402 BRB, which arrived in May 1956 as fleet number 9. The other two arrivals during the year were rather longer in the tooth. In August Hulleys bought a former PMT Tiger TS7 bus with a Brush B36F body from a dealership. Unbeknownst to Hulleys 'HVT 919' (as it proclaimed itself to be) was actually 1935 Tiger BEH 963 which had been the victim of an 'identity swap' while at the dealership. It became fleet number 20. In December it was followed into the fleet by JTB 965, a 1948 Crossley SD42/3 with Trans-United C33F bodywork. This had been new to Barnes of Rawtenstall, later migrating to Scarlet Band in County Durham. In June 1956 it had passed to Castle Coaches of Bolsover who sold it to Hulleys six months later as fleet number 10. It ran until September 1960.

Two more ex-PMT Tigers arrived during 1957. Both were (genuine) 1937 models which had received new Burlingham B35F bodies in 1949. TS8 variant FEH 812 arrived in May and became fleet number 23, while TS7 EEH 132 appeared in June as the new fleet number 20. The 'old' number 20 (the bogus HVT 919) was then returned to its vendor while its two PMT cousins remained at Baslow for another five years. In July another Guy Arab III coach with a Meadows engine joined the fleet in the shape of KTC 511 which (like Hulley's own NEH 155) carried elegant Windover Huntingdon bodywork. New to Harrop of Newton-le-Willows in 1949, the Arab had two further owners before its arrival at Baslow as the new fleet number 25. The 'old' number 25 (KRA 939) was then re-numbered 15. KTC 511 survived until May 1965.

There were no vehicle purchases at all in 1958, but a total of five in 1959. The first arrival, in March, was by far the most impressive. MWJ 197 was an AEC Regal IV coach with 39-seat Windover

Kingsway bodywork, new to Sheffield United Tours in 1950. It was also Hulleys first underfloor-engined vehicle and became fleet number 11, remaining in the fleet until August 1965. The other purchase in March was less ambitious. GJW 884, a Bedford OB with Mulliner DP28F bodywork new to Worthington of Wolverhampton in 1949, was acquired as a source of spares for the existing OBs in the fleet. In many ways 1959 might be considered Hulleys 'classic year' from an enthusiast's viewpoint. May saw the purchase of Arab III/Burlingham bus LHN 574. Unlike the Arab III coaches it had a Gardner 5LW engine and had been new to Darlington Triumph in 1949, passing with that operator to United subsidiary Durham District Services. Hulleys gave it fleet number 27 and it served until August 1965.

One of the company's most famous vehicles was acquired in June 1959. Alexander-bodied Guy Otter coach NTB 403 had started its life with Monk of Leigh in 1951, passing to Knightsbridge of Burnley in December 1954, and then to MacFarlane of Balloch during 1955. Returning to England as Hulley's No 2 it was usually found on service 2 to Tideswell until being withdrawn from use in July 1965. That was not the end of its story. In November 1969 the Otter was returned to active service and was finally retired two years later. The final enthusiasts' delight of the year came in July when Hulleys bought Sentinel STC4/40 bus NDE 555 to become fleet number 16. The company's first underfloor-engined service bus, it had been new to Morrison of Tenby in 1951. In December 1958 it passed to Bellis of Buckley before moving on to Baslow where Hulleys used it until July 1964.

Into the 1960s

The first acquisition of the new decade came in March 1960 when a third Bedford OB/Duple Vista coach joined the fleet as No 6. JNN 174 had been new to Barton Transport in 1947, passing to Thomas of North Muskham ten years later and from them to Hulleys. It outlasted the Scout pair, remaining in use until August 1969. The next arrival (in July) was another underfloor-engined coach in the shape of AEC Reliance/Burlingham Seagull KBN 90, Hulley's fleet number 12. New to Knowles of Bolton in 1956, it stayed at Baslow until August 1970. The final acquisition of the year was something more traditional with local connections. RC 9673, a Willowbrook-bodied AEC Regal I bus, had been new to Trent in 1947. It arrived at Baslow in December 1960 as fleet number 14 and gave eight years of loyal service to the firm.

Three coaches were bought during 1961. In March Daimler CVD6/Burlingham Sunsaloon GAW 672 arrived as fleet number 17 and lasted until November 1965. It had been new to Whittle of Highley in 1950 and Hulleys was its fifth owner. In the following month an Arab III (6LW) with stylish Harrington FC35F bodywork, FCO 187, arrived at Baslow but this was acquired for spares use and never entered service. It had been new to the Basil Williams group in 1949. The final coach purchase of the year, Bedford SB3/Duple TWP 967, went into service in September as fleet number 10. The vehicle had been new to Broadway Coaches in 1957. Hulleys replaced its petrol engine with a Bedford 330 diesel unit in July 1970 (many of the company's other petrol-powered SBs were similarly modified), and then in October 1973 removed its 41 coach seats and replaced them with 40 bus seats. Thus modified the vehicle stayed in service until June 1976.

More well used coaches arrived in 1962, starting with AEC Regal III/Plaxton FC39F NTF 514 in April which replaced KRA 939 as the new fleet number 15. The Regal had been new to Kia Ora of Morecambe in 1952, and Hulleys was its fifth owner (a phrase that could be used for many of the company's purchases in the 1960s). It remained in service until February 1967. The second arrival of the year was also a fully-fronted vehicle built in 1952, PS2/13 Tiger MUP 641 which carried a 37-seat Burlingham Sunsaloon body. It had been new to Wilkinson of Sedgefield, became Hulley's No 22, and stayed until June 1966. The other two purchases made in 1962 were both Bedford SBGs. The older of the two was an early 1953 example with Yeates bodywork, EBV 850, which had been new to Batty-Holt of Blackburn. Like the Tiger/Sunsaloon it arrived in May, becoming fleet number 4 and surviving until February 1969. The other SBG, JCK 826, carried Plaxton Venturer bodywork and had been new to Premier of Preston in 1956. It came to Baslow in June as fleet number 5 and was withdrawn in August 1975.

Something Completely Different

In late 1962 Hulleys decided that it needed to make a comprehensive transition to underfloor-engined vehicles for its service bus fleet. Intent was one thing, availability of suitably cheap vehicles another. With underfloor Leylands and AECs out of its price range the company chose to take the path less trodden. Few independent operators had dared to buy surplus stock from Midland Red as they were powered by engines designed and made by the company itself and had little commonality of parts with those of commercial manufacturers. The unpopularity of the vehicles meant that Hulleys could buy them for little more than scrap value and in early 1963 decided to give them a try. Two were acquired in January, both 44-seaters. HHA 697 (fleet number 20) was an S6 model dating from 1947 while LHA 358 (fleet number 26) was an S9 built in 1949. They were proudly repainted in full Hulley livery and put to work on route number 1. Another S9 from the 1949 batch, LHA 400, arrived in May 1963 as No 19, followed by a 1948 vintage S8, JHA 836, which came to Baslow in June 1964 as fleet number 18 and replaced the Sentinel which went for scrap. The first of the Midland Red buses to be withdrawn was HHA 697 in February 1965. The fleet number 20 was then transferred to LHA 358 so that the remaining trio formed a group in the fleet list. JHA 836 and LHA 358 were withdrawn during 1967, with LHA 400 surviving until August 1968.

Only a month after the arrival of the fourth Midland Red vehicle a machine of more orthodox origins came onto the market at a reasonable price. Yorkshire Traction had started to dispose of its fleet of Brush-bodied Royal Tiger buses, new in 1951, and DHE 348 came to Hulleys as fleet number 23. In May 1965 it was followed by two more examples from the same batch, DHE 350 and 353, which took fleet numbers 24/5. All three lasted until 1968. In June 1965 the company bought FMJ 766 as fleet number 21. This was a PS1/1 Tiger coach delivered to Seamarks of Westoning in 1948 with a half-cab Thurgood body. In 1954 they replaced the original body with a fully-fronted Plaxton FC35F unit and the rebodied vehicle gave good service to Hulleys (especially during the annual Bakewell Shows) until its withdrawal in June 1970. The final purchase of 1965 was DGV 974, a 1952 Bedford

Bedford SBO/Duple (Midland) B42F bus PET 100 was new to Maltby Miners' Home in 1957, passing to Andrew of Sheffield in August 1969 before resale to Wigmore's Excelsior of Dinnington two months later. Hulley bought it in August 1971 as their fleet number 6. Withdrawn from use in October 1979, it passed into preservation in 1980 and was advertised for sale quite recently. Bring it home! *(John Holmes)*

Fanfare 6171 WJ again, in the company of a far more interesting vehicle. BMMO CS5 coach 795 GHA had been new to Midland Red in 1959. It arrived at Baslow in May 1971, initially on hire from Midland Red, but was officially purchased in January 1972 as fleet number 14. Sold in April 1973, it went on to an after-life as a stock-car transporter. *(John Holmes)*

Leopard/Fanfare 1505 WJ was new to Sheffield in 1959 and was sold to Hulley in July 1971 as fleet number 16. Alongside is Bedford SB5/Duple (Northern) Firefly coach BHL 525C, new to West Riding in 1965. It came to Hulley from its third owner, Saxton of Heanor, in September 1973 and received fleet number 15. The Fanfare lasted until May 1976, the Firefly until February 1979. *(John Holmes)*

Plaxton Embassy III bodywork was only available in 1964 and thus much rarer than its two predecessor designs. This example, EVX 325B, was new to Roydonian Coaches and was fitted to a petrol-engined Bedford SB3 chassis. It served with later owners in Rochdale and Salford before acquisition by Hulleys as fleet number 11. They fitted it with a Leyland O.350 diesel (as in the SB8 model) before placing it into service in September 1976. *(John Holmes Collection)*

SB coach with Gurney Nutting bodywork which had been new to Towler of Brandon. It arrived in Baslow in September, was painted up as fleet number 3, but never actually entered service.

There were no additions to the fleet in 1966, and only three 'pre-owned' coaches in 1967/8, so the withdrawal of the last three Midland Red vehicles and all three Yorkshire Traction Royal Tigers meant that very old coaches were operating most of the stage carriage mileage, despite the withdrawal of service 9 during 1967. None of the vehicles which arrived in 1967/8 were particularly suitable for stage work, but were very economical. In August 1967 Bedford SB3/Duple NFV 296 was acquired as fleet number 11. It had been new to Enterprise of Blackpool in 1958 and served with Hulleys until August 1975. The next arrival was equally long-lived. Bedford SB3/Yeates Europa 903 CPT had been delivered to 'Favourite No 2' in County Durham in 1959 and went through another four owners before arriving at Baslow in January 1968 as fleet number 3. It remained in service until October 1975. Hulleys fans waiting for something more interesting were rewarded in April 1968 when the company bought a rare Guy Warrior coach with Plaxton Consort bodywork, JBV 234, which became fleet number 1. The Warrior, new to Batty-Holt of Blackburn in 1957, had gone on to serve with Hopley of Mount Hawke in Cornwall and Webb of Wincle in Cheshire. Hulleys fitted it with a Bedford engine before placing it into service, still in the basic blue and grey colour scheme of Batty-Holt. It finally received the red and grey version of Hulleys livery in early 1969 and gave a total of four years service to the firm. It then disappeared without trace giving rise to persistent rumours that it might still exist somewhere. Check your nearest barn.

Fanfares for the Family

The final decade of family control began with the acquisition of two more Bedford coaches in January 1969. ROU 22, Hulley's fleet number 7, was a Leyland (diesel) engined SB8 with Duple bodywork and had been new to Liss & District in 1957. OBK 310 was of similar age and carried identical bodywork but was an SBG with a Bedford petrol engine. It had been new to Byng of Southsea and became Hulley's No 8. Both machines lasted until July 1973.

On the 22nd of March 1969 Henry Hulley's oldest child, James, passed away at the age of 74. He had been the senior voice in the family's discussions since the founder's death in 1955, a position now assumed by the next oldest of the brothers, Thomas Hulley. After a respectful interval vehicle acquisitions resumed in September 1969 when AEC Reliance/Strachans Everest coach MOR 597 arrived at Baslow to become the new No 15. The Reliance had been new to Aldershot & District in 1954 and came to Hulleys after a short stay with an operator in Ellesmere Port. It ran from Baslow until September 1972. The final acquisition during 1969, Bedford SBG/Duple B40F bus LBL 702, arrived in November as fleet number 4. New in 1955 to the UK Atomic Energy Authority at Harwell, its bodywork had been built at the former Nudd Bros & Lockyer factory a year before the operation moved to Loughborough. The SBG bus survived with Hulleys until September 1973 despite its radioactive past.

In July 1970 service 3 (Baslow-Freebirch-Chesterfield) was withdrawn, having been unprofitable for the best part of a decade. Times were hard. Only one vehicle was bought during 1970, and even that one did not immediately join the operational fleet. Bedford SB1/Yeates Fiesta coach XNV 3 had been new to KW Services of Daventry in 1961 and was sold to Hulleys in March 1970. It was then parked in the yard as a static exhibit until November 1972 when it finally entered service as the new No 2.

The stage carriage network started to expand again during 1971 as the North Western Road Car Co abandoned several of their routes in the Bakewell area. In January Hulleys assumed responsibility for most journeys between Bakewell and Over Haddon using service number 11 (the record shows no use of the service number 10 by the company), and in December replaced North Western on school-day journeys from Bakewell to Tideswell and Saturday workings along the same route as far as Monsal Head. North Western had used the service numbers 185/186, but Hulleys preferred the number 12.

Thomas Hulley died on the 6th of April 1971 at the age of 71. With the two oldest brothers now gone control of the business passed to a triumvirate of Jack, Benjamin, and their sister Nina who had served as company secretary for many years. Despite the loss of Thomas the firm seemed to experience a revival of its fortunes during the year as routes which had made a loss for North Western proved to be profitable for Hulleys. The first vehicle to arrive was in a way a tribute to Thomas who had been a strong advocate of the Midland Red 'S type' purchases. 795 GHA came from the same source but was a C5 coach, very few of which 'escaped into the wild' when Midland Red had finished with them. It arrived at Baslow in May (operating 'on loan' until Hulleys officially bought it in January 1972) and became fleet number 14, retaining its basic Midland Red livery. After withdrawal in April 1973 it was sold for use as a stock car transporter. The next arrival was quite mundane by comparison. Bedford SBO/Duple coach ODL 48 had been new to Southern Vectis in 1957 and then served with United Counties in 1967/8 before passing to a Lincolnshire coach operator and then to Hulleys in July 1971. Originally earmarked for use as a source of spares, it was found to be in better condition than had been thought and eventually joined the operational fleet in August 1973 as No 9. Two years later its 37 coach seats were replaced by 40 bus seats and it remained a regular performer on the stage services until its sale to a preservationist in July 1979. Sadly, in the long term, it did not survive.

Another purchase in July 1971 provoked little comment at the time but proved to be a portent of things to come. The new arrival was 1505 WJ, a 1959 Leyland L1 Leopard with Weymann Fanfare C41F bodywork, and it came from Sheffield's 'B' fleet. Vehicles from this part of the Sheffield inventory were used quite frequently on the 'C' fleet services as well, so the coach had frequently passed through Baslow (and Tideswell) with its original owner. Hulleys gave it fleet number 16. The surprise came in the following month when Hulleys bought five more ex-Sheffield Fanfares from their second owner, Midland Red. These were 1960 machines registered 6170-4 WJ and received fleet numbers 17-21. No 19 never entered service and was used as a source of spares, while No 21 entered the active fleet rather belatedly in February 1973. The five operational Fanfares were withdrawn from use between 1975 and 1978 having filled a sizeable hole in the company's armoury of equipment.

August 1971 also witnessed the arrival of one of Hulleys best-known vehicles of the era. PET 100 was a Bedford SBO with Duple (Midland) B42F bodywork and received fleet number 6. New to the Maltby Miners Home Transport in 1957, it had seen further use with Excelsior Coaches of Dinnington before turning up at Baslow. 'Pet', as it was usually known, replaced the Guy Otter as the regular vehicle on the Tideswell route but also appeared on the remaining Grindleford services. Three months after its arrival the Otter was sold for preservation, but fate was cruel and this marvellous machine ended up as scrap metal. 'Pet' remained in service until October 1979 when it too was sold to a preservationist and is believed to survive, having been offered for sale as recently as 2014.

After nine additions to the fleet in 1971 it was unremarkable that few were made during 1972. Two vehicles arrived in April. Leyland L1 Leopard/Burlingham DP41F 5906 W, new in 1961, was another refugee from the Sheffield 'B' fleet and became Hulley's fleet number 22. The second acquisition was another of Hulleys 'celebrity' vehicles. 2626 UP was a Bedford SB5 with a modified chassis and a Yeates Pegasus B45F body, new to Armstrong of Ebchester in 1962. It passed from its original owner to Raisbeck of Bedlington in 1967, and then to Bartle of Outwood in January 1970. They withdrew the vehicle in April 1971 and sent it to a scrapyard which is where Hulleys found it a year later. Jack Hulley's judgement that the Pegasus was fundamentally sound was borne out by the fact that it remained in service until August 1978 despite being involved in a rear-end collision shortly after its arrival at Baslow. It was sold (for a nominal amount) to a preservation group who moved it to the premises of Webster of Hognaston (qv) but it survived for barely 18 months before ending up as scrap. Hulley's vehicles have not done well in preservation.

The Pegasus was followed by three well-used Bedford SB coaches. The first, 514 PML, a 1958 SB8 with Duple bodywork arrived in June 1972 as fleet number 12 and lasted until January 1975 when it was scrapped after being side-swiped by a lorry. The next was XNA 11, an SB3 with Plaxton Consort bodywork new to Finglands of Manchester in 1959. It came to Baslow in February 1973 as fleet number 14 and was withdrawn from use in August 1977. After sitting in the yard for a few years it found new employment with a morris-dancing troop in the Stockport area. Another SB3/Plaxton, 1961 model

The largest PSV user of Bedford VAL buses was A&C Wigmore of Dinnington, near Sheffield. This VAL70/Willowbrook B56F example, VWW 982F, was new to them in 1968. In October 1971 it passed to Blankley (Gem) of Colsterworth, and then to Hulley in December 1975 as fleet number 12. Acquired for schools contracts, it was withdrawn in March 1979 after this work was transferred to double-deckers. *(Derek Crawford Collection)*

New to Sheffield in April 1962, Leopard L1/Park Royal bus 616 BWB passed to South Yorkshire PTE in April 1974. Hulley's bought it in May 1976 (along with sister machine 618 BWB) and placed it into service seven months later as fleet number 24. Withdrawn from use in June 1978, it passed to a dealer but found no further user. *(John Holmes Collection)*

3455 WA, was acquired from Drabble of Sheffield in March 1973 for use as spares.

An eighth ex-Sheffield Leopard joined the fleet in July 1973 as number 23. A Weymann Hermes-bodied bus new in 1960, 6310 W gave exactly five years of service to the company. The final arrival of 1973, in September, was Bedford SB5/Duple (Northern) Firefly coach BHL 525C. This had been new to West Riding in 1965, making it relatively young by Hulley's standards, and it operated as fleet number 15 until February 1979. Another fairly modern coach arrived in September 1974 when 1966 Bedford VAM14/Plaxton GNL 713D joined the fleet as No 16, lasting until May 1980.

From School Runs to Retirement

Changes in government education policy in the 1970s brought new opportunities for independent bus and coach operators. The school leaving age was raised, meaning that more pupils were in the system at any given time, and many smaller schools were closed with their former inmates transferred to larger schools further afield. In most cases the contracts for schools services went to the lowest bidder so this was a cut-throat business. Hulleys entered it cautiously and ended up with various journeys to Lady Manners School in Bakewell among others. Higher capacity equipment was needed for some of these trips and in November 1974 a Ford R226 with Strachan DP53F bodywork was acquired to meet the demand. NPM 315F was one of a batch which had been bought by Wallace Arnold subsidiary Evan Evans in 1968 for use on hotel/airport transfer work. It came to Baslow from its second owner, GB Coaches of Longton near Preston, and stayed until August 1978 as fleet number 4. It was rarely seen on the stage carriage services.

Little then changed until October 1975 when yet another SB coach turned up at Derwent Garage. EVX 325B, fleet number 11, was a 1964 SB3 model with Plaxton Embassy III bodywork and was used until March 1979. The next new arrival was a second vehicle acquired specifically for the schools contracts, this time a three-axle Bedford VAL70 with a densely seated Willowbrook B56F body. VWW 982F had been new to Wigmore of Dinnington in 1968, passing to Blankley (Gem Coaches) of Colsterworth in October 1971 and then to Hulleys as fleet number 12 in December 1975. It remained in use until March 1979.

A third Hulley brother, Lancelot, died in 1976 and the three siblings who ran Hulleys began to consider the future of the firm. Nina was by then 68 years old while Jack was 65 and Benjamin 63. None of the men and women in the next generation of the family had shown any interest in replacing them at the helm, so the three Hulleys had no option but to consider selling the business to another operator. Trent showed very little interest but Chesterfield Corporation was prepared to make an offer when the time was right. Their first suggestion of a suitable price was considered to be derisory and the Hulleys decided to stay on for another year or two.

Another brace of ex-Sheffield L1 Leopards were acquired in May 1976. Fleet numbers 24/25 (616/8 BWB) had been new in 1962 and carried Park Royal B45F bodies. Their stay was comparatively brief and they were withdrawn during 1978. The only other vehicle acquired in 1976 was a 1963 Bedford VAL14 with Duple Vega Major bodywork, 9805 UK, bought as an engine donor for VAM14 No 16 in June. The following year was similarly quiet. In August 1977 the company bought its first 36ft PSU3/1R Leopard, 400 RRR, which became fleet number 19. The vehicle had been new to East Midland in 1963 and carried Willowbrook B53F bodywork. An identical machine, 402 RRR, was acquired in October 1977 as fleet number 20 but proved more troublesome than its twin. It finally entered service with Hulleys in June 1978 and was withdrawn just two months later, 400 RRR out-lasting it by four years.

Negotiations continued with prospective purchasers, making the acquisition of further vehicles seem unwise. Hulley's ageing fleet and high turn-over rate soon caused problems as numbers dwindled with every 'retirement' of an existing asset. In the short term services were maintained by hiring vehicles from Chesterfield. The corporation's L1 Leopard/Park Royal 9022 R was fitted with a destination blind which included Hulley's routes for this work as were Chesterfield's Reliance No 29 and Panther No 81 and possibly several others.

It had seemed almost inevitable that a deal would be done with Chesterfield, but at the last minute the Hulleys decided to accept an offer from another independent operator. On the 11th of August 1978 Henry Hulley & Sons Ltd was sold to JH Woolliscroft & Son of Darley Dale, which traded as Silver Service (qv). The family decision meant that the three principals could enjoy life in retirement, an option unavailable to James and Thomas who had both died 'in harness'. Benjamin passed away in 1987, Jack in 1993, and Nina in 1996.

Under New Ownership

Nobody could accuse the Woolliscrofts of failing to invest in their new subsidiary. By the end of August many of the less roadworthy Hulley vehicles had been retired and replaced by an influx of newer rolling stock. These included the first double-deckers ever owned by the Hulley company, five Bristol FLF6G/ECW Lodekkas which had previously served with Western SMT. VCS 366-8/70/5 (Hulley's fleet numbers 26-30) were 1963 vehicles and – with the exception of No 28 which never entered service – were mainly used on schools runs. The stage services were also in dire need of fresher vehicles and the new owners provided two 1965 PSU3/3RT Leopards with Alexander Y-type C49F bodywork which had been new to North Western but later operated for National Travel (North West) and then East Yorkshire. DDB 155/6C received Hulley's fleet numbers 36/7.

Optimism was in the air again, and in December 1978 the company introduced its first entirely new stage carriage service since 1956. Route 14 ran from Baslow to Chatsworth House and Beeley, twice each weekday, mainly for the benefit of staff at the stately home. In April 1979 Chesterfield Leopard/Park Royal 9022 R (which already had Hulley's destinations on its blind) officially joined the fleet as No 40. It might be argued that the dual doors of this vehicle made it less than ideal for rural operations, but compared to what followed the Leopard was a dream machine. After a month or two of expensive vehicle hiring from East Midland (including a double-deck Albion Lowlander which appeared on the Tideswell route!) the Woolliscrofts signed a contract with T&W Bus Sales of Clay Cross involving the leasing (or hire purchase, sources vary) of a fleet of Leyland Panther buses. The vehicles in question had been new to Liverpool Corporation in 1968/69 and carried MCW B47D bodywork. Most of them were sent to Baslow, arriving between April 1979 and April 1980. Fleet numbers 41-3 were allocated

to FKF 924/901/922F while fleet numbers 48-51 went to RKA 957G/FKF 902F/RKA 955G/RKA 971G. They were awful in every respect, but mercifully short-lived. Most were withdrawn during 1982 although fleet number 42 soldiered on as a bus of last resort until March 1984.

In June 1979 the Woolliscrofts decided to try a Leyland National, receiving ex-Plymouth example SCO 418L on loan from the Ensign dealership. It was allocated to Hulleys as fleet number 46, but its inadequate engine and dual-door configuration made it few friends. After two months of intermittent service it was returned to Ensign. Half way through its brief stay the Woolliscrofts had been forced to transfer Reliance/Plaxton coach LMD 543C from the Silver Service fleet to Hulleys to cover for its bouts of unreliability. This machine had been new to Frames of London and kept its Silver Service fleet number of 17 after transfer to Baslow.

From 1 to 170

In 1980 Derbyshire County Council (which subsidised many of the rural bus routes, including those of Hulleys and Silver Service) decided to number all of the county's bus services into a single sequence without duplication. The scheme was to take effect from the 25th of May, and the Woolliscrofts chose the same date to make some changes of their own. The Chesterfield to Bakewell section of Hulleys service 1 was linked with Silver Service's route from Bakewell to Matlock via Winster to produce an hourly through service from Chesterfield and Baslow to Matlock. This became the 170 in the new Derbyshire-wide numbering system and was jointly licensed to Hulley's and Woolliscroft's with each providing two vehicles. The other section of route 1, from Bakewell to Youlgreave and Middleton, became new service 171. Route number 2 to Tideswell became the 172, with most journeys curtailed at Baslow but still offering connections and through ticketing on the 170. The remaining services to Grindleford were withdrawn, but the Mondays only short workings on service 5 between Eyam and Bakewell survived as new service 175. Service 6, which ran on summer Sundays only to Hartington, was re-routed via Monyash, extended into Dovedale, and renumbered 176, while service 11 from Bakewell to Over Haddon became the 178. Service 12 had already vanished, its workings

These three Bristol FLF6G Lodekkas (VCS 375/370/367, Hulley fleet numbers 30/29/27 respectively) were new to Western SMT in 1963. Acquired for schools journeys in August 1978, they also appeared on the Chesterfield-Tideswell and Bakewell local services when demand was high. After withdrawal in mid-1980 fleet number 30 went to Top Deck Travel for use on long distance motor-home tours, and number 27 was exported to Zambia. Number 29 got no further than a Yorkshire scrapyard. *(Derek Crawford Collection)*

Leopard PSU3/Willowbrook B53F bus 400 RRR was new to East Midland in April 1963 and carried an interim version of 'Federation' bodywork with double-curvature front windscreens but a rounded rear dome. Hulleys bought it in August 1977 as fleet number 19 and kept it until February 1982. In this late 1979 shot the Leopard is still in red and pale cream while Lodekka VCS 366 has received the Woolliscroft red and beige livery. *(John Holmes Collection)*

absorbed into the timings of other operators, and service 14 from Baslow to Beeley was replaced by new service 179 which ran from Bakewell to Rowsley via Pilsley, Chatsworth, and Beeley.

A third PSU3 Leopard/Y-type coach arrived in Baslow in March 1980 as fleet number 59. CAG 494C had been new to Western SMT in 1965 and its acquisition allowed LMD 543C to return to Darley Dale. In June 1980 the Woolliscrofts bought four 1970 Ford R192s with Plaxton Derwent B45F bodywork from Midland Red. The name of the bodywork style was a happy coincidence. Fleet numbers for Silver Service and Hulley's vehicles was now in a common sequence and YHA 319-21/77J became fleet numbers 55-8. The first two were allocated to Baslow and carried Hulley's legal lettering, but while 55 was painted in traditional Hulley's red, sister bus 56 was painted in Silver Service blue. It was a sign of things to come. Two months later another double-decker was placed on Hulley's 'O' licence in the shape of ex-Glasgow Atlantean/Alexander UGA 218H. This also carried full Silver Service livery despite its Hulley's legal lettering.

The truth of it was that the monstrously inappropriate ex-Liverpool Panthers had given Hulleys a bad name for the first time in its history, and the Woolliscrofts had decided that the easiest solution was to present all of its vehicles in Silver Service livery with Silver Service fleet-names. Henry Hulley & Sons Ltd remained a separate corporate entity with its own operator's licence and vehicle allocation, but by 1982 had vanished as a name on the side of the buses. The red livery used at Baslow was also phased out with all surviving Hulleys vehicles being repainted in blue and beige.

Renaissance

We are now well past our cut-off point of 1980 so further fleet details would trespass on the territory of a future author. There is, however, a happy ending to the Hulleys story. By 1987 the Woolliscroft family had divided into two factions. Selwyn Woolliscroft wanted to sell the group's stage carriage services to concentrate on more remunerative coaching work. His brother John and their mother Nancy were equally determined to keep the buses running and decamped from Darley Dale to the Baslow office to make the point. The two sides eventually agreed that the bus services, Baslow garage, and the Hulleys name would be sold off, but only to a buyer acceptable to all of the Woolliscrofts. The original version of this plan imagined selling the bus operations to an employee buy-out, but before this could take place an offer was received from the two senior managers at Baslow, Arthur Cotterill and Peter Eades, and accepted by the Woolliscroft directors. Hulleys duly re-emerged from the shadows.

Arthur Cotterill retired in 2001, leaving Peter Eades in control. He had started his PSV driving career with White of Calver (qv) in 1959, moving to Hulleys in 1961 and ultimately becoming Assistant Traffic Manager until John and Nancy Woolliscroft moved into his office. He was also the grandson of Stanley Eades who had sold his business to Henry Hulley in 1930. Under his direction the company regained its reputation for reliability, adopting a new blue and pale cream livery cheekily stolen from South Notts who sold several (later model) Leyland Nationals to the resurrected Hulleys. Peter Eades passed away in 2013, aged 74, but the business continues under the expert supervision of his son, Richard.

Further Reading

The definitive book about the Hulley company is also one of the most elusive books on the second-hand market. "Hulleys of Baslow" by John Bennett (Robin Hood Publishing, 1988) sold out quickly and few enthusiasts have been willing to part with their copies. In the 28 years since publication I have never seen a single copy on a second-hand stall. If you have better luck make sure that you buy it while you can.

My Lady of Crich

See Taylor of Crich

Pashley of Bradwell

Bradwell is a village of just over 1,200 residents on the road from Buxton and Tideswell to the Hope Valley. Lead mining was the traditional local industry, although this declined from Victorian times onward. In 1894 the Midland Railway opened a line from Manchester to Sheffield via Chinley and Dore and a station was opened at Hope, two miles to the north of Bradwell. The new station was sub-titled 'For Castleton and

Bradwell' and both villages were connected to it by horse-drawn conveyances. After the First World War these were replaced by motor vehicles, and by 1930 the Castleton station bus was being operated by Jennie Paine (who later sold out to North Western) while the bus to Bradwell was maintained by Messrs Edgar & Pashley of that village. They also offered a taxi service.

Nothing has been discovered about Albert Edgar, who left the partnership before the Second World War. William Edwin ('Billie') Pashley then became the sole proprietor. The first recorded vehicle (there may have been earlier ones) was 14-seat Morris RA 8755, new to Edgar & Pashley in June 1929. Another new vehicle, a Commer Centaur with Reeve & Kenning B20F bodywork registered RB 8899, arrived in July 1933 and was known locally as 'the Big Bus' with the Morris then down-graded to being 'the Little Bus'. The firm was based at Brookside Garage in Bradwell and also undertook petrol sales and motor repair alongside the bus and taxi business.

In 1938 the original Morris was replaced by a new Morris 14-seater registered FNU 369. No prizes are available for guessing what the villagers called it. The two vehicles continued the service throughout the war years. After the end of hostilities Billie Pashley decided to expand his fleet to service the demand for excursions andprivate-hires. In March 1946 he managed to secure a brand-new Bedford OB/Duple Vista coach, JRA 580, even though such vehicles were like gold dust at the time. The arrival of another brand-new coach, Austin CXB/Mann Egerton 29-seater NRA 96, in July 1949 took the fleet strength up to four.

The Austin would be Pashley's last new vehicle. In May 1951 the ageing Centaur was replaced by a 1938 vintage Commer PN3 with a 21-seat coach body by Waveney of Lowestoft, AFW 92. This vehicle had been new to Premier of Scunthorpe, passing to Enterprise & Silver Dawn in 1940 and then to Ford of Killamarsh before arriving in Bradwell. In July 1953 Morris FNU 369 was withdrawn from service and not replaced.

The Commer PN3 lasted for just over three years before being replaced in September 1954 by a government surplus Morris CV11 with a rather basic Jones B15F body. LYL 25 had been new in 1951 and had previously operated for the Ministry of Works. The next arrival was more impressive.

Bedford SBG/Duple C36F CEN 535 had been new to Auty's Tours of Bury in May 1954 and came to Bradwell in June 1956, replacing the Bedford OB which was sold to Bull of Tideswell (qv). While the SBG took care of excursions and most of the private-hire work, the Austin was dedicated to the station service, and the Morris was available for small-scale private-hires such as transporting pub darts teams to away fixtures.

In 1952 Pashley had married Grace Major who worked at a boarding house in the village. She was ten years younger than him and he began to think about lessening his business commitments. These thoughts finally turned into action in July 1958 when he sold the PSV part of his operations to Sheffield United Transport. Exactly why such a large operator should bother is unrecorded, although SUT did continue to use the Bradwell garage as an out-station for several years. It might have been seen as a way to avoid 'dead mileage' on eastbound excursions from the Hope Valley area, although the Bradwell based vehicle also operated a short schools journey during term-time.

For more than six months SUT was also responsible for the Hope Station service, operating it with a centre-entrance Reliance/Duple Elizabethan coach which was poorly suited to the task. In 1959 service 72 from Sheffield to Castleton, operated jointly by North Western and Sheffield JOC, was diverted to serve Bradwell (it already passed Hope Station) and the separate local service ended. The taxi and motor business continued until Billie Pashley's death in 1972. His wife Grace then ran the taxi service for another ten years before retiring. She died in 2006, aged 89.

Silver Service of Darley Dale

James Henry Woolliscroft was born in 1881 at Rocester in Staffordshire, to the south of Ashbourne and close to the Derbyshire border. The village was later to become world-famous as the home of JCB excavators, but in those simpler times James's father found employment as a cowman. He later became a tenant farmer, but the farm could not possibly support all of his seven children. James was the seventh of them and so had to look elsewhere to earn a crust. He apparently found his way to the Derwent valley, as in 1903 he married Daisy Watson of Rowsley and the couple took up residence in the nearby

Chesterfield's Leopard L1/Park Royal B42D bus 9022 R, new in December 1963, had been loaned to Hulleys during 1978 and their destinations were added to its route blind. The corporation sold it to dealer Wombwell Diesels in November 1978 who passed it back to Hulleys (complete with compatible blind) in April 1979. Given fleet number 40 it lasted until February 1982. *(Derek Crawford Collection)*

Fleet number 41 went to the first of the ex-Merseyside Panthers, FKF 924F. New to Liverpool in October 1968, it carried an MCW B47D body. Clay Cross dealer T&W procured it in January 1979 and three months later it went into service with Hulleys. Drivers, engineers, and passengers were united in their dislike of these vehicles. Bedford TK tow-truck LOG 383F (which replaced the 'Big Bedford' shown on page 39) sits alongside, waiting for the next call from a broken Panther. *(Derek Crawford Collection)*

Pashley of Bradwell's best known vehicle was this Austin CXB/Mann Egerton coach, NRA 96, new to the operator in July 1949 and seen here at Hope Station on the stage carriage service. In 1958 it passed with the business to Sheffield United Tours but was not used by them, passing immediately to a dealer and then to a new career as a mobile shop. *(Omnibus Society - Roy Marshall)*

In May 1951 Pashley's 1933 vintage Commer service bus was retired and replaced by this slightly more modern Commer PN3/Waveney C21F coach, AFW 92. New to a Lincolnshire operator in December 1938, it came to Pashley from Ford of Killamarsh and lasted until its sixteenth birthday at the end of 1954. Its replacement was a three year old Morris CV personnel carrier with only 15 seats acquired from a government surplus auction. *(Trevor Weckert Collection)*

village of Darley Dale, three miles from Matlock on the main road to Bakewell and beyond.

By 1911 they had a greengrocer's shop in the village, with James making door-to-door deliveries with a horse and cart. Just after the First World War these were replaced by a Ford Model T van, and to help pay for his new vehicle Woolliscroft fitted it with rudimentary seating in the evenings and at weekends and opened an informal bus service between Darley Dale and Matlock. In 1920 the unidentified Ford had its van bodywork permanently removed and replaced by a 12-seat char-a-banc body. Jim Woolliscroft had found something more interesting than lettuces and rhubarb.

The first purpose-built bus was NU 4909, a brand-new Reo Speedwagon with Spicer B14F bodywork delivered in December 1924 as fleet number 1. Its arrival enabled a regular service to be maintained over an extended Rowsley-Darley Dale-Matlock route. Fleet number 2 followed in May 1925 in the shape of NU 6502, a Reo type W with an 18-seat char-a-banc body which replaced the Model T on private-hire and excursion duties. At first Woolliscroft used the fleet name 'Reliance' for his new enterprise.

Almost all of Woolliscroft's vehicles were bought new until the Second World War. The first exception to this rule was EH 6135, a 1925 all-Dennis 20-seater which came from Dawson of Hanley in May 1926. It remained in use until 1934 but never acquired a fleet number. Instead the number 3 went to RA 480, a Reo Pullman with Lewis & Crabtree B26F bodywork new in September 1926. During 1927 the 'Reliance' fleet name was abandoned and the four vehicles then in use received 'Silver Service' branding. A second stage carriage service, from Matlock to Bakewell via Winster and Birchover, was inaugurated and certain journeys on the first service were extended beyond Rowsley to Youlgreave. Woolliscroft also provided a works service from Matlock to the brickworks at Friden.

The Golden Years of Silver Service

Jim Woolliscroft's son James Watson Woolliscroft ('Jim Junior'), born in 1907, joined the family firm almost from the cradle and by 1928 was a driver and mechanic. In that year the business moved from its original (rented) premises in Stancliffe Yard to a new garage in Hackney Lane. Two more Reo Pullmans arrived in May and July 1928. RA 5578 and RA 6505 received fleet numbers 4 and 5 and also carried Lewis & Crabtree bodies, but were C24F coaches. Number 4 had a very respectable life-span, being withdrawn in 1947, but number 5 received a new Willowbrook C24F body in June 1937 and then remained in use until April 1957! By then it was easily the last of its kind to be licensed as a PSV in Great Britain and it is a great shame that it went for scrap after 29 years of loyal service to the business.

In September 1929 the Woolliscrofts decided to try something different and bought an AEC 660 Reliance with Bond B32F bodywork, RA 8740, as fleet number 6. Another marque of vehicle came into the fleet in February 1930 with the acquisition of fleet number 7 (RB 771), a BAT Cruiser with Eaton C20F bodywork, while a second AEC arrived in April 1931 as fleet number 8. This was RB 3954, the company's first AEC Regal, and carried a Cravens B32F body. It replaced fleet number 1, leaving numbers 2-8 plus the Dennis in the company's inventory at the time of Road Service Licence hearings in 1931/2. The Woolliscrofts came away with licences for all of their existing stage carriage routes, despite loud and persistent objections from North Western, Trent, and the LMS Railway. They were also licensed for their seasonal 'period return' express service from Holloway, Matlock, and Darley Dale to Blackpool, despite similar objections and the fact that the service had only commenced on a timetabled basis in 1930.

Three more new vehicles arrived in 1934 to replace older stock. A second No 3, ANU 483, was delivered in March and was a Leyland SKP3 Cub with Willowbrook C26F bodywork, while the new No 1 (ARB 816) was a Dodge KB with a Willowbrook C20F body and went into service in December. Between the two, in July 1934, Silver Service took delivery of the most famous vehicle in its history. ARA 475, a side-engined AEC Q with a formidable Willowbrook C37C body, received fleet number 10 and was the regular vehicle on the seasonal express to Blackpool from 1934 until 1940 when the service was suspended for the duration of the war. The government had no interest in requisitioning such an unusual vehicle, so the Q spent the war years in storage at the premises of H Strange & Son of Tansley – a Matlock area coach operator run by a close friend of Jim Woolliscroft. After the war its visits to Blackpool were infrequent as younger vehicles came into use, but it continued to find work on private-hires until its withdrawal in October 1961 at the age of 27. It then remained at the depot as an informal museum exhibit until acquired for preservation in May 1970.

Three more vehicles were taken into stock before the outbreak of the Second World War. Fleet number 11 was taken by CRA 757, an AEC Regal with Willowbrook C35F bodywork which arrived in May 1936. Up to this point all of Woolliscroft's vehicles had been petrol-engined, but in June 1938 the firm decided to try its first diesel. Surprisingly, fleet number 12 (FNU 271) was not an O662 Regal but a Gardner-engined Daimler COG5/40 with a Willowbrook DP39F body. Having realised that diesels were a good idea, Woolliscroft returned to the AEC fold in January 1939 with the purchase of FRB 122, an O662 Regal/Willowbrook DP35F which replaced the 1929 Reliance as fleet number 6.

War, a Wedding, and a Travel Boom

Only one vehicle from the fleet was requisitioned by the government. In early 1940 Regal No 11 was taken by the War Department. It failed to return in 1945 but was apparently in good enough condition to serve six more owners before its final withdrawal in 1955. Silver Service received two second-hand vehicles during the conflict. In 1942 a TS7 Tiger with a Weymann C28F body, WN 7754, became the new No 8. The vehicle had been new to South Wales in March 1935. Its original body was replaced by a new Willowbrook DP35F unit in April 1949, and in May 1961 it was fitted with an AEC 7.7 engine which continued to confuse Leyland enthusiasts until its eventual withdrawal in May 1965 when the chassis was 30 years old. The other wartime arrival (in 1943) was CWA 353, a 1936 petrol-engined Regal with a Cravens C32R body which had been new to Beauchief Coaches in Sheffield. It became the new fleet number 11 and lasted until April 1959.

Two other events which took place during the war are worthy of mention. In August 1941 James Watson Woolliscroft married Nancy Millington. He was 34 and she was 23. The new Mrs Woolliscroft would go on to produce two sons, John and Selwyn, who (along with their mother) were to play important roles in the future drama of the Silver Service group. With 'Jim Jr' married and approaching middle-age it was time to formally recognise his contribution, and in July 1943 the business was incorporated as JH Woolliscroft & Son Ltd, having previously operated as a sole proprietorship of the founder. He was by then 62 years old and gradually withdrew from his eponymous enterprise until retiring completely during 1948.

With JW Woolliscroft in charge the firm entered the post-war era in style. The first two purchases were both brand-new Regal Is. JRA 446 arrived in June 1946 as fleet number 2 and carried a Duple C35F body, while the similarly registered KNU 446 was delivered to Darley Dale four months later as fleet number 4 and was fitted with Willowbrook DP35F bodywork. With some of the pre-war vehicles on their last legs, Silver Service decided to buy on the second-hand market as well as from the production line. A 1934 Guy BB with Brush B26F bodywork (FA 5447) was acquired from Burton-on-Trent Corporation in November 1947 and became fleet number 17. It lasted around four years.

The other two deliveries in 1947 (in December) were a matching pair of AEC Regal IIIs of the more powerful 0962 variant which carried Duple A type C33F bodies. LRA 907 (No 14) and LRB 62 (No 15) became the half-cab flagships of the fleet and were soon nicknamed 'The Heavenly Twins'. No 14 ran in its original form until May 1970, but No 15 lost some of its heavenly charm in 1959 when Yeates fitted it with a particularly unsympathetic full front. Rather than disguising its age this merely disguised its attractive design, and it left the active fleet in August 1969.

Both purchases in 1948 were pre-war in origin. In October Silver Service bought diesel-engined Regal/Trans-United C33F coach HTB 700 from Kia Ora of Morecambe. The registration had been issued in July 1947 but the Regal had been new as a petrol-engined variant delivered to Timpson of London SE6 in February 1939. In its original form (registered FLM 386) it had carried a Harrington C32F body. Kia Ora bought it from a dealer, fitted it with a diesel engine, and had it rebodied. Why they decided to sell it only 15 months later after all that expenditure remains a mystery. The mutton dressed as lamb (given fleet number 16) did well for itself at Darley Dale and lasted until November 1967.

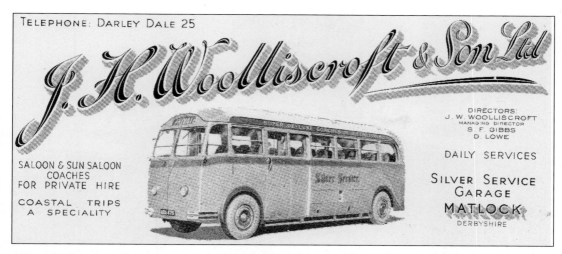

A Silver Service letterhead from the days when telephone numbers were short and 1934 AEC Q/Willowbrook coach ARA 475 was still the pride of the fleet, despite being more than 12 years old at the time the letterhead was produced - the clue is in the listing of the founder's son as managing director. *(John Dixon Collection)*

Silver Service's Reo Pullman RA 6505 (fleet number 5) was delivered to Darley Dale in July 1928 and originally carried a Lewis & Crabtree C24F body. Nine years later it received a Willowbrook C24F body (as seen here) and remained in service until April 1957. Sold to a showman, it was last licensed in June 1959. What a pity that it was not preserved to sit alongside the AEC Q as a tribute to the company's history. *(John Holmes Collection)*

AEC Regal/Cravens B32F bus RB 3954 was new to Silver Service in April 1931 as fleet number 8. By 1943 the body was disintegrating and the chassis was sold to Green Luxury Coaches of Walton-on-Thames who fitted it with a pre-war Duple C32F body. After moving on to the Bryn Motor Co of Pontllanfraith in May 1947 it was scrapped in 1954. *(JH Woolliscroft & Son)*

Fleet number 9 was allocated to RB 9013, a Dennis Lancet with Willowbrook DP32F bodywork delivered to Silver Service in July 1933. Originally a petrol vehicle, it received an AEC 7.7 litre diesel engine in April 1946. After withdrawal in December 1955 it remained at Darley Dale until being sold for scrap in November 1960. *(JH Woolliscroft & Son)*

The other purchase in 1948 was EWA 538, a Leyland TD5 new to Sheffield Corporation in 1937 with a Cravens double-deck body. Silver Service bought the chassis from a dealer after its original body had been scrapped and fitted it with a new Willowbrook DP35F body in April 1949. It then entered service as fleet number 18. By 1959 its Leyland engine had gone, replaced by an AEC 7.7, and it remained in use until April 1961.

The Fifties and Sixties

There were no arrivals in the fleet between April 1949 and March 1952 when Silver Service bought a pair of brand-new underfloor-engined coaches. PRA 865/6 (fleet numbers 19/20) were AEC Regal IVs with elegant, if slightly bulbous, Willowbrook C41C bodies. They served until 1966/67 with No 20 going to an after-life in Australia where it was fitted with a new body in 1970. Its ultimate fate is unknown.

Another long pause between acquisitions was broken in October 1956 by the arrival of Bedford OB/Duple Vista coach GVJ 190. This had been new to Llangrove Coach Service of Llangarron in 1949 and became Woolliscroft's fleet number 3. Three months later another Welsh OB/Vista coach was acquired. JTG 280 had been new to Starkey of Pentre (also in 1949) and took fleet number 1 at Darley Dale. The OBs out-lasted most of their species in the stage carriage sector, with No 3 remaining in service until December 1972 and No 1 until August 1971. Both were later sold into preservation, although No 1 was scrapped within a few years.

May 1959 saw the purchase of a three year old Reliance with Duple Britannic C41C bodywork from Lily Coaches of Cockfosters. Registered 26 HMD, it became fleet number 21 and was withdrawn in December 1974. Another coach from the same operator arrived in April 1960 in the shape of Reliance/Harrington Wayfarer 149 UMP. This vehicle was less than a year old and took fleet number 22. Despite being four years younger than its Lily Coaches compatriot it left the Silver Service fleet before it, in June 1974. The Woolliscroft's final purchase of a traditional half-cab bus came in April 1961 when 1946 Regal I/Weymann saloon KEH 602 arrived from PMT. When new this had carried a Weymann B34F body, but in July 1956 it was fitted with

a 1949 Weymann B39F unit from another PMT bus. It remained in service at Darley Dale until October 1966.

In November 1963 JH Woolliscroft & Son acquired the business of H Strange & Son of Tansley, the coach operator which had looked after Silver Service's AEC Q during the war years. The sale included two petrol-engined Bedfords with Yeates Europa C41F bodywork, a 1957 SBG (950 DNU) which became Silver Service's No 17, and a 1958 SB3 (893 FRB) which took fleet number 18. Both remained in Strange's red and cream livery (but with Silver Service legal lettering and fleet names) for several years after the take-over. The next two arrivals were also Bedford SB variants, but of a frighteningly spartan design when compared to the luxurious Europa coaches. Brand-new diesel-engined SB5s DRB 10/11C (fleet numbers 11/12 – the fleet number 10 was still worn by the immobile Q) were delivered in March 1965 and carried Strachans Pacesaver B39F bodywork. This design had originally been produced as a low-cost option for sale to military or governmental customers, and the word 'utilitarian' is really too kind. I rode on one once and never cared to repeat the experience. The pair tended to be confined to the Matlock-Rowsley service as they were incapable of keeping to schedule in the steeper terrain of the Matlock-Bakewell run. No 12 was sold to a building contractor in Derby in 1972, hopefully for use as a site-hut, but No 11 stayed in the fleet until 1977 before vanishing from view. Oddly, I now wish that somebody would find it intact!

There was only one new arrival in 1966, but it was a real head-turner. CDK 410C was a Bedford VAL14 with an imposing Harrington Legionnaire C52F body. It had been new in April 1965 to the famous Yelloway of Rochdale fleet, which put it to work on the long express routes operated jointly with Premier Travel from Clacton-on-Sea to Cambridge, the East Midlands, Manchester, and Blackpool. This was all rather too much for a VAL14, designed as they were for small coach operators with low vehicle utilisation, and in April 1966 the machine celebrated its first birthday by moving to Darley Dale as fleet number 23. It was Silver Service's first 36ft long vehicle and stayed in the fleet until November 1972, later passing to Thornes of Bubwith for a final year of service.

The VAL14 provided a drastic contrast to the next arrival, in January 1967. This was a 1963 Albion Nimbus/Weymann B31F, RJX 252, which had been new to Halifax JOC but then quickly discarded along with the rest of its kin after the type's shortcomings with reference to hills became apparent. It became Silver Service's No 2 and was kept away from the steepest gradients on the route-map until its withdrawal in June 1974. Another arrival in January 1967 was CTE 721B, a Bedford SB5/Duple Bella Vega coach which had been new to Gay Line Coaches (yes, really!) of Lytham St Anne's in 1964. It came to Darley Dale from its second owner, Mascot Coaches of Norwich, was allocated fleet number 19, and stayed until May 1970. The third and final acquisition during 1967 took place in March when fleet number 20 (549 EAC), a 1963 Bedford VAS1/Duple Bella Vista 29-seater arrived from Gray Line of Bicester – not to be confused with Gay Line. The VAS remained in service until December 1979, found further employment as a caravan, and was then converted into a mobile cafe. In this latter guise it could often be found at the side of the A6 in Rowsley, very much still a part of the local scene.

Having absorbed Strange & Son in 1963 without any ill effects, Silver Service decided to buy the business of Taylor of Crich (qv) in October 1969. Gervase Taylor had decided to retire and the sale included 1950 Bedford OB/Duple Vista coach ORB 45, Bedford VAS1/Duple Bella Vista coach VNL 51, and two stage carriage services. A service from Crich to Derby operated on Fridays only (with one journey in each direction), while on Saturdays a Crich to Ripley service operated at hourly intervals. The OB never received Silver Service livery or a fleet number and remained in Taylor's two-tone brown colour scheme (with his 'My Lady' fleet name in the eyebrow aperture) until its withdrawal in November 1970. It moved very little during its short stay at Darley Dale, although it was hired for a railway enthusiasts' excursion to Haworth in the West Riding on one occasion and barely made it back to base. The VAS became fleet number 16 and stayed until February 1979.

The Reign of the Brothers

James Watson Woolliscroft, son of the founder, died in March 1970 aged 62. The company continued under the stewardship of his widow, Nancy, and his two sons, John and Selwyn. In May they refreshed the coaching stock by adding a Bedford VAL70 with a stylish (and then quite rare) Caetano C52F body, UYC 799G, to the fleet as No 24. It was only 14 months old at the time and came from R&S Travel of Minehead, whose registerd office was actually in London W8. Despite its modernity it only stayed at Darley Dale for eight months before moving on to Danson of Bolton in Lancashire. The next arrival had an even briefer stay. OTT 96 was a 1953 Bristol LS6G/ECW coach which had been delivered to Southern National for use on the Royal Blue network. Retired by them in 1969, it passed to the dealer North of Sherburn and North's hired it to Silver Service for three months from June to September 1970 to meet additional demand during the Peak District tourist season. It received no fleet number and operated in 'as it came' livery minus fleet names.

The final arrival of 1970 was more significant than either of its predecessors. AEC Reliance/Roe B45F bus 8625 DT had been new to Doncaster Corporation in 1961 and came to Silver Service in September as fleet number 5. It became a stalwart of the route to Bakewell until its withdrawal exactly three years later. January 1971 saw the arrival of LMD 543C, a 1965 Reliance with Plaxton Panorama C41F bodywork which had been new to Frames Tours of London WC2. It became fleet number 17 and stayed until April 1979 when it was transferred to the (by then associated) Hulley fleet at Baslow. The only other arrival during 1971 was XTG 383H, a 1970 Ford R226 with a Duple Viceroy C53F body, which came in February and replaced the Caetano-bodied VAL70. It remained in the full livery of its previous owner, Bebb of Llantwit Fardre, until its departure in June 1972, and never received a Silver Service fleet number.

In January 1972 another ex-Doncaster Reliance (8629 DT) turned up as fleet number 6. Identical to No 5, its belated arrival is explained by an interim career with Golden Miller of Feltham. It was withdrawn shortly after its twin in November 1973. The next delivery to Darley Dale was a far more expensive piece of kit, being a brand-new AEC Reliance/Willowbrook Expressway C53F coach which replaced the Bebb Ford in June. It arrived with the registration mark DUR 974K (having

Leyland SKP3 Cub/Willowbrook C26F coach ANU 483 was delivered to Silver Service in March 1934 as fleet number 3 and served for more than 22 years before sale to Aston of Marton for spares use. *(WJ Haynes)*

An off-side view of AEC Q coach ARA 475, revealing the location of its engine behind the driver. The vehicle was delivered to Silver Service in July 1934 as fleet number 10 and carried a Willowbrook C37C body. Withdrawn from use in October 1961, the Q was parked outside the garage until May 1970 when it passed into preservation. *(John Holmes Collection)*

The Q in company with a Trent Atlantean at the Dovedale terminus of their route 30 from Derby. The high frame and floor height of ARA 475 is immediately apparent – most of the breed were built as buses and were thus considerably lower as the engine could be mounted beneath a longitudinal bench seat. On a coach this was not an option. *(John Holmes)*

After the brave choice of the Q in 1934 Silver Service turned back to more conventional vehicles. FNU 271 was a Daimler COG5/40 with a Willowbrook DP39F body and was new to the company in May 1936 as fleet number 12. Withdrawn in January 1961 it was scrapped on site at Darley Dale. *(John Holmes)*

been registered by a dealer) but after two months at Darley Dale this was changed to XRA 876L which made the vehicle look younger than it actually was. For some reason the authorities allowed this change and the vehicle remained in service as fleet number 24 until July 1981.

Two more coaches were acquired in November 1972, both coming from Hebble of Halifax. BJX 75C (Silver Service fleet number 19) was a run-of-the-mill Reliance with a Plaxton Panorama body and stayed in the fleet until February 1975. The other Hebble exile was also a 36ft Reliance but carried an Alexander Y-type DP49F body. TCP 900 (Silver Service No 23) was made even more unusual by being one of the few Y-types not to feature a 'roof box' destination display, its rounded front dome giving it an entirely different appearance to others of its clan. It stayed with Silver Service until April 1976.

In November 1973 a 1963 vintage Ford Thames with Plaxton C41F bodywork, 7616 UK, arrived at Darley Dale. It had been new to Don Everall in Wolverhampton but came to Darley Dale from its third owner, St Albans City Coaches of Hertfordshire. Despite receiving full Silver Service livery and fleet number 15 it was actually registered to John Woolliscroft as an individual rather than to the company until December 1977. It was withdrawn seven months later.

Another brand-new coach was acquired in June 1974. TNU 647M was a late-model Bedford SB5 with Plaxton C41F bodywork and became fleet number 18. In March 1977 it was sold to Warrington of Ilam. The only other vehicle purchase during 1974, a six year old 12-seat Ford Transit minibus registered YRB 617G, arrived in December and was allocated fleet number 22. In February 1975 the brothers were on the look-out for a good second-hand coach and decided to try a Bedford YRT with an all-metal Duple Dominant coach body. GRH 909L had been new to Kingston International Travel of Hull in 1973 and gave service to the Woolliscrofts as fleet number 19 until January 1977. Within weeks of its arrival at Darley Dale an order was placed for a brand-new example of the same combination and this turned up in November 1975 as KWE 144P, fleet number 21. Both Dominants were 53-seaters.

In March 1976 the company bought the business of Wagstaffe of Matlock along with a 1965 Albion VT21L Victor/Duple (Northern) Firefly coach,

HWB 944C, and a 1970 Ford Transit 12-seater, ONE 587H. The Albion remained in the Silver Service fleet for 18 months but never received a fleet number. In contrast the humble Transit became No 14 and was used until March 1979. Two months after selling his original operation to the Woolliscrofts, Mr Wagstaffe went back into the coaching business in Matlock, suggesting that Silver Service's solicitors had done a less than perfect job when drafting the sale agreement.

A pair of second-hand Reliances joined the stage carriage section of the fleet in April 1976. WEE 237/8 came from Grimsby-Cleethorpes Transport and carried dual-door Willowbrook B42D bodies. They became fleet numbers 9/10 and were sold on to Webster of Hognaston (qv) in late 1979. The fifth and sixth vehicles acquired during 1976 were a pair of Bedford YRT/Duple Dominant C53F coaches, JVS 931/2N, which arrived in December and took fleet numbers 31/32 to match their registrations. New in 1975 to Fox of Hayes (probably best remembered for providing the coach for the Beatles 'Magical Mystery Tour'), they gave exactly two years of service to the Woolliscrofts.

February 1977 brought the purchase of a three year old Bedford CF/Deansgate C17F mini-coach, YNC 805M, which became fleet number 30. It was followed in March and April by two second-hand 36ft Ford coaches; a Plaxton-bodied R1114 from Bullock of Cheadle (HFM 808N, fleet number 34), and a Duple-bodied R226 from Smith of Shenington (MUE 657L, fleet number 33). The R226 was sold in April 1979, but the R1114 lasted until 1984. The next arrival was FUM 943K (fleet number 35), a 1972 Bedford VAS5 coach with Duple bodywork which came from Fallas of Leeds in May 1978. It left two years later.

The Silver Service Group

As already recorded the Hulley family sold their bus company to JH Woolliscroft & Son in August 1978. By then the Hulley fleet was in poor condition and several vehicles were taken off the road immediately after the sale. The imminent start of the school contract season forced the Woolliscrofts to buy replacements quickly and five FLF Lodekkas were acquired from Western SMT to fulfil these duties. They were already in a close approximation of Hulley's livery and could be pressed into service without a repaint. Hulley's depleted stage carriage fleet was buttressed by the addition of two 36ft Leopards with Alexander Y-type bodywork. Apart from these new arrivals little changed at Baslow at first, with vehicles continuing to operate in Hulley's livery, with Hulley's fleet names and legal lettering, on Hulley routes.

The coaching fleet at Darley Dale was not forgotten during these monumental changes and in December 1978 Silver Service acquired two brand-new Ford R1114/Duple Dominant 53-seaters. YKY 840/1T became fleet numbers 38/39 and replaced the two Bedford YRTs acquired from Fox of Hayes. The Silver Service bus fleet was in need of an additional vehicle too, and this materialised in May 1979 in the form of an Albion Nimbus with Harrington DP30F bodywork, TUH 14. This had been new to Western Welsh in 1960, passing to Smith of March in September 1966 and then to Booth & Fisher of Halfway (see Part Two) in July 1968. It went with the business to South Yorkshire PTE in August 1975, and they sold it to Silver Service who gave it fleet number 45. The Woolliscrofts had apparently forgotten how gutless their previous Nimbus had been, but they were quickly reminded of the type's limitations and sold it on after just five months. The other arrival during May 1979 was another Ford R1114/Plaxton coach from Bullock of Cheadle, this one a 1976 model registered RCA 556P which became fleet number 44.

In August 1979 several vehicles at Darley Dale and several more in the Hulley fleet at Baslow were taken off the road after inspections. The Woolliscrofts did their best to fill in the gaps in the Darley Dale roster by short term hiring from other operators. Finglands of Manchester provided Ford R1114/Duple Dominant coach MND 737P for a month while Lancaster City Transport offered the services of two rear-engined saloons, a Panther with East Lancs B53F bodywork (LTC 109F, new to Lancaster Corporation) and an AEC Swift with Northern Counties B50D bodywork (UTJ 908H, formerly of Morecambe & Heysham). The latter two vehicles operated in full Lancaster livery at first, but in November 1979 Silver Service decided to buy them both as fleet numbers 53 (the Panther) and 54 (the Swift). They replaced the GCT Reliances which were sold on to Webster of Hognaston (qv). Two months

earlier, in September 1979, fleet number 52 had arrived. This was an AEC Swift with MCW B41D bodywork, DPD 505J, which had been new to London Country in 1971. In September 1978 it had passed to T&W Bus Sales of Clay Cross and then sat in their yard for a year before being hired to the Woolliscrofts. It was returned to T&W in May 1980 as part of the Merseyside Panther deal. A hire which lasted for considerably longer was that of XBR 657R, a 1977 Ford R1114/Plaxton coach which arrived in October 1979 and stayed until March 1981. Despite its long visit it remained without Silver Service livery or fleet number.

From 1980 onwards the Hulley fleet name and livery began to disappear. Many vehicles were still officially registered to Henry Hulley & Sons Ltd and carried legal lettering to that effect, but most gradually acquired Silver Service's new stage carriage fleet livery of light blue and beige and wore 'Silver Service' or 'Silver Service Group' titles. This change began in May 1980 when the main stage carriage services of the two companies were merged into a single route. The new 170 left Chesterfield for Baslow and Bakewell on the mileage of Hulley's route 1 and then continued from Bakewell to Matlock via the Silver Service route through Birchover and Winster. The hourly frequency was maintained by two vehicles from Baslow and two from Darley Dale. The Woolliscrofts decided that it was better to market the new through service under a single fleet-name. If that had been the only consideration it might have made more sense to choose the Hulley name, as they were more widely known in most of the operating territory, but by May 1980 the word Hulley had become synonymous with Merseyside Panthers and unreliability.

By 1982 the word Hulley had disappeared from the vehicles (except for their legal lettering) and all operations were marketed under the Silver Service name. The Merseyside Panthers were disposed of as quickly as possible and replaced by a variety of more appealing equipment. A quartet of Ford R192/Plaxton Derwent buses from Midland Red was followed by a veritable host of Bristol RE variants during the early 1980s. ECW-bodied examples came from PMT and East Midland, two Marshall-bodied specimens came from Ribble and ten more REs (with an eclectic mix of East Lancs, Northern Counties, and Pennine bodywork) were acquired from Burnley & Pendle.

Leyland TS7 Tiger WN 7754 was new to South Wales Transport in March 1935, carrying a Weymann C28F coach body. Requisitioned by the Ministry of Supply in July 1940, it was fitted with four extra seats and then allocated to Silver Service in 1942 as fleet number 8. In April 1949 it received a new Willowbrook DP35F body (as seen here) and in May 1961 the Leyland engine was replaced by an AEC 7.7 litre diesel unit. In 1965 it was sold for preservation but ended up being scrapped in 1972. *(John Holmes)*

Silver Service's fleet number 16, a pre-war AEC Regal, had a complicated history. New to Timpson of Catford in February 1939, it originally carried a Harrington C32F body and bore the registration FLM 386. After the war it found its way to Kia Ora of Morecambe who scrapped the Harrington body, fitted it with a new Trans-United C33F unit and a diesel engine, and re-registered it in July 1947 as HTB 700. Silver Service bought the vehicle in October 1948 and kept it until November 1967. The scrap-man then came calling. *(John Holmes)*

Leyland TD5 Titan EWA 538, fleet number 18, was equally interesting. New to Sheffield in December 1937 with a Cravens H31/24R double-deck body, it suffered shrapnel damage during the Second World War. Sold to a dealer as a chassis only, it passed to Silver Service in 1948 and was fitted with a new Willowbrook DP35F body in April 1949. By 1959 it had been fitted with an AEC diesel engine and after its withdrawal in April 1961 this engine was transferred to WN 7754. The engineless hulk was scrapped in March 1963. *(John Holmes)*

This AEC Reliance with rare Duple Britannic C41C bodywork, 26 HMD, was new to Lily Coaches of Cockfosters in February 1956. The Britannic model was only sold during 1956 – from the following year until production ceased in 1962 central entrance examples shared the Britannia name with their front entrance siblings. Silver Service bought the coach in May 1959 as fleet number 21, and it remained in service for 15 years before sale as a mobile caravan. *(Derek Crawford Collection)*

AEC Regal I KEH 602 was new to PMT in 1946 with a Brush B34F body. In July 1956 the chassis was lengthened to 30ft and fitted with a Weymann B39F body transferred from another PMT machine. Silver Service acquired the vehicle in April 1961 as fleet number 7 and kept it for five and a half years. *(Chris Rischer Collection)*

Two contrasting Silver Service coaches seen at Darley Dale. LRB 62 (fleet number 15) was one of a pair of AEC Regal IIIs with Duple A type C35F bodies new to the company in 1947. In 1959 it received a new 'full front' from Yeates and remained in service in this form until August 1969. Bedford SBG/Yeates Europa C41F coach 950 DNU had been new to Strange of Tansley in February 1957 and passed with that business into Silver Service ownership in November 1963. It received fleet number 17 but kept Strange's red and cream livery for at least four years, lasting until July 1970. *(Peter Roberts via John Holmes)*

The other Strange of Tansley vehicle acquired by Silver Service, 1958 Bedford SB3/Yeates Europa 893 FRB, received fleet number 18 and had been repainted into Silver Service livery by the time this photograph was taken in 1967. It remained in the fleet until November 1973. *(John Holmes)*

This Bedford VAS1 coach with a Duple Bella Vista C29F body, 549 EAC, was new to Grayline of Bicester in December 1962. It passed to Silver Service in March 1967 as fleet number 20. After withdrawal in December 1979 it became a mobile caravan, and then re-appeared as a road-side cafe on the A6 at Rowsley in the early 1980s. *(Peter Roberts via John Holmes)*

VNL 51 was a Bedford VAS1 coach with a Plaxton C29F body which started its career with Armstrong of Westerhope in February 1962. In March 1966 it moved to Shropshire with Jones of Market Drayton, and in July 1967 passed to Taylor of Crich. When Gervase Taylor sold his business to the Woolliscrofts in October 1969 the vehicle became Silver Service fleet number 16. Withdrawn in February 1979 it migrated to Northern Ireland. *(John Holmes)*

AEC Reliance/Roe B45F bus 8625 DT was new to Doncaster in November 1961 and sold to Silver Service in September 1970 as fleet number 5. In September 1973 it was sold on to Osborne of Tollesbury for use as a source of spares. *(John Holmes)*

Silver Service bought this brand-new AEC Reliance 6U3ZR with Willowbrook Expressway C53F bodywork from a dealer in June 1972, already registered as DUR 974K. It received fleet number 24, and two months after delivery was re-registered as XRA 876L despite having been in revenue earning service under the original (more accurately dated) marks since its arrival. Sold in July 1981, it was later converted into a horse transporter. *(Colin Anderson Collection)*

Alexander Y-type coaches without a roof-box destination display always looked a little bit odd. This is TCP 900, an AEC Reliance 2U3RA with a DP49F body new to Hebble of Halifax in May 1964. Silver Service bought it in January 1972 as fleet number 23, and kept it until April 1976. *(Colin Anderson Collection)*

Although we are in the deregulation era by this point, a few other vehicles are worthy of mention. AEC Merlin AML 569H had been new to London Transport in 1970 as MBS 569 and originally carried 32 seated passengers plus numerous standees. Silver Service bought it in September 1981 as fleet number 65. In December 1982 it was sent to Willowbrook to have six more seats added and remained in service until August 1987, providing welcome relief to the swarm of RE types. The Merlin narrowly avoided transfer to the revived Hulleys, but many of the Bristol REs were destined to make the transition. Also included in the buy-out were a trio of Bedford YMTs with Wadham Stringer Vanguard bus bodies (MKP 180/2/3W). They carried 61 people by using '3+2' seating in the rear half of the interior, and were acquired by Silver Service during 1987 from Maidstone Borough Transport in Kent.

Postscript

Profits from the Silver Service Group's stage carriage services were never that great and Selwyn Woolliscroft attempted to diversify into more profitable activities. The excursion and tours side of the business was deliberately expanded, including many more trips to Europe, and an ambitious seasonal express service to resorts in Devonshire and Cornwall was inaugurated in 1984. The allocated vehicle spent a week in Cornwall before returning to Darley Dale, and the company used the new deregulated environment to start offering excursions at the Cornish end. This was not a great success and it might have been better to send the coach there and back every weekend with an overnight break for the driver.

More coaching activity was taken on board in 1985 when Silver Service became a participant in the X67 express service. This had originally operated between Chesterfield and Manchester via Baslow and Tideswell, but by 1985 had been extended at both ends to run from Lincoln to Liverpool. It was still losing money and in an attempt to keep it going the existing operators had persuaded Silver Service to join in. The former Hulley route 172 from Chesterfield or Baslow to Tideswell was withdrawn on weekdays and the X67 diverted via Eyam and the other villages it had served. In this way a short route which lost money (the old 172) became a very long

route which lost quite a lot more. The Liverpool extension was soon dropped, and the Lincoln extension cut short at Mansfield.

Despite the rather mixed results on the coaching side Selwyn continued to argue that this was the only way forward, a position that hardened still further after the full implications of the 1985 Road Traffic Act had been understood. Meanwhile, Nancy and John Woolliscroft remained committed to providing bus services to local people, arguing that the year-round income provided a measure of stability to the firm's cash-flow, and were refusing to consider the possibility of a sale to a larger operator such as East Midland. By 1987 the atmosphere had become so adversarial that Nancy and John had moved from the offices at Darley Dale to Baslow to escape the constant tensions within the family. In August of that year the Hulley name began to be painted on the sides of buses again, and the subsequent sale of the stage carriage services to Arthur Cotterill and Peter Eades in 1988 has already been covered under the 'Hulley of Baslow' heading.

After the split Silver Service continued as a coach operator, but its remaining days were numbered. On the 1st of May 1990 the Fuel Oil Supply Co (Silver Service's main provider of diesel) presented a petition to the High Court for a receiver to be appointed with a view to the liquidation of JH Woolliscroft & Son Ltd. In the absence of any realistic settlement plan from Silver Service the petition was granted and the company ceased to trade. It was a very sad end for such a fascinating story.

Steeples of Parwich

The Steeples family were well-known in the small village of Parwich, four miles to the north of Ashbourne and a mile or so to the east of the main road to Buxton. In the 1891 census William Steeples was listed as the local policeman, while Herbert Steeples was noted as a bricklayer. At around this time public transport to Parwich was provided by Joseph Twigge who ran a horse and cart into Ashbourne on market days.

Meanwhile, another branch of the Steeples family was resident in the nearby village of Hognaston where they had the tenancy of Bridge Farm. Robert Henry Steeples was born on the 3rd of March 1896, and after acquiring skills as a motor mechanic during the First World War decided to try his hand as a haulier and motor-bus operator. The first two vehicles were a Ford Model T van and a Maxwell lorry, neither of which have been identified. They were both new in 1920 and were used as goods vehicles during the week and as 14-seaters at the weekends. The Maxwell was replaced by a similarly unidentified 20-seat Reo in 1925, and the Ford by an anonymous Albion 20-seater in 1929. The Reo gave way in its turn to a 20-seat Chevrolet in 1931.

RH Steeples original service ran from Hognaston to Ashbourne, bringing him into conflict with the Webster family's operation over the same route. The Websters were very important people in the Hognaston area and William Webster had established an outpost in the neighbouring village of Parwich. In April 1932 a deal was done whereby RH Steeples would sell his Hognaston operations to Edwin Webster and Albert Carnson in exhange for William Webster's services from Parwich along with a garage and filling station in that village at Creamery Lane.

The first fully identified vehicle came in July 1936 when brand-new Commer PN3/Waveney C20F coach CRB 259 arrived in Parwich. It replaced the Albion. In December 1938 the Chevrolet was converted into a lorry and its place in the bus fleet taken by a brand-new Bedford WTB/Thurgood C26F coach, EJH 956, which had been registered by its body manufacturer in Essex.

There were no additions to the fleet during the Second World War. By December 1949 the Commer was on the way out and was replaced by a Mulliner-bodied Bedford OB bus. This vehicle, ORE 359, had been new to Warrington of Ilam (just across the Staffordshire border from Parwich) in September 1947. It was quickly put to use on the Parwich-Ashbourne route (which operated on Tuesdays, Thursdays, and Saturdays) and on a Monday-Friday works contract which connected Parwich and other villages to the Tatton family's textile mills at Mayfield. The Friday only service to Derby was normally operated by the WTB until its sale in August 1951. Its replacement was LNW 830, a Bedford OB with a relatively unusual ACB C28F body. This vehicle had been new to Kelsall Coaches in Leeds in 1947 and came to Parwich from Parkin of Borrowash.

The proprietor had done most of the driving up to this point, but the addition of the works

contract had taken the number of hours beyond his personal capabilities. Fortunately, a candidate was at hand as one of RH Steeples four daughters had married Ron Twigge, a descendant of the original village carrier. Another of Mr Steeples' daughters, Mrs Eileen Ellis, recalls hard winters days dispensing petrol at the garage in this era, and also her father's tales of the late evening run from Ashbourne to Parwich on Saturdays. The final departure was frequently over-loaded and on at least one occasion two well-oiled passengers decided to sit on the bonnet with their feet resting on the Bedford's mudguards. Fortunately, neither was killed.

The ACB-bodied OB was sold in April 1959, succeeded by another OB with the more usual Duple Vista body. ECL 190 was a 1951 model and had been new to Broadland in Norwich, passing to Pooley of Long Sutton before moving westwards to Parwich. Three years later the ex-Warrington's OB was sold on to another Ashbourne area operator, Allen of Roston (see Part Three), and not replaced, leaving ECL 190 as the only vehicle in use. Mr Steeples passed the age of 70 in 1966 and found driving more difficult and routine maintenance work becoming next to impossible. He decided to retire and gave notice to the Traffic Commissioners that he would cease to trade at the end of November 1967. The OB was officially sold to Hartle of Buxton in October, but continued to operate the Parwich routes 'on hire' for another month.

The Derby service was lost, but North Western acted quickly to restore a diminished schedule to Ashbourne. This provision was achieved by diverting journeys on route 109 (Matlock-Ashbourne) into the village, but this was limited to one departure in each direction on Thursdays and two on Saturdays. Even at the very end Steeples had offered one round-trip on Tuesdays and Thursdays and six on Saturdays. RH Steeples enjoyed a long retirement and died in March 1983, aged 87.

Taylor of Crich

Gervase Edward Taylor was born in Tansley in 1894. His father (also called Gervase) had the tenancy of Spout Farm and by 1911 the younger Gervase was working as an apprentice waggoner for a neighbouring farmer, moving to Crich in

Mulliner-bodied Bedford OB bus ORE 359 was new to Warrington of Ilam in September 1947, migrating across Dovedale (and the county boundary) to Steeples of Parwich in December 1949. Steeples sold it to yet another Ashbourne area independent, Allen of Roston (see Part Three) in April 1962. *(Anthony Moyes)*

Associated Coach Builders bodywork was uncommon outside of the firm's north-eastern heartland, and even more so when mounted on Bedford OB chassis. LNW 830 (a C28F coach) was new to Kelsall Coaches of Leeds in December 1947, but Steeples bought it from Parkin of Borrowash (Luxicoaches) in August 1951. Its next move was to Burrows of Grantham in April 1959. *(Anthony Moyes)*

This Bedford OB/Duple Vista coach, ECL 190, was new to Broadland of Norwich in March 1951, making it a very late production example. It later served with Pooley of Long Sutton before migrating to hillier terrain with Steeples of Parwich. Seen in the background of this Ashbourne bus station view are Warrington's OB/Vista EDB 535, an unidentified OB/Vista in the livery of Webster of Hognaston, and two Trent vehicles. *(Anthony Moyes)*

Another view of ECL 190, this time parked outside Steeples' garage on Creamery Lane in Parwich. After Mr Steeples decided to retire the OB was sold to Hartle of Buxton, but rented back to him for three weeks while North Western sought approval to provide a replacement service. *(Anthony Moyes)*

1916 after his marriage to a local girl. Like so many other young men he gained driving and motor repair skills during the First World War (in his case while serving with the Devonshire Regiment), and in 1919 bought an army surplus Dennis 30cwt lorry which could be converted into a makeshift bus using wooden bench seating and a hoop-and-canvas roof. This vehicle was used to deliver coal from Monday to Friday, but on Saturdays had its seats installed and operated several trips between Crich and Ripley. In 1920 a seven year old Ford Model T with a van body was acquired and this could also be equipped with basic seating.

In 1921 the first purpose-built bus arrived in the shape of a new Dennis char-a-banc with 16 padded seats. This allowed the first Dennis to become a permanent lorry. The char-a-banc carried the name 'My Lady', a branding which would be used (albeit somewhat sporadically) until the end. Another Dennis was acquired in 1923 but was fitted with a 16-seat saloon body built by the chassis manufacturer. Its purchase was the result of Mr Taylor obtaining contracts to carry miners to the Oakerthorpe and Swanwick collieries. In 1925 the Ford Model T was replaced by a brand-new Reo with a 14-seat Sanderson & Holmes body. Like all of Taylor's vehicles before 1929 it has defied identification.

In May 1929 Mr Taylor bought a Willys Overland chassis and transferred the body from the Reo to his new acquisition which was registered RA 8532. The Reo was then converted into a lorry and replaced the original Dennis on coal delivery duties, while the Willys operated the Ripley market-day service on Saturdays, a new return trip to Derby on Fridays, and was available for private-hire at other times. Some reports suggest that its second-hand body was later replaced by a Wilkinson unit, also with 14 seats.

The Willys (by then the only bus in the fleet) was sold to Brookes of Derby and its replacement was a brand-new Dennis Ace with a 26-seat Willowbrook body registered ANU 833. The Ace proved itself to be good value for money, lasting until November 1947 and then being sold for further service with Allen of Roston (see Part Three). The Ace's replacement was a factory-fresh Bedford OB/Duple Vista coach, LRB 158.

In September 1950 the fleet doubled in size with the arrival of a second brand-new OB/Vista coach, ORB 45. The two bonneted Bedfords

remained in use until July 1967 when LRB 158 was sold to Slade of High Bullen and replaced by a third-hand Bedford VAS1/Plaxton Embassy C29F coach, VNL 51. This whiff of modernity had started its career in February 1962 with Armstrong of Westerhope in Northumberland, passing to Jones Coachways of Market Drayton, Shropshire, in March 1966, and then to Taylor.

The proprietor was already 73 years old when the VAS1 was purchased and began to feel his age. In October 1969 he decided to retire and sold his two vehicles and the 'goodwill' of his stage services to JH Woolliscroft & Son Ltd of Darley Dale, trading as Silver Service (qv). The VAS1 was quickly repainted into Silver Service livery and stayed with the fleet for more than nine years, but ORB 45 was left in Mr Taylor's two-tone brown livery complete with 'My Lady' eyebrow sign and saw little use before being de-licensed in November 1970. It then rotted in the grass for a while before being scrapped on site at Darley Dale. Silver Service continued the Derby service until 1978 and the Ripley route until 1983. Both are now covered by other operators on a daily basis thanks to the considerable extra patronage provided by visitors to the National Tramway Museum.

Webster of Hognaston

In 1666, the year of the Great Fire of London, the Webster family was mentioned as being in the haulage business for the first time. Operating from a stables in Hognaston they ran a team of pack-horses which carried agricultural products out of the village and then brought manufactured goods into the area on the return leg. By 1856 the family had moved over to horse-drawn traction and had expanded its business activities to include the sale of grain and flour. The village bakery was another Webster enterprise.

During this period the mastermind of the family's commercial expansion was Joseph Webster, born in Philadelphia (USA) in 1825. His American birth remains unexplained, but by 1856 he was back in Hognaston and had married Fanny Cowley from the nearby village of Mugginton. They produced ten sons and three daughters to replenish the family stock. The sons included Joseph Jr (born 1857), William (1858), John (1860), Thomas (1863), Phillip (1864), James (1865),

For most bus enthusiasts this vehicle, Bedford OB/Duple Vista coach ORB 45, was inseparable from any mention of Taylor of Crich. New to this micro-operator in September 1950, it trundled backwards and forwards between its home village and Ripley almost every Saturday for 19 years. In October 1969 it passed with the business to Silver Service. *(Omnibus Society - Roy Marshall)*

ORB 45 was never repainted into Silver Service livery nor allocated a fleet number. It saw little use with its new owners and was last licensed in November 1970. This lovely little machine then rotted in the grass at Darley Dale for a while before being scrapped. *(John Holmes Collection)*

Samuel (1868), Isaac (1870), Edwin (1871), and George (1873), while the daughters were Fanny Jr (1861), Lucy (1867), and Eliza (1872). Equipped with this home-grown army of employees the business became extremely competitive. A general grocery store and the village post office were soon added to the family's empire.

Each member of the family was allocated responsibility for a particular part of the business. Joseph Sr and Jr oversaw the grain and flour trade and the bakery (assisted at the latter by Isaac), Fanny Sr was in control of the post office, and William and Edwin took responsibility for the transportation activities which included coal deliveries to local residents. By 1891 passengers were being carried on the Websters' horse-drawn wagons with regular trips to Derby (on Tuesdays and Fridays) and to Ashbourne (on Saturdays). A competing village carrier, Noah Lamb, operated passenger schedules to Wirksworth (on Tuesdays) and to Ashbourne (on Saturdays, in competition with Webster's), but he had disappeared before the end of the century and Webster's network had been extended to include Wirksworth.

After the First World War the family moved from horse and steam power to the internal combustion engine. The first known (although unidentified) motor vehicle was a Ford Model T lorry-bus which arrived in 1920. It was followed by R 7923, a Garner Busvan (did what it said on the tin) which could be fitted with up to 22 seats. This was new in January 1922. In 1925 it was joined by a Dennis 30cwt bus with an 'NU' registration (the rest of its identity is concealed in the only known photograph) and in 1927 an unidentified Chevrolet with a 14-seat Wilkinson body replaced the Garner. The Dennis was then replaced by RA 4695, a brand-new Guy BA with a Guy B20F body which was delivered in January 1928. New market-day services to Bakewell (on Mondays) and Matlock (on Tuesdays) were started during the late 1920s.

With regulation of the bus industry on the horizon Edwin Webster and his sons (William had retired) decided that they needed to persuade some of their competitors to stand down in order to remain profitable in the new business environment. The services of TW Woolley and Albert Carnson (Edwin Webster's son-in-law!) were acquired outright, adding new journeys with slightly different routes to both Ashbourne

and Derby. Shortly before the Road Traffic Act of 1930 came into force a deal was done with RH Steeples (qv) which involved trading his Hognaston routes for W Webster's two services from Parwich. Licences for all of Webster's routes (including the recent acquisitions) were duly granted by the Traffic Commissioners, and this led to the arrival of a brand-new 20-seat Morris Director (RB 5727) in March 1932 which took the PSV fleet to three.

In July 1935 a new Bedford WLG chassis was obtained and fitted with the Wilkinson B14F body previously carried by the Chevrolet (which then became a lorry). Edwin Webster was impressed by the WLG and went on to buy two brand-new Bedford WTB coaches with Duple bodywork, CRA 993 in July 1936 and FNU 875 in July 1938. Both lasted until March 1956, paying for themselves many times over. The second of the pair replaced the Guy BA, meaning that Webster's entered the Second World War with four passenger-carrying vehicles.

A new OWB with Mulliner utility bodywork, HRB 75, was allocated to Webster's in May 1943 and replaced the Morris Dictator. The first two deliveries after the end of the war were a pair of Bedford OBs with Duple Vista C29F bodywork. JRB 953 was delivered in July 1946 and LRA 310 in October 1947. They were followed into the fleet by another Bedford OWB bus, FTG 179, which had been new to Morris of Pencoed in 1945 and arrived in Hognaston in May 1948. This took the fleet strength to seven.

A third brand-new OB/Vista coach arrived in March 1950 as ONU 972 and increased the fleet to eight. The next acquisition was an almost new Crossley SD42/7 coach with a 33-seat Yeates body, HWY 664. This came from Kitchin of Pudsey in September 1950, when less than twelve months old, and replaced the 1935 Bedford WLG with its (by then decrepit) 1927 Wilkinson body. Bedford OWB bus HRB 75 left the fleet in 1953, but was belatedly replaced in March 1954 by a fourth OB/Vista coach, MTB 533. This vehicle had been new to Lamb of Upholland in 1950 but came to Webster's from Les Gleave of Audlem.

The post-war coaching boom was well past its peak by the mid-1950s and when the two pre-war WTBs were retired in March 1956 they were replaced by a single new vehicle, Commer Avenger III/Duple C37F coach 640 BNU. At around the same time the service to Matlock was abandoned, although existing journeys on the route were continued as far as Wirksworth. In October 1959 the Crossley was sold and its place taken by 1954 Bedford SBG/Plaxton Venturer coach KVN 150, and two months later Bedford OB coach JRB 953 was replaced by similar machine NNU 461. This had been new to Doughty of Brimington in 1949 and when the Doughty business was sold to Chesterfield Corporation in November 1959 the new owners had declared it redundant.

After seven years without a new vehicle the Webster brothers (Edwin Jr – known as 'Young Eddie' and Henry) decided to splash out on a modern Bedford SB5 with Duple Bella Vega C41F bodywork and an unusual registration, 887 R. The new coach arrived in March 1963 and replaced OWB bus FTG 179. Bedford OB coach LRA 310 was the next to go, its place taken in December 1965 by a Bedford SB1/Yeates Europa C37F, UNR 146, which had been new to Gibson of Barlestone in 1960. Another second-hand coach, 1964 Bedford SB5/Duple Bella Vega 230 HFR, arrived from Enterprise of Blackpool in January 1967 and replaced the Commer Avenger III, while in June 1968 Bedford OB coach ONU 972 was retired and its place went to 1960 Bedford SB1/ Duple Super Vega JEF 559. An identical 1960 Super Vega, WBD 777, was acquired in April 1971 to replace SBG/Plaxton KVN 150.

The penultimate Bedford OB/Vista coach, NNU 461, was also retired in April 1971 and not immediately replaced although the arrival of a 1966 Bedford CALZ30/Martin Walter C11F mini-coach in December 1971 (HPN 116D) brought the fleet strength back to seven vehicles. A much grander acquisition was made in May 1972 when brand-new Bedford YRQ/Willowbrook Expressway C45F coach VNU 75K arrived in Hognaston. It was briefly an eighth vehicle until the final Bedford OB, MTB 533, was retired at the end of the year.

The YRQ was also the last coach to be acquired by the Webster brothers who were now in their seventies and intent upon retirement themselves. They agreed to sell the business to one of their drivers, Alan Ward, and the deal was done in June 1973. Seven vehicles were included along with the garage at Hognaston, the 'goodwill' of the stage carriage services, and the trading name 'Webster's of Hognaston', which the new owner continued to use. In October 1973 Mr Ward

went into partnership with Mr G Beeley, who had previously operated coaches from Allestree near Derby. Mr Beeley brought two vehicles into the new partnership, a 1962 Bedford SB5 with Yeates bodywork which had been new to Felix of Stanley (3 XRA), and a 1967 Ford R226/Plaxton C52F which had originally been delivered to Don Everall in Wolverhampton (LUK 583E). The partnership lasted for less than two years, but Mr Beeley's two coaches remained in the Webster's fleet after its dissolution.

The next arrivals were a quartet of very interesting coaches. Bedford VAL14/Plaxton 52-seater BMX 296A arrived in April 1975. It had been new to Hume of Hockley in 1963 and was one of less than 100 British PSVs to carry an 'A' suffix registration. A more elegant coach was acquired in September 1976 in the shape of AEC Reliance/ Harrington Cavalier 43-seater 83 VPP, new to Red Rover of Aylesbury in 1962. This displayed fleet number 12, although it appeared that Webster's had only operated 10 previous vehicles while under Mr Ward's stewardship. Several of these older vehicles were given single digit fleet numbers during 1976, but any hope that the numbering system would be logical disappeared in April 1977 when the next arrival became fleet number 16. This was allocated to EOD 31D, a 36ft Reliance with Harrington's equally stylish Grenadier bodywork which had been new to Devon General's Grey Cars fleet in 1966. Another coach with Western Traffic Area origins followed it to Hognaston. Or, more accurately, was towed there behind a recovery vehicle. RDG 306G was a Daimler Roadliner with Plaxton bodywork, new to Black & White Motorways of Cheltenham Spa in 1969. It had more recently served with B Cabs in Stoke-on-Trent and came to Webster's with serious accident damage. Any intention to restore it to working order quickly evaporated.

The last of the three arrivals during 1977 was even more interesting, being Webster's first ever double-decker. The Bristol FLF6B Lodekka with ECW H38/32F bodywork, 508 OHU, had been new to the Bristol Omnibus Co and arrived in December to begin work on a schools contract in January 1978. The New Year brought another major change in Webster's operations when its Hognaston-Ashbourne and Hognaston-Wirksworth services were combined into a new through route subsidised by Derbyshire

This Bedford OWB with Duple 'relaxed utility bus' (soon to be known as Mk II) bodywork, FTG 179, was new to Morris of Pencoed in October 1945. In May 1948 it passed to Webster of Hognaston, surviving with them until March 1963. *(Anthony Moyes)*

Websters preferred Bedfords, so the purchase of this Crossley SD42/7 coach with a Yeates C33F body was somewhat out of character. HWY 664 had been new to Kitchin of Pudsey in August 1949 and passed to Webster only one year later. It stayed at Hognaston until October 1959. *(Anthony Moyes)*

Bedford OB/Duple Vista coach MTB 533 was new to Lamb of Upholland (near Wigan) in July 1950. Webster bought the vehicle in March 1954 and kept it in everyday use (latterly on schools runs) until the end of 1972. In this view it is about to leave Hognaston for Ashbourne. *(Geoff Lumb)*

This OB/Vista was briefly in the ownership of a municipal operator. NNU 461 was delivered to Doughty of Brimington in May 1949, staying with that business until its acquisition by Chesterfield Corporation in November 1959. Three Bedford OBs were included in the deal, but were rapidly resold without being operated, this example passing to Webster before the end of the year. NNU 461 was only briefly out-lasted by MTB 533 as it was finally withdrawn in April 1971. *(Anthony Moyes)*

County Council. This was numbered 411 and effectively replaced the old North Western route 109 which had expired some years earlier. After deregulation the new 411 was extended beyond Wirksworth to Matlock on Tuesdays and Saturdays, bringing Webster's stage carriage vehicles back into that town for the first time in more than 30 years.

The County Council expected certain standards from its bus operators, and soon made it clear that they expected Webster's to obtain a 'proper' bus for the 411. This materialised in March 1978 when Reliance/Willowbrook B42D saloon 495 ALH arrived on loan from Chesterfield Corporation. It had been new to London Transport in September 1960 as RW1, the first of three acquired as tentative RF replacements. LT decided to modernise its RFs instead and all three passed to Chesterfield in November 1963. The Reliance kept its Chesterfield livery throughout its eight month stay at Hognaston along with its corporation fleet number of 18. The green livery and the fleet number were both appropriate for Webster's at the time.

Another famous bus turned up at Hognaston during 1978, but not as part of the Webster fleet. Henry Hulley's well-known SB5/Yeates Pegasus, 2626 UP, had been retired at the time of the Woolliscroft take-over and was then acquired by a preservation group who kept it at Webster's premises for six months or so. Sadly, it did not survive for very much longer, a tragic loss to the area's transport heritage.

In November 1978 the loan of the Chesterfield Reliance came to an end and Webster's was once again without a service bus. The firm got away with using coaches for a year or so before the County Council made threats about the continuation of the 411 contract. A solution was finally found in October 1979 when two Reliances similar to 495 ALH were acquired from Silver Service at Darley Dale. WEE 237/238 had been new to Grimsby-Cleethorpes Transport in September 1963 as fleet numbers 9/10 and carried Willowbrook B42D bodies. In April 1976 they passed to Silver Service with the same fleet numbers (and very little change to their livery), and were still in basic GCT colours when they arrived in Hognaston. WEE 237 was used for spares to restore its twin to reasonable health, and WEE 238 entered service on the 411 in January 1980.

There were two other acquisitions in late 1979, both of them Bedford coaches with Duple Dominant bodywork. BUX 217L was a 1973 YRQ 45-seater and UNW 37M a 1974 YRT with 53 seats. The following year saw the purchase of another former Black & White Motorways vehicle, 1972 Bristol RELH6G/Plaxton 47-seater ADG 332K. This arrived in June 1980 from Black & White's successor firm, National Travel South West, and stayed until April 1982 when it passed to North Somerset Coaches. In early 1981 it was joined at Hognaston by a 1968 Leyland Leopard with Alexander Y-type C49F bodywork, KJA 260F. This had been new to North Western but arrived in National Travel white and was not repainted during its stay with Webster's, although it did receive fleet number 22.

The next arrival (in February 1981) was a vehicle which would become Webster's stage carriage workhorse for the following eight years. PNV 434M was a Bedford YRQ with a Willowbrook 001 B45F body and had been new to United Counties in 1973. It replaced Reliance WEE 238 on the Ashbourne-Wirksworth/Matlock route and proved to be outstandingly reliable when compared to most of the elderly vehicles operated since the change of ownership at Hognaston.

In the deregulation era Webster's continued to maintain the 411, the weekly run to Derby (given the route number 414), various tendered routes (notably the 133 from Ashbourne to Belper), and its schools service commitments. The Lodekka had been withdrawn in 1980 and no further double-deckers had been acquired, the schools runs being operated by second-hand coaches. In December 1983 Webster's bought two 1976 Bedford YMTs with Plaxton bodywork from Barton Transport (MTV 508P and RRR 513R), and the next purchase of any real interest came in 1988 when the YRQ service bus was replaced by a trio of Fords which had been new to Northern Scottish in 1977. USO 160/1S were R1014s with 45 seats and USO 168S was an R1114 with 53 seats. All three carried attractive Alexander AYS bodywork and were used both on the 411 and on the schools journeys.

In 1991 Alan Ward decided to retire and sold the company to Patrick Brown of Hulland Ward. Mr Brown moved the business from Hognaston to his home village and traded as Express Motors rather than Webster's. The ex-Scottish Fords were

In December 1965 Webster bought this Bedford SB1/Yeates Europa C37F coach, UNR 146, which had been new to Gibson of Barlestone in February 1960. It lasted long enough to be one of the vehicles transferred to new owner Alan Ward in 1973. *(Eric Wain)*

The last vehicle acquired during the founding family's ownership of Websters was this Bedford YRQ with Willowbrook Expressway C45F bodywork, VNU 75K, new in May 1972. It became the regular performer on the Friday only service to Derby, but was disposed of relatively quickly by the new proprietor in exchange for two older machines. *(Colin Anderson Collection)*

Not all of Alan Ward's acquisitions for Websters were old bangers – some were genuine classics. One such was KJA 260F, a 36ft Leyland Leopard PSU3/3RT with Alexander Y-type C49F bodywork, new to North Western in 1968. It arrived in Hognaston in early 1981 as fleet number 22 and remained in the bland overall white livery applied to NBC coaches throughout its final years. *(Colin Anderson Collection)*

Bedford YRQ/Willowbrook 001 B45F bus PNV 434M was new to United Counties in 1973 and was acquired by Websters in February 1981. It retained its NBC corporate livery of leaf green and white as this was reasonably similar to (although much less stylish than) Websters' traditional colour scheme. The YRQ spent the best part of a decade on local stage services before being replaced by a trio of Ford/Alexander buses in 1988. *(Colin Anderson Collection)*

gradually replaced by more modern vehicles including Bristol LHs and Leyland Nationals, painted in an attractive blue and white livery. In 2002 Express Motors ceased to trade, bringing to an end a story that went all the way back to 1666.

White of Calver

The village of Calver stands at the cross-roads of two important routes, the east-west axis running from Chesterfield towards Manchester and the north-south line from Sheffield to Bakewell. To the north of Calver the Sheffield road bifurcates briefly, becoming joined into a single road again at Fox House, three miles further on towards the city. The western fork passes through Grindleford while the more easterly trajectory takes in Froggatt on the opposite side of the Derwent Valley. Grindleford acquired a railway station in 1894 with the opening of the Midland Railway's line from Manchester to Sheffield, but the station was located more than a mile from the village. By 1905 a regular (horse-drawn) wagonette service was meeting the more important trains to take passengers on to Grindleford village, Calver, Stoney Middleton, and Eyam. The fare was six old pence each way (2.5p in today's currency).

Arthur Goddard of Calver Sough operated the connecting service, and continued it throughout the First World War despite losing two of his sons during the closing stages of the conflict. Arthur Sr (born in 1864) and his younger son Arthur Jr (born in 1901) persevered through their grief and in 1919 traded their horses in for a military surplus Crossley 'RFC', which could accommodate 14 passengers on makeshift seating. A second, larger, military surplus vehicle (possibly a Daimler) was acquired in 1921 and fitted with a char-a-banc body for a far more ambitious enterprise. This was a new route from Eyam, Stoney Middleton, Calver, and Froggatt to Sheffield, terminating on private ground at Tomlinson's garage on Ecclesall Road to avoid the attentions of Sheffield Corporation's Watch Committee.

Competition was not long in coming. In April 1922 AF Hancock started a service from Sheffield to Buxton, following Goddard's route as far as Eyam and then continuing via Tideswell. Hancock had the advantage of using a city centre terminus (the char-a-banc parking ground at Moorhead), obliging Goddard to transfer his

service to the same site. In September 1922 the larger of Goddard's two vehicles was involved in an accident at Froggatt and this seems to have been the death knell for his Sheffield route. The Grindleford Station service continued.

Hancock faced fresh competition on the Froggatt side of the valley from April 1924 when Murdock MacKay of Bakewell started a Bakewell-Ashford-Great Longstone-Calver-Sheffield service. In April 1925 a separate Bakewell-Ashford-Great Longstone route was inaugurated and the Bakewell-Sheffield service was diverted to run via Hassop, Calver, and Grindleford, providing a more direct route (and a new competitor on the Grindleford side of the valley), but three months later MacKay sold the revised service to Sheffield Corporation which gave it route number 40. In October 1927 the municipality acquired the stage carriage routes of AF Hancock, bringing Sheffield vehicles into Froggatt, Eyam, and all points to Buxton for the first time.

On the Grindleford side of the valley Goddard's vehicle had already been competing with another operator for almost a year before MacKay's intrusion. In May 1924 Maurice Kenyon of Grindleford had bought a 14-seat Ford Model T and used it from Grindleford Station to Calver and Baslow. A second (Monday only) service from Grindleford to Bakewell began shortly afterwards. As a result both White and Kenyon were rather disturbed when Sheffield Corporation decided to divert the (ex-Hancock) service to Buxton to run via Grindleford rather than through Froggatt. If allowed to stand this alteration would have doubled Sheffield's presence in Grindleford and could easily have led to the disappearance of the services run by local operators. It would also have left the village of Froggatt without any bus service at all. After appeals from all the disadvantaged parties Bakewell Rural District Council voiced their displeasure to Sheffield, and the Buxton service returned to its original route through Froggatt in February 1928.

White of Grindleford

Some of the more rustic independents were marginalised by the Road Traffic Act of 1930, and somewhat dumbfounded by the paperwork necessary for continued operation. There is no evidence that Arthur Goddard had any literacy problems, but by 1931 he had passed retirement age and decided that the new regulated environment was not for him. He put the word out that a business opportunity existed and offered the service to AF Hancock who was still operating his coach fleet. Hancock had no wish to antagonise Sheffield Corporation, but happened to mention the offer to the man who rented the house next to the Hancock grocery store in Grindleford, Edward Thomas 'Teddy' White. Mr White (who did some driving for Hancock) was very interested, applied for the licence, and bought a brand-new 20-seat Bedford WLB bus to replace the unidentified vehicle latterly used by Goddard. Maurice Kenyon objected to White's licence application, as did Sheffield, but the Traffic Commissioners accepted that White had inherited the 'grandfather rights' to the licence from Goddard and the WLB (registered RB 5882) went into service on the Grindleford to Eyam route in March 1932.

A second 20-seat WLB was acquired in 1934. VL 3210 had been new to a Lincolnshire operator in 1931 and was one of the first batch of Bedfords ever built. The fleet doubled in size again in 1936 with the delivery of a brand-new WLB/Duple C20F coach, BWB 369, and the acquisition of a three year old Bedford WHG 14-seater, RB 8731, previously owned by Stoppard of Clay Cross. In 1938 a new Bedford WTB/Duple C26F coach, ERB 289, joined the fleet and replaced VL 3210, while in March 1939 White's very first WLB was traded in for AAY 105, a 1937 WTB/Duple C26F coach which had been new to Farrow of Melton Mowbray.

In May 1939 Maurice Kenyon decided to retire due to ill-health and sold his business to Henry Hulley of Baslow (qv). Hulleys acquired two vehicles and the services from Grindleford to Baslow and Bakewell. For the next three decades a red Hulley machine would sit alongside the blue White's vehicle waiting for the trains at Grindleford.

White of Calver

White's original premises (a yard in Grindleford) could not adequately accommodate the growing fleet, and in 1941 Mr White acquired Flint House Garage in Calver to act as his new base. The Bedford WHG expired in September 1943 and the firm was allocated an OWB utility bus as its replacement. By the time this vehicle, JNU 732, materialised in July 1945 Hitler was dead,

Germany had been defeated, and the bombing of Hiroshima was only weeks away. Nevertheless it provided welcome additional capacity.

The first post-war vehicle arrived in September 1946; a brand-new Bedford OB/Duple Vista coach registered KNU 857 which took the fleet strength to five. This momentarily dipped to four in December 1947 when WTB/Duple AAY 105 was withdrawn, but went up to six in January 1948 with the arrival of two more new OB coaches. KWB 334 was another example with a Duple Vista body while LRB 284 carried less common (on an OB) Yeates bodywork. A third, rather mysterious, OB also joined the fleet during 1948. ESG 236 had been new to an unknown operator in 1946 and its registration document proclaimed it to be chassis number 12080. That unit was actually exported. Its 25-seat coach body was another unknown, although one source has suggested that it might have been built by Plaxton and originally fitted to an unspecified WTB. This confusing machine only stayed with White's until December 1949.

Other withdrawals during 1949 included BWB 369 in July and (rather more surprisingly) 1946 OB/Duple KNU 857 in December. Three additional vehicles joined the fleet to make up for the losses. First came NNU 183, an Austin CXB with Mann Egerton C29F bodywork new in April 1949. Next was NNU 761, a new Bedford OB with SMT's version of Duple Vista bodywork, which arrived in May. The third addition was HYF 971, a 1947 OB/Vista which had been new to the British South American Airways Corporation, acquired from a dealer in September.

Two new vehicles arrived in time for the 1950 summer season. A Dennis Lancet III with Yeates C33F bodywork (ONU 417) was delivered in January, and another Bedford OB/Duple Vista (ORA 281) in April. This took the fleet strength to nine until Austin NNU 183 was sold in September after less than 18 months at Calver. With eight vehicles in use at the end of the year, it will be apparent that the stage service to Grindleford (which required one under-utilised vehicle) had become a distant second to the business's coaching and contract activities. To give White's due credit they continued to provide a perpetually unprofitable bus route for the benefit of the local community when others might well have walked away from the task.

White & Sons

White's first Bedford SB, a brand-new example with a Duple Vega C33F body registered RNU 284, arrived in January 1952. It replaced the second-hand Bedford OB HYF 971, and in September OWB bus JNU 732 was also sold, reducing the fleet to seven. For the following nine years all of the firm's purchases would be additional SB models, starting with URB 247 in March 1954. This was a new SBG with a Yeates Riviera C36F body and replaced Bedford OB/Yeates coach LRB 284 which was sold to Bull of Tideswell (qv). The last surviving pre-war Bedford, ERB 289, had been de-licensed the previous April without replacement. Changes in the fleet were reflected by changes in management. The founder's sons Edward Jasper White (born in 1917) and Harry Ronald White (born in 1922) had been involved in the coaching business since their adolescence, and in May 1955 their contribution was acknowledged when the family firm was incorporated as ET White & Sons Ltd.

Another brand-new vehicle, Bedford SBG/Duple C41F coach 179 BNU, was delivered in March 1956. Its arrival was followed by the sale of Bedford OB/SMT NNU 761 and Lancet III/Yeates ONU 417. This left the fleet with just three SBs and the two surviving OBs (KWB 334 and ORA 281), all of them bought new by White's. The reduction in fleet size was partly illusory – the five vehicles left in use could carry more passengers than eight of their smaller predecessors – but the post-war coaching boom had definitely gone and the Suez Crisis of 1956 caused further problems to the private-hire sector due to fuel rationing.

This down-turn in business led the firm's directors to choose good quality second-hand coaches for the best part of a decade. In October 1958 a 1957 Bedford SBG with Duple C41F bodywork (545 BTC) was acquired from Walls of Wigan, and replaced Yeates-bodied URB 247. An almost identical 1956 SBG/Duple, WWB 462, came from Hirst & Sweeting of Sheffield in May 1960, replacing 1952 SB/Vega RNU 284. The fleet strength went down to four when OB/Duple KWB 334 was withdrawn in April 1961 and not replaced. The private motor car was now in its ascendancy, but, fortunately for the Whites, they had developed a petrol station and shop at their Flint House premises so it was a case of swings and roundabouts.

The first non-Bedford purchase since 1950 took place in January 1962 when 1960 Ford 570E/Duple C41F coach 854 JPT arrived from Trimdon Motor Services in County Durham. It replaced the second-hand SBG/Duple 545 BTC. The other second-hand Bedford, WWB 462, was replaced in November 1962 by 1961 Bedford SB8/Duple 518 BXK which came from JM Coaches in London. This had a diesel engine (as did the Ford) and the two gave much better fuel economy than their SBG predecessors.

The sole remaining Bedford OB, ORA 281, covered the Grindleford Station route until July 1963 when it was replaced by MWD 908, a 1953 Bedford SB/Duple Vega C35F which was short enough to manoeuvre in the station yard although less than perfect for a stage carriage route. It came from Hill of Stockingford. In January 1964 SB8/Duple coach 519 BXK arrived from JM of London, more than a year after sister machine 518 BXK, and eliminated the final petrol-powered Bedford SBG, 179 BNU. Two smaller vehicles arrived during the year. The first was a 12-seat Morris J2 minibus, AND 975B, bought new from a Manchester dealership in September 1964. Far more interesting was XJO 211, a 1955 Bedford AZ2 (a bonneted model more usually seen as an ambulance) with a Spurling B14F body. It arrived at Calver in November 1964 from its third owner, Frostways of Hull, and saw occasional use on the Grindleford service.

The two vehicles acquired during 1965 were at opposite ends of the price range. In January brand-new Bedford SB5/Duple Bella Vega C41F coach DNU 601C was delivered, becoming White's first new full-size coach since 1956. Rather cheaper was 1950 Albion FT3AB Victor/Duple C31F coach ONU 140, acquired from Strange of Tansley in September for the Grindleford route. It was 18 inches shorter than the 1953 Bedford SB which had encountered some problems in the confines of the station yard – especially if a Hulley vehicle was already in position.

Fleet strength had now crept back to eight vehicles, although two were minibuses. Bedford SB/Duple Vega MWD 908 was withdrawn in May 1966 and replaced by 1956 vintage SB/Plaxton Venturer C41F coach FSN 134. When new this had been a petrol-engined SBG but had later been fitted with a Bedford 300 cu in diesel engine as in the SB1 variant. It came to Calver from Julia Coaches of Great Houghton, its fourth owner.

Despite the Sheffield registration marks, Bedford OB/Duple Vista coach KWB 334 was new to White of Calver in January 1948. It gave more than 13 years to the firm, much of it on the stage service from Grindleford to Eyam, before being sold to Askew (a member of the Keswick-Borrowdale consortium in the Lake District) in April 1961. *(Chris Rischer Collection)*

Albion FT39 Victor/Duple C30F coach ONU 140 was new in 1950 to Strange of Tansley and passed to White of Calver in September 1965. Seen here at the operator's base, it was a regular performer on the station service until withdrawn at the end of 1967. It was then exported to the Republic of Ireland where it became FCI 308 with Burgin of Abbeyleix. *(Robert F Mack)*

The only acquisition during 1967 was a new 12-seat Ford Transit minibus, PRA 919E, which replaced the Morris J2. The following year saw the withdrawal of three vehicles and the delivery of one. The withdrawals were of the Albion Victor in January 1968 (it found further use in the Republic of Ireland), the solitary Ford 570E in May, and the Bedford/Spurling 14-seater in June. The new arrival was WRB 534F, a Bedford VAM70 with Duple Viceroy C45F bodywork. By this time Grindleford Station yard had been re-organised, allowing 30ft long coaches to turn around safely, and FSN 134 became the regular vehicle on the stage service.

The 1967 Ford Transit minibus was swapped for a new one (LVR 268G) in August 1969, and the following year saw the arrival of a new Bedford SB5/Plaxton Panorama C41F coach, HNU 553H. The pendulum swung back to Duple in July 1972 with the delivery of a new Bedford YRQ with relatively rare Viceroy Express C45F bodywork, VRB 899K. The Viceroy Express variant was suitable for both coach and bus work, and would prove its value to White's as larger operators began to reduce their services through the area.

By 1971 the old Hancock service to Buxton (Sheffield/North Western route 84) had dwindled from five journeys per day to two. After the closure of Sheffield JOC and the dismemberment of North Western it passed to Trent and in the summer of 1974 was combined with the route from Buxton to Hanley as service 28. This brought PMT in as a joint operator, but the length of the new route made its reliability variable and the Buxton-Tideswell-Eyam-Sheffield section was separated again as Trent service 208. This suffered more cuts during the 1980s and was ultimately reduced to one journey each way with the revised service number 244. A through service from Hanley to Sheffield via Buxton was later revived by PMT as their service X23, but this ran via Bakewell and Baslow rather than through White's territory.

These reductions led to the introduction of a new stage carriage service, the X65 from Buxton to Sheffield, operated by White's and usually the preserve of the Viceroy Express for the first few years before it was usurped by a pair of younger Bedfords with Duple Dominant bodywork.. The new service took the old Hancock/Sheffield route from Buxton to Calver, but then continued through Grindleford to Fox House and Sheffield. It ran four times each day from Monday to Saturday and three times on Sunday, almost matching the frequency of the old SJOC/NWRCC 84. The only losers were in the village of Froggatt which was left with one bus per day in each direction, Monday to Friday only, and timed to be completely impractical for journeys towards Buxton which did not involve an overnight stay. In the opposite direction the 244 arrived in Sheffield at 0910 and left at 1710, making it virtually useless for all Froggatt residents except commuters who could be late for work or students.

Meanwhile, the original service from Grindleford to Eyam continued alongside the X65, using Derbyshire County Council allocated route number 274, and offering three or four journeys on Monday to Friday and just one on Saturday. Between them the two White's services provided half of the scheduled timings between Grindleford and Calver, with the other half being operated by South Yorkshire PTE route 240 – the successor to Murdock MacKay's revised service of 1925.

By 1993 the White family was making a very good living from the filling station and shop at Flint House Garage, and much less impressive margins from the coach and bus business despite the acquisition of Bull of Tideswell (qv) in 1988. Chesterfield Transport, by then owned by its employees and sporting a bold new blue/yellow/white livery, made an offer for White's during the summer of 1993 and after some fine-tuning the bid was accepted. White's vehicles were repainted into Chesterfield livery but retained 'White's of Calver' fleet names and legal lettering. This all came to an end in July 1995 when the Stagecoach group, which had already acquired East Midland Motor Services, bought Chesterfield Transport. A reminder of the firm's final incarnation can be found at preserved bus rallies in the shape of PRA 109R, an Alexander-bodied Leyland Leopard which started life with Trent and later served with Lancaster City Transport before moving to Chesterfield's Retford & District subsidiary and then to White's. It is unquestionably a fine machine, but what a pity that none of White's Bedford OBs (or even the Albion) have survived to help us remember the days when White's were truly independent.

JH Woolliscroft

See Silver Service of Darley Dale

PART TWO
NORTH-EASTERN
DERBYSHIRE

While north-western Derbyshire has long had an economy dominated by agriculture, quarrying, and tourism, the north-east of the county has traditionally been a coal-mining area. That is no longer true, of course, but the story of how that happened is too sad and controversial to be told here. All one can do is ask the reader to imagine a landscape of grime, pollution, and subsidence, but also to imagine offset the relative prosperity and communal spirit of the many thriving mining villages.

The largest settlement by far in this part of the county is Chesterfield with more than 100,000 inhabitants. Despite its size and importance as a regional centre it remained a borough rather than a city, as did Derby itself until 1977. To the north of Chesterfield, on the main route to Sheffield, the small town of Dronfield had around 15,000 residents and proceeding clockwise from here a traveller would pass through the pit villages of Eckington (11,000), Killamarsh (9,000), Clowne (6.000), Staveley (18,000), Bolsover (12,000), and Clay Cross (10,000). The latter lies to the south of Chesterfield and roughly half way to the town of Alfreton (22,000). Although an old market town Alfreton had also prospered from the coal-field and there were two substantial mining villages to the east of the town, South Normanton (10,000) and Pinxton (6.000). The coal-field continued across the county boundary towards the Nottinghamshire town of Mansfield, and to the north of that town a kink in the Derbyshire border enclosed the pit village of Shirebrook (10,000).

There were other employers besides the coal mines, but these tended to be in coal or colliery related industries. Eckington had the Sitwell family's iron-works and other iron foundries could be found in Staveley and Clay Cross. The ironworks in the latter village had been founded by the Stephensons, of railway engineering fame, but was sold to the locally based Jackson family in 1871 and remained in use until the 1960s.

While the iron-works needed coal and coke to feed their furnaces, the coal mines needed iron

for a multitude of purposes. The pits needed other commodities too, and Alfreton became a centre for the production of high-strength ropes which attracted orders from across the UK and further afield. Other firms in the area produced drainage pipes, machine tools, and chemicals. As coal mines were closed employees of these suppliers suffered alongside the miners, as did those employed in local shops and hostelries. The past might have been a dirtier and more brutal time in north-eastern Derbyshire, but it was also a happier time for most in the villages.

Lest the picture seem too monochrome, I should add a little local colour. At the heart of one of the pit villages lay Bolsover Castle, a magnificent structure erected after the English Civil War by the Cavendish family (which included assorted Dukes of Devonshire, Earls of Shrewsbury, and the famous Bess of Hardwick). An earlier Norman castle had occupied the site since the 12th century. Now owned by the National Trust, the castle is a significant tourist attraction and for several years in the present century a 'heritage' bus route run by a Cosy Coaches Bedford OB served it in style.

The other major tourist attraction is a work of nature which is also of major historical importance. Creswell Crags is a limestone gorge on the Derbyshire/Nottinghamshire border, and caves in the area were home to Neanderthal humans as long ago as 58,000 BC. The local Neanderthal population fled the growing ice-sheets, but the caves were again in use (by later human variations) at around 32.000 BC and then continuously from 15.000 BC onwards. The caverns contain the only known prehistoric cave art in England and provided archaeologists with 'The Ochre Horse', a realistic image of a horse's head carved into a horse bone. It dates from around 10,000 BC.

The pit village of Clowne was the birthplace of the company which became East Midland Motor Services, while Chesterfield Corporation expanded its sphere of influence to include surrounding mining communities such as Bolsover, Clay Cross, Dronfield, and Staveley. Only in the far north of the region were there opportunities for an independent operator (Booth & Fisher) to develop a network of services. Truman of Shirebrook had services to both Mansfield and Worksop, but the other three independents which survived until the 1950s were basically single route operations from a stage carriage viewpoint. Every one of the operators listed in this section made a far larger proportion of its annual revenue from colliery works journeys than from its stage services. As the coal mines disappeared so did they.

Booth & Fisher of Halfway

Joseph Booth was born in the mining village of Killamarsh in 1889 and by the end of the First World War was employed in the offices at West Kiveton colliery. In 1919 he set up his own coal delivery business using a one-ton Langham lorry acquired from a Chesterfield haulier. Booth kept his colliery job until he was certain of success and the vehicle was driven by his brother Fred. Things went well, two more lorries were acquired (a Dennis and a W&G), and then in 1921 a Daimler CC chassis was purchased which could be fitted with either a lorry or a 26-seat char-a-banc body depending upon the task of the day. This machine was registered WA 2369.

In 1922 three more passenger carrying vehicles were acquired, an unidentified 14-seat Guy, a 14-seat Oldsmobile (R 7786), and another Daimler CC registered W 3201. This latter purchase had been new to Sheffield Corporation as fleet number 1 in 1913, equipped with an open-top double-decker body built by Dodson and offering 36 seats. There is some doubt as to whether it served Booth in this configuration or did so after being fitted with a single-deck body (as were several other former Sheffield double-decker chassis sold to independent operators). One correspondent suggests that its original body was swapped for the B27R body from Sheffield fleet number 2 before its sale to Booth. In the absence of photographic evidence we may never know.

Considering Booth & Fisher's later renown, the details of its early fleet have remained remarkably sketchy. In 1923 an unidentified W&G char-a-banc was placed into service (which may or may not have been a former W&G demonstrator), while another example of that marque (registered NU 5090) turned up in 1925. The same year saw the arrival of four unidentified Crossley RFCs from military surplus (at least some of which were fitted with 14-seat bodies) and these inaugurated Booth's first regular bus service, from Killamarsh to Worksop in Nottinghamshire via Woodall, Harthill, and Thorpe Salvin. This operated on

Wednesday, Friday, and Saturday only and while not losing any money failed to make very much.

The growing fleet of buses and lorries required a reliable engineer, and late in 1925 Joseph Booth gave that job to Donald Fisher from the nearby village of Ridgeway. Fisher, born in 1900, had been a mechanic in the Royal Naval Air Service towards the tail end of the First World War and became an invaluable part of the company. Five years later Joseph Booth would help to finance Fisher's own business enterprise, a motor repair shop, as a way of rewarding him and ensuring his continued availability. Skilled mechanics were becoming harder to find.

From Garner to Bedford

In 1927 the Killamarsh to Worksop service was re-routed via Wales, Kiveton Park, Harthill, and Thorpe Salvin, and passenger figures began to improve despite direct competition from Kirkby of Harthill. Daily operation soon followed. A new Morris Commercial, WB 8295, was acquired in February 1927 and fitted with a 20-seat bus body by Firth, but its existence as a bus would be short-lived. Later in the year Joseph Booth became a franchised dealer for Garner bus and lorry chassis, and in March 1928 placed a 20-seat Garner coach (WE 1368) into his own fleet. It was followed in November by another Garner (WE 3452) which was fitted with the Firth body from the Morris Commercial. WB 8295 then became a coal lorry.

A four year old Morris Commercial bus with 18 seats, RR 308, was acquired from Kendal of Worksop in January 1929, and this was followed in March by another brand-new Garner registered WE 4439. With the additional capacity Booth opened a second bus route in July 1929, running from Killamarsh to Sheffield via Eckington, Apperknowle, Coal Aston, and Dronfield. At the city end this terminated on private ground at Battey's Garage on Ellin Street. Battey had previously operated a service from Sheffield to Bakewell via Baslow, but had sold that route to the corporation in 1924. Booth used the 'return ticket' arrangement on his new Killamarsh route. As no tickets were sold within the Sheffield boundary no licence was required from the city's notoriously hostile Watch Committee. Sheffield's officials kept a close eye on all independents operating into the city, and Booth's service was noted on its second day of operation. The municipal men were

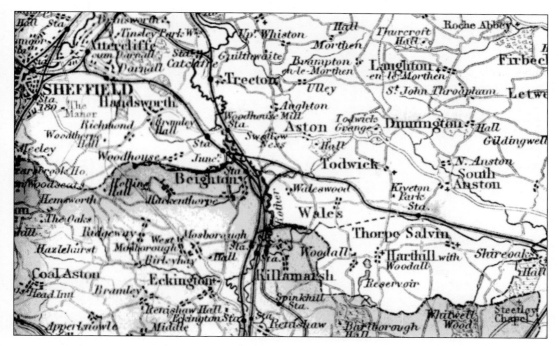

This map from the first decade of the 20th century shows most of Booth & Fisher's operating territory. The only exceptions are the major town of Worksop (just beyond the eastern edge of the map, to the right of the village of Shireoaks) and the Derbyshire town of Dronfield (immediately to the west of Coal Aston and Apperknowle). Also missing is Halfway – then still known as Holbrook and presumably omitted to avoid confusion with the 'other' Holbrook.

New to the Royal Navy in 1945, this Bedford OWB with a Mulliner body was one of a pair acquired by Booth and Fisher in 1947. Ten years later KRB 599 received a Perkins diesel engine, and lasted until January 1960. After withdrawal it became a mobile shop in the Killamarsh area. *(Omnibus Society- Roy Marshall)*

Bedford OB/Barnard coach LRB 750 was acquired by the Sheffield Omnibus Enthusiasts Society in August 1969. After ownership by several other preservationists the machine is now earning its keep again, available for rental from a Todmorden company which specialises in film and TV work. *(Les Dickinson)*

The three OB/Barnaby coaches were followed by a dozen OB buses with the bodywork order evenly divided between two Yorkshire firms, Allsop of Sheffield and Woodhall Nicholson of Halifax. MNU 80 (fleet number 13) was one of the Allsop B29F examples and arrived in May 1948. It is seen at Sheffield Station on a regular contract. It was withdrawn from use in January 1968 and then scrapped. *(Les Dickinson Collection)*

not beyond the tactic of entrapment and Booth was fined in September 1929 for operating without a licence after a 'passenger' surreptitiously left money on a vehicle as a 'fare'. He treated this with the contempt it deserved and continued the service, extending it at the Killamarsh end to High Moor before the end of the year.

A fourth Garner, WE 8161, joined the fleet in March 1930 and carried a 20-seat coach body. The Crossleys and various other older vehicles had gone by then, leaving the company with six passenger machines (the other two being W&G NU 5090 and second-hand Morris RR 308). Applications to the new Traffic Commissioners during 1931 resulted in Road Service Licences for both routes despite numerous objections from third parties. Surprisingly, Sheffield Corporation was not among them, having had a last minute change of heart which resulted in Booth (and Wigmore of Dinnington) receiving licences from the city's Watch Committee.

By 1933 Garner was on its last legs and Booth acquired one final example of the breed, WJ 5583, before abandoning the dealership franchise. This machine was delivered as a lorry but was soon fitted with a 14-seat bus body and replaced the Morris. With no more Garners available the company was forced to look elsewhere. In June 1933 a brand-new Dennis Lancet with a 32-seat Reeve and Kenning coach body arrived at Killamarsh as WJ 7012. It was officially registered to Joseph Booth, but had been financed by Donald Fisher who wanted to expand from motor repair into long distance coaching work. As Booth's vehicles rarely strayed far from their home turf there was no direct conflict of interest and the Lancet was made available for hire from either of the two businesses.

November 1933 saw the arrival of a vehicle more suitable for the stage carriage services. WU 8618 was a 1926 all-Leyland PLSC1 Lion with 31 bus seats. It had been new to short-lived Derbyshire independent Unity Motor Services of Clowne, passing with that business to Sheffield Corporation in October 1927, and later to the newly established Sheffield JOC. They traded it in to Leyland in September 1933 and the Lion was refurbished before sale to Booth. It became the vehicle of choice for the Sheffield route, being too large for the narrow lanes on the way to Worksop.

The Worksop route was catered for by the next second-hand purchase, a 1931 Chevrolet 20-seater registered WJ 1454, which arrived at Killamarsh in August 1935. Three months later the Leyland Lion was withdrawn after a major mechanical failure and a replacement was desperately sought. It materialised in early 1936 in the shape of another 1926 all-Leyland Lion, 32-seater HC 6043, which had been new to Eastbourne Corporation. In July 1936 another new coach jointly operated by Messrs Booth and Fisher was delivered. CWB 60 was an Albion PK115 Victor with a 25-seat Reeve & Kenning body. The vehicle survived the war and ran until 1951.

It seems that the 1931 Chevrolet made a good impression at Killamarsh as the (essentially similar) Bedford range became the default option from 1936 onwards. Three new 26-seat WTB coaches were acquired before the start of the Second World War. The first two, DWJ 543 (delivered in July 1937) and EWE 60 (delivered in January 1938), had Thurgood bodies while the third, EWJ 99 (delivered in April 1938), carried Duple bodywork. A fourth WTB, 1936 machine CRA 222, joined the fleet in early 1939 from Leah of Mosborough and had a Reeve & Kenning C26R body.

Wartime Arrivals

With the outbreak of war production of coal was drastically increased by 24 hour working at many pits, and this created a higher demand for public transport in the north Derbyshire coalfield. Joseph Booth received two 1932 vintage Leyland Lions towards the end of 1939 to help deal with this additional traffic. HL 5224 was an LT3 with Roe B32R bodywork which had been new to West Riding, while OD 1829 was an LT5 with a Weymann B31F body previously operated by Devon General. The same company had been the original owner of OD 5864, a 1933 LT5/ Weymann B30F bus which came to Booth from its second registered keeper, Valliant of London, during 1940.

For reasons which are not readily apparent at this distance in time the company's first two Bedford OWB utility buses were initially registered to Donald Fisher rather than to Joseph Booth & Co, although they were transferred to the main Booth fleet shortly after delivery. HRB 188/9 arrived in July 1943 and carried the Roe version of the 32-seat utility body. A more seasoned vehicle joined the fleet in October 1943 when TS2 Tiger VF 7677 arrived at Killamarsh. It had been new to United Automobile Services in 1930 and carried a United B30F body. The final addition during the war was another Bedford OWB (JNU 184), which had the Duple version of the body and arrived in January 1945. Two more Duple-bodied OWBs (JNU 957/8) were delivered after the end of the war, in October 1945, and at some point during the year an additional OWB (1943 machine HRB 168 with a Roe body) was acquired with the business of Barker of Eckington.

In November 1945 the long-time collaboration between Joseph Booth and Donald Fisher was finally acknowledged by the proclamation of a formal partnership. The legal lettering on the vehicles was changed accordingly and the company began to trade as 'Booth & Fisher'.

A Profusion of OBs

Buses were hard to find during 1946 and the only addition to the fleet was WS 8042, a 1936 Leyland LZ2 Cheetah with a fully-fronted Alexander FB36F body which had been new to SMT in Scotland. It replaced 1932 Lion OD 1829 which had been withdrawn in December 1945. Two more of the pre-war Leylands (VF 7677 and HL 5224) were withdrawn during 1947 along with the last surviving Garner (14-seater WJ 5583). This disposal of antiquities was occasioned by the delivery of four Bedfords, three of them pre-owned. The first to arrive (in March 1947) was KRB 318, a new OYL goods chassis which had acquired a wartime Duple utility bus body from an unidentified OWB. The next two were genuine OWBs with Mulliner bodies which had been new to the Royal Navy in 1944/45. Sold to Booth & Fisher in April 1947, they received the civilian registrations KRB 598/9. The final Bedford of the year, GXD 639, had carried a civil registration mark since new in 1943, being one of a fleet of Duple-bodied OWBs used by the top secret code-breaking establishment at Bletchley Park. It arrived at Killamarsh in December 1947.

Booth & Fisher sold its lorries to the state-owned British Road Services in early 1948, receiving generous compensation which was put to use in the remaining bus and coach operations. Two more ex-Navy Bedford OWBs were acquired in February 1948 as LNU 7 and LNU 178. They were both 1944 machines with Mulliner bodywork. During 1947, knowing that nationalisation of the haulage industry was imminent, Booth & Fisher had placed an order for no fewer than 15 new Bedford OBs and these began to arrive in March 1948 with the last being delivered in October. For the first time in the company's history (and the last!) fleet numbers were allocated. Numbers 10-12 (LRB 749-51) carried Barnaby C29F bodywork, while numbers 13-18 (MNU 80/79/81-84) had 29-seat bus bodies by Sheffield coachbuilder Allsop and numbers 19-24 (MNU 686-690/MRA 599) were fitted with DP29F bodies made by Woodall Nicholson of Halifax. It was an enormous investment for an independent operator of Booth & Fisher's size, and made all the more remarkable by the fact that only one older machine (a WTB) was withdrawn during 1948 in exchange for the 17 newcomers to the fleet. Booth & Fisher had grown to three times its former magnitude. The reason for this was the establishment of the National Coal Board and the introduction of free transportation for many coal-miners. Independents elsewhere (see Truman of Shirebrook in this section) experienced similar growth spurts until the new Conservative government abolished free travel concessions for colliery workers in 1951.

The multiplication of the fleet meant a search for larger premises, and the company moved from Killamarsh to Holbrook Colliery in the village of Halfway. The village had also been known as Holbrook at one time, but had changed its name to that of a local pub to avoid confusion with 'the other Holbrook' in the south of the county. The colliery had closed in 1944 and a part of the site with several out-buildings provided more than enough room for the armada of Bedfords. There were no fleet additions in 1949, but in 1950 the Bedford fleet grew even larger on the strength of new colliery contracts. Between January and July six more second-hand Bedford OWBs arrived at Halfway. Three (CNR 241/CNR 454/DRY 537) came from Gibson of Barlestone, two (CDT 206/EWW 602) from Billie's Coaches of Mexborough, and one (GAL 33) from Wright of Newark. All had Roe bodywork except for EWW 602 which was a Duple machine.

Underfloor Engines

In 1950 the main Killamarsh-Worksop service was extended to Beighton, where it executed an

Booth & Fisher's first underfloor-engined vehicle was SNU 234, a Leyland PSU1/15 Royal Tiger coach with Leyland C41C bodywork. New in July 1952, it was sold to Cherry of Beverley in the East Riding in March 1963. *(RHG Simpson)*

After a pair of AEC Monocoaches (one of which is illustrated in Part Four) Booth & Fisher turned to the AEC Reliance as its standard work-horse. Reliance MU3RV/Roe DP41F dual-purpose vehicle 352 BNU was delivered in May 1956. After withdrawal by B&F in October 1974 it was sold to Gunstone Bakery of Dronfield as a staff bus – Gunstone had long been a destination for B&F works journeys. *(John Holmes)*

In 1957 Charles H Roe was too busy to supply B&F with bodywork at the required time and so passed the order to its ACV sister company Park Royal in London. Reliance MU3RV/Park Royal B45F bus 19 DRA was delivered in April 1957 and lasted long enough to pass into South Yorkshire PTE ownership in February 1976. It never received an SYPTE fleet number as it was sold for scrap in August 1978. *(RHG Simpson)*

Reliance 2MU3RV/Roe DP41F dual-purpose vehicle 864 KNU was new to Booth & Fisher in May 1959 and differed from earlier deliveries in being equipped with front dome and cantrail windows. It became SYPTE fleet number 1084 and was sold for scrap in 1980. *(John Holmes)*

anti-clockwise loop around the village's roads before returning to Killamarsh and points east. A new variation of the Worksop service was also introduced, running from Limetree Avenue in Kiveton Park. The following year was devoid of vehicle acquisitions, but in July 1952 Booth & Fisher entered the underfloor-engined era with the acquisition of two brand-new Leyland Royal Tigers. SNU 234 was a PSU1/15 coach variant with Leyland's own C41C bodywork, while SNU 235 was a PSU1/13 bus with a B44F body, also by Leyland.

Kirkby of Harthill's competing service from Wales to Worksop was acquired in 1953 and blended in with Booth & Fisher's existing route variations on the way to the Nottinghamshire town. Kirkby remained in business as a coach operator and vehicle dealership. A second Royal Tiger bus, URA 601, was delivered in January 1954. The chassis was identical to that of SNU 235, but the bodywork had been built by Duple at the former Nudd Bros & Lockyer works near Kegworth. In spite of this third Royal Tiger delivery Booth & Fisher had found the type less than ideal due to its heavy steering, inadequate brakes, and poor fuel economy. On the other hand Leyland's light-weight successor to the Royal Tiger, the Tiger Cub, had a relatively tiny (350 cu in) engine and was also far from suitable for the company's territory. As a result the next order for new vehicles went to AEC. This in itself was hardly a surprise as many other Leyland customers turned to AEC for the larger (410 cu in) engine in their lightweight designs. The really surprising thing was that Booth & Fisher went for the integrally constructed AEC Monocoach, much rarer than the orthodox AEC Reliance design which involved a separate chassis and the customer's choice of bodywork.

The company's two Monocoaches (with standard Park Royal bodies) materialised as WRA 11/12 in December 1954/January 1955. Most Monocoaches ended up with Scottish Bus Group subsidiaries, and Laycock of Barnoldswick was the only other customer for the type among English independent operators. Neither Booth & Fisher nor Laycock came back for more. Booth & Fisher's next order was for two Reliances with Roe DP41F bodywork, delivered as 352/3 BNU in May/June 1956.

The company's older OWBs were starting to wear out, and the narrow lanes on the Worksop route (and on many of the colliery services) meant that more second-hand Bedfords were the only option for their replacement. A 1946 vintage OB/Mulliner B30F was bought from military (RAF) surplus in October 1956 and received the registration mark 691 CRA. Three more new Reliances followed, 19 DRA (with a Park Royal B45F body) in April 1957, and 517/8 GRA (with Roe DP41F bodies) in May 1958. A trio of time-expired OWBs were withdrawn during 1958 and replaced by Mulliner-bodied OB buses. GEW 58, built in 1948, arrived from Chiltonian Coaches in July, and was followed by 1950 vintage KXW 644/635 in September and December respectively. The 1950 machines had been new to London County Council as 'non-PSV' welfare buses. Two more new Reliances with Roe DP41F bodywork were delivered in May 1959 as 863/4 KNU, and there were also two more used OBs in that year, KGY 270 and KXW 646, both of them Mulliner-bodied buses previously used by London County Council.

Enter the Nimbus

The supply of good quality Bedford OBs was beginning to dry up and the two partners were acutely conscious of the need for an 'OB replacement'. Like the more famous concept of a 'Douglas DC-3 replacement' this existed in the abstract for many decades before finally becoming a reality, and in those intervening years operators were forced to make do with imperfect approximations of what they were actually looking for. The first real (albeit unsuccessful) pretender to the OB throne was the Albion Nimbus, an underfloor-engined design for 29-31 passengers introduced in the mid-1950s. The original MR9 version was basically a variation on Albion's Claymore lorry chassis and made very few friends outside of its native Scotland. An improved NS3N model was launched in 1959 and Booth & Fisher decided to try a couple. 363/4 MRA arrived in January/February 1960 and carried Willowbrook B31F bodywork. I once asked a driver for his opinion of these machines and he thought for a moment before saying 'they fit down the lanes'. This was the extent of his enthusiasm for the type.

As might be expected the company hedged its bets and managed to find another four second-hand Bedford OB buses to join the fleet during

1960. Mulliner-bodied JAD 832 had actually been acquired the previous year, but entered service in May. New in 1949 to Flint of Nettleton it had gone to Alderson of Settle before coming to Booth & Fisher. The other three acquisitions all carried Beadle bodies and had been new to Southern National in 1949. HUO 680-2 were bought from Wakefield dealership Comberhill Motors in September 1960 and entered service in September/October/November respectively. They replaced the last three Bedford OWBs.

The first vehicle to be delivered in 1961 marked a change in attitude toward coaching activity, being only the second 'full size' coach ever bought new –and its predecessor had been Donald Fisher's Lancet in 1933! Ford 570E Thames Trader 3893 WA arrived in April and carried Duple Yeoman C41F bodywork. The full size element of the bus fleet was topped up in November 1961 by the delivery of 843 URB, another AEC Reliance with Roe bodywork. Unlike the earlier deliveries it was of dual doorway configuration and its seating capacity was thus reduced to 42. The centre exit was specified so that Booth & Fisher could experiment with driver-only operation on the Sheffield route, but the experiment came to a sudden end in September 1963 when the Reliance was involved in a serious accident which left its bodywork beyond economic repair.

The New Garage

In January 1962 the company bought the business of Plant of Mosborough along with an ageing 1952 Bedford SB/Duple Vega C33F coach, KWY 559. It remained in the fleet for two years. A second new Ford 570E/Duple Yeoman coach, 884 XNU, was delivered in May 1962, but the major event of the year was the opening of a new purpose-built garage at Halfway to replace the tumbledown premises at Holbrook Colliery. As well as accommodation for the bus and coach fleet the new site included a filling station and a base for the company's PSV/HGV driving school. There were also changes to the Sheffield route during the year, with most journeys operating via the new Holmesdale Estate to the east of Dronfield. Short workings on the route which had previously operated between Sheffield and Apperknowle were also diverted into Holmesdale, later being extended to form a one way loop through the eastern half of Dronfield.

Two more Ford 570E coaches arrived in 1963. The first, 3725 R, was delivered in April and carried a Duple (Northern) Firefly body, while 5889 R (new in May) had Duple's Hendon-designed Trooper bodywork. Both seated 41. A more interesting purchase was a third Albion Nimbus with Willowbrook B31F bodywork, 537 JTC, which arrived in December. This vehicle had been new as a Leyland demonstrator in June 1959 (Leyland marketed its subsidiary Albion's designs in England and Wales) and was then sold after a year to Barrie of Balloch, trading as the Loch Lomond Bus Service. Barrie kept it for just over three years before selling it on to dealership Millburn Motors who sold it to Booth & Fisher.

The following year remained quiet on the vehicle front until June when two Bristol SC4LK buses with mandatory ECW B35F bodywork were acquired from a dealer. Both had been new to Eastern National, 612 JPU in 1957 and 9575 F in 1958. No more were bought but the two ex-ENOC machines remained in service at Halfway for almost six years. The only other purchase of 1964 was Booth & Fisher's first 36ft long vehicle, Ford 676E Thames 36/Harrington Legionnaire C49F coach ARA 534B. The Legionnaire body was relatively uncommon and the distinctive vehicle served as the flagship of the company's coaching fleet for more than nine years.

Joseph Booth was 76 years old in 1965, and this was also the year in which Donald Fisher passed state retirement age. Booth's eponymous son had also become active in the business, but even he was in his mid-fifties. It was time to consider things such as potential death duties which might cripple the business, and as a result the partnership became incorporated as Booth & Fisher (Motor Services) Ltd. The other major problem was the company's need to replace more time-expired Bedford OBs. In February 1965 Booth & Fisher bought a batch of five 1959 Albion Nimbuses from Great Yarmouth. They carried Willowbrook B31F bodies more or less identical to those on the company's existing three examples and entered service in March (CEX 492), April (CEX 494), September (CEX 491), November (CEX 493), and April 1966 (CEX 490). A larger capacity vehicle joined the stage carriage fleet in September 1965 in the shape of a new AEC Reliance, HNU 786C. This carried a dual-doorway Marshall B52D body and was the company's first 36ft long bus.

Booth & Fisher's first Albion Nimbus was 363 MRA, an NS3N with a Willowbrook B31F body bought new in January 1960. It became SYPTE fleet number 1056 and was sold to a dealer in August 1978. *(Terry James Collection)*

Booth & Fisher continued to buy second-hand Bedford OBs after the arrival of the first Nimbuses. In September 1960 three 1948 examples with Beadle B29F bus bodywork were acquired from Southern National, among them HUO 680. It gave almost nine years of service to the company. *(Terry James Collection)*

When Reliance 2MU3RA bus 843 URB was delivered to Booth & Fisher in November 1961 it carried a dual-door Roe B42D body. This structure was demolished in an accident in September 1963 and the sad remains of the vehicle were stored at Halfway depot. In April 1966 the chassis was sent to Marshall of Cambridge to receive the new Marshall B43D body shown here and re-entered service three months later. It became SYPTE fleet number 1089 and was withdrawn from use in August 1979. *(RHG Simpson)*

The company took a greater interest in private-hire work from the early 1960s onwards. Ford 570E/Duple Trooper C41F coach 5889 R was new in May 1963 and remained in the fleet until May 1974 when it was sold to Griffiths of Nantwich. In the following year it migrated to Northern Ireland for use by a church. *(RHG Simpson)*

Albion NS3N Nimbus/Willowbrook B31F bus 537 JTC was new as a Leyland Motors demonstrator in June 1959. In July 1960 it passed to Barrie of Balloch (Loch Lomond Bus Service) and then to Booth & Fisher in December 1963. Withdrawn from use in July 1977, it never received an SYPTE fleet number. *(RHG Simpson)*

Having reservations about the performance of its Nimbuses, Booth & Fisher decided to try a couple of second-hand Bristol SC4LK/ECW B35F buses in June 1964. Both had been new to Eastern National This example, 612 JPU, lasted until June 1970. No more of the type were acquired. *(Terry James Collection)*

The decision to send 843 URB to Marshall for rebodying was probably influenced by the arrival of AEC Reliance 4MU4RA/Marshall B52D bus HNU 786C in September 1965. It became SYPTE fleet number 1093 and was sold to a dealer in 1980. *(John Stringer)*

Great Yarmouth Corporation was clearly impressed by the Nimbus as it ordered five for delivery in 1959, all with Willowbrook bodies identical to those supplied to Booth & Fisher. This made them attractive to the Halfway operator which acquired the entire batch when it was offered for sale in March 1965. CEX 493 entered service with B&F eight months later and was sold to a dealer in November 1978. *(RHG Simpson)*

Since September 1963 the wreck of Reliance 843 URB had been a sad fixture in the yard at Halfway, but in January 1966 the remains of its Roe body were removed and the (almost undamaged) chassis sent to Marshall for rebodying. It would return six months later with a B43D body similar to, though shorter than, that of HNU 786C and give many more years of service. Other additions to the fleet during 1966 included a brand-new Ford R192/Duple (Northern) Viscount C45F coach (LNU 238D, delivered in April), a ninth Albion Nimbus (1963 example RJX 251, which carried a Weymann B31F body and came from Halifax in June), and another new 36ft long service bus (Ford R226/Strachan MNU 387D, delivered in July).

A more ominous change came in the New Year when the Sheffield city boundary was extended to include the Derbyshire villages of Halfway and Beighton. Although this posed no immediate threat to the company's existence it meant that the Halfway base would soon fall into the area of the South Yorkshire Passenger Transport Executive, and the new PTEs were to prove rather intolerant of anomalous independent operators doing business within their boundaries.

The Nimbus tally rose to ten in March 1967 with the acquisition of TUH 7. This carried a Harrington DP30F body and had been new to Western Welsh in 1960. It was followed in May 1967 by two more brand-new Ford R226 service buses, PWB 948/9E, although these examples carried Duple (Midland) DP49F bodies rather than the Strachan DP51F design used on MNU 387D. A second ex-Western Welsh Nimbus, TUH 8, was acquired in October 1967 (from Wood of Pullington), and a third example from the batch (TUH 14) came from Bluebell Coaches of March in July 1968.

The last of the original swarm of 15 Bedford OBs, Barnaby-bodied LRB 750, was withdrawn from use in November 1968. It had outlasted all of the second-hand examples except for the three former Southern National machines with their rather ungainly Beadle bodies. The company's very last OB was HUO 680 from this batch which was finally retired in July 1969. After 21 years and 3 months as a Bedford OB operator the 'bonneted bus' era had come to an end. In total 47 had been operated, made up of four pre-war WTBs, 17 OWBs, one OYD masquerading as an OWB, and 25 OBs. Few of these found further employment as PSVs, but at least 18 of them were converted into mobile shops, remaining a part of the local scene for several more years. The fleet of 12 Nimbuses could not hope to compete with this record.

Two more Ford service buses were delivered in March 1970. DWA 401/2H were of the shorter R192 design and carried Willowbrook DP45F bodies. Like the R226 buses (sold in 1973) they were quite a short-lived element in the fleet. DWA 402H was sold in May 1974 and DWA 401H in June 1975. A longer presence was maintained by two 1961 Reliance/Roe B45F buses, 8628/30 DT, acquired from Doncaster in September 1970. Two more new Fords arrived in May 1971 as JWE 896/7J, but these were 36ft R226s with Duple Dominant C53F bodywork. Despite having coach seating they could also be used on 'driver only' stage carriage work and often appeared on the Sheffield-High Moor service.

The Passing of Giants

Joseph Booth died in January 1972 at the age of 82. It soon became clear that the Fords had been his idea as no more were bought and all subsequent acquisitions were AEC Reliances. A 1962 example with Marshall B45F bodywork, TCY 662, came from South Wales Transport in June 1972. A month later the company took delivery of two brand-new 36ft Reliances with Plaxton Elite Express C51F bodywork, PWE 713/4K, and similar vehicles would be bought in July 1973 (WWA 931L and WWB 233L), August 1973 (WWJ 608/9M and XWB 295/6M), April 1974 (BWA 260M), and May 1975 (HWG 421N). They could be used on either bus or coach work and replaced all of the Fords.

In the meantime a new route had been introduced in May 1973 at the urging of (and with financial support from) the local authority in Dronfield. This connected Coal Aston and the new estates on the east side of the town with the main shopping area and the Gosforth Valley estate to the west. The service was jointly licensed to the three existing operators in Dronfield (Sheffield, Chesterfield, and Booth & Fisher), but in reality it was a single vehicle operation and worked almost exclusively by Booth & Fisher. This was of no great advantage as the service was poorly patronised, despite several attempts to increase its appeal, and it soon became clear that most people on the estates wanted to travel to Sheffield, not Dronfield. The route was finally withdrawn in June 1975.

Some of the oldest Reliance service buses were in need of replacement by June 1973 and the solution was to acquire two 1961 examples with Weymann DP40F bodywork (334/6 NKT) which had previously served with Maidstone & District. Two more from the same batch were added in May 1974 (340 NKT) and September 1975 (332 NKT), and all four would eventually go to Silver Star in Caernarvonshire after their time with Booth & Fisher.

Donald Fisher died in January 1975, aged 74, and his death signalled the beginning of the end for the company he had done so much to build. After his demise only four more vehicles were bought, HWG 421N and 332 NKT which have already been mentioned, and a pair of new Reliances with Duple Dominant C51F bodywork which arrived in November 1975 (KHL 667P) and in December 1975 (KKY 63P). By the time of their delivery the surviving members of the Booth and Fisher families were in negotiations with South Yorkshire PTE, which was eager to buy the business.

The take-over took effect on the 13th of February 1976, although the company remained as an operating subsidiary with its own depot, vehicles, and livery. The fleet at the time of the take-over was composed of Monocoach WRA 12 (sister vehicle WRA 11 had been withdrawn after colliding with a fallen tree), 10 Nimbuses (TUH 7/8 had been sold during 1975), 14 'short' Reliances (from 19 DRA onwards), and all 12 of the 36ft Reliances. The damaged Monocoach (WRA 11) had been sold to a preservation group before the take-over, but was later found to be beyond reasonable repair and when WRA 12 was withdrawn in 1977 it entered preservation in lieu of its twin. WRA 11 was then scrapped.

In March 1978 the remaining Booth & Fisher vehicles received SYPTE fleet numbers, and one month later Reliance 517 DRA (now fleet number 1081) became the first Booth & Fisher vehicle to receive the PTE's brown and cream livery. By the end of the year the company's licences and vehicles had been officially transferred to the PTE, but many of the Nimbuses and older Reliances remained in Booth & Fisher livery until their withdrawal in 1979/80. The newer Reliances

with Plaxton Elite and Duple Dominant bodywork were gradually repainted, with LHL 667P being the last to succumb, in early 1981. The garage at Halfway was retained for many years by the PTE and its successors until First Group closed it as an economy measure in 2007. Five years later it became the main base for TM Travel (previously of Staveley), and is now conveniently located close to a tram terminus and Park & Ride facility.

Some Booth and Fisher vehicles have also survived. Bedford OB/Barnaby coach LRB 750 was once well known on the rally circuit, still in Booth & Fisher livery, but is currently owned by Brian McNeill of Todmorden who uses it in a generic maroon and cream colour scheme as part of his 'Rollingpast Action Vehicles' fleet which provides old coaches, ambulances, and the like for film and TV productions. Monocoach WRA 12 is safely on display at the South Yorkshire Transport Museum, while Nimbus TUH 7 has been repainted into Western Welsh livery by a preservationist in north-east England. TUH 14 is also still with us, but unlikely to survive in the long term as it is being used as a source of spares for another Western Welsh Nimbus. At one stage (in 1988) ex-M&D Reliances 334/40 NKT were also recorded as being in preservation, but they seem to have vanished and may have been scrapped. The memory of this great operator will be far more enduring.

Flint of Carr Vale

In 1920 Charles Flint was listed in a Bolsover area trade directory as a 'carter', without clarifying whether his conveyance was horse-drawn or motor-powered. It is known that he found most of his work in the local collieries during the week, but also offered passenger rides from the mining village of Carr Vale into Bolsover town centre in the evenings and on Saturdays. His first identifiable motor vehicle came in July 1925 when brand-new Chevrolet NU 6935 was delivered to his premises in Carr Vale. No details have survived, but the Chevrolet is believed to have been equipped with a van body with removable bench seating positioned facing inwards. A second new example of the same design, RA 632, was delivered in October 1926 and with this doubling of the fleet it became possible to offer a Monday-Friday daytime service from Carr Vale to Bolsover.

Booth & Fisher became a magnet for second-hand Nimbuses in much the same way that Dan-Air Services acquired a monopoly of second-hand Comet jets. RJX 251, an NS3AN model with a Weymann B31F body, had been new to Halifax in June 1963 and was sold to B&F exactly three years later. It became SYPTE fleet number 1059 and by May 1979 was in use with Chesterfield Cricket Club as a 'non-PSV'. It was scrapped four years later. *(John Holmes)*

Other Nimbuses came from Western Welsh, the type's largest operator. TUH 14 was an NS3N with a Harrington DP30F body, new to Western Welsh in July 1960. In September 1966 it passed to Bluebell Coaches of March and then in July 1968 to Booth & Fisher. As SYPTE fleet number 1058 it was withdrawn in February 1979, passing to Silver Service of Darley Dale three months later. *(Terry James Collection)*

The exact pedigree of this vehicle is hard to ascertain. The chassis of AEJ 590 is a Commer Q4, probably from government surplus stock after the end of the Second World War. The C30F coach body is stated in some sources to be by Abbott, suggesting that it had been donated by a pre-war machine. First registered to Lloyd-Jones of Pontrhydygroes, it came to Flint of Carr Vale in March 1953 and stayed for four years. *(Omnibus Society - Roy Marshall)*

This 1949 Bedford OB/Plaxton C29F coach, GNT 517, was new to Greatrex of Stafford despite its Shropshire registration (the dealer was in Shrewsbury). Flint of Carr Vale bought the vehicle in April 1957, keeping it for two years before replacing it with a Plaxton-bodied Commer Commando of similar vintage. *(Chris Rischer Collection)*

In January 1930 a third vehicle joined the passenger fleet, a new Ford 14-seater registered RB 402. This stayed for just over six years before being traded in for a 1929 Chevrolet LQ 14-seater, VO 696, which had previously been operated by Stone of Worksop. The two original Chevrolets were sold shortly afterwards, leaving the LQ as the only passenger carrying vehicle in the fleet, but its dominance at Carr Vale was short-lived as in August 1938 it was replaced by a much larger machine, 1930 vintage Leyland TS3 Tiger/Duple C26R coach GH 7029. This had been new to Premier of Slough passing to the London Passenger Transport Board in 1933 for use on Green Line work. For several months it was the only PSV in the fleet until the arrival (in early 1939) of CH 8125, a 1929 SOS M type with a Brush B34F body which had previously run for Trent.

The only addition during the war years was RA 8058, a 1929 Maudslay ML3B with a United B32F body, which arrived from Henry Hulley of Baslow in 1943. It provided back-up for the SOS on works services to local collieries while the Tiger coach maintained a much reduced service from Carr Vale to Bolsover and was also used on longer distance military contracts. After the end of the hostilities Mr Flint (like every other coach operator in the country) tried to find as many additional vehicles as possible to meet the public demand for leisure. Dates remain uncertain, but 1946/47 saw the arrival of 1929 LT1 Lion/B32F bus RB 159 (ex-Midland General), similar 1929 LT1/B35F bus VB 3555 (from an unknown source), 1930 LT1 Lion/Brush B30F bus HE 4749 (ex-Yorkshire Traction via Rowe of Cudworth), and 1932 Commer Centaur/Willowbrook B20F bus TL 2241 (once with Hulley of Baslow). These vehicles were also used on an increasing number of restricted 'works' journeys as Flint had secured a contract to carry miners from Bolsover to Glapwell Colliery.

Further additions to the fleet during 1948 were a 1938 Bedford WTB/Willmott C26R coach from Crown of Birtley (JR 8280), a 1931 all-Leyland LT2 Lion/B30F bus which had been new to Yorkshire Woollen but had later served with Newbury & District (HD 4371), and a 1932 LT5 Lion/Roe B32F bus from County Motors (VH 4000). The Commer Centaur TL 2241 and Lions VB 3555/HE 4749 were withdrawn in July 1949 after failing inspections, and were partly replaced by two early model Leyland Tigers. SC 4366 was a 1929 vintage TS2 with a Cowieson C30F coach body, while GO 1043 was a 1930 TS1 with an unidentified 31-seat coach body.

There was another major cull of superannuated rolling stock during 1950 which saw the departure of the SOS, the Maudslay, Tiger coach GH 7029, and Lions RB 159, HD 4371, and VH 4000. Slightly newer motive power was needed to replace them and in May 1950 a 1936 TS7 Tiger/Park Royal C32R coach, JG 6524, arrived at Carr Vale. It had been new to East Kent but came to Flint via Wye Valley of Hereford and Monico of London. Another Tiger, 1933 vintage TS6c/MCCW B32R bus RB 9311, had been acquired from Truman of Shirebrook (qv) in March but had proved to be unfit for service. Truman had bought it from its original owner, Chesterfield Corporation, in 1946. Undeterred by this hiccup Flint went back to Truman for two additional vehicles later in 1950, buying 1937 Bedford WTB/Duple coach ENU 497 (which had been new to Truman) and similar vintage TS7 Tiger/Burlingham C32F coach BTJ 358 (originally delivered to Warburton of Bury). Another purchase with Lancashire origins, 1946 Bedford OB/Duple Vista HTB 80, came from Kia Ora of Morecambe in October 1950.

The founder became ill during 1951 and sadly died early in the New Year, control of the firm's assets passing to his widow Mrs Elizabeth Flint in May 1952. As was understandable there were no additions to the fleet in 1951/52, although Tigers SC 4366, GO 1043, and BTJ 358 were withdrawn during the latter year after unsuccessful inspections. Ridership on the Glapwell Colliery service had plummeted after the withdrawal of free travel concessions so the Tigers did not really need to be replaced. The first acquisitions during Mrs Flint's proprietorship took place in March 1953 when 1934 Dennis Lancet/Willowbrook C34F coach AVO 387 arrived from Wright of Newark, followed by Commer Q4/Abbott C30F coach AEJ 590 from Lloyd-Jones of Pontrhydygroes near Aberystwyth. They replaced Tiger JG 6524 and WTB JR 8280 respectively.

Bedford WTB coach ENU 497 was sold in May 1954 and not replaced due to the gradual down-turn in private-hire work. The Dennis Lancet was next to go, replaced in May 1955 by

Bedford OB/Duple Vista coach GTB 564 which had been new to Battersby of Morecambe in 1947. Two years passed before the next fleet reshuffle in April 1957. The 1946 OB coach HTB 80 and the solitary Commer Q4 were withdrawn and replaced by two 1950 Bedford OBs, GNT 517 with Plaxton C29F bodywork (new to Greatrex of Stafford), and HOU 863 with Duple Vista C29F bodywork (new to Hants & Sussex).

The fleet had now shrunk from its maximum size of ten (in 1948) to just three Bedford OBs. It briefly surged back to four in August 1958 with the acquisition of 1948 Lancet III/Whitson C33F coach AXG 54 from Scarlet Band of West Cornforth. This vehicle only stayed until October 1959. Meanwhile, all three of the Bedford OBs had been withdrawn in May 1959 and replaced by a very varied trio of vehicles. FWW 435 was a 1947 Commer Commando with Plaxton C29F bodywork (new to Bolton-by-Bowland), ONU 338 was a 1951 Commer Avenger with a Churchill C33F body (acquired from Cope of Heanor), and EWH 647 was a 1952 Bedford SB with Duple Vega C33F bodywork from Slater of Bury.

The Commer Commando departed in June 1961, reducing the fleet to two for the first time since 1930. The Commer Avenger went in June 1963, replaced by a 1955 Bedford SBG with Yeates Riviera C36F bodywork (WRB 625) acquired from Sharpe of Beighton, and in September 1964 the fleet size bounced back to three with the addition of 1955 Bedford SBG/Duple C36F 'Fishmouth' Super Vega 361 FRE from Hogg of Bennington. In September 1965 Bedford SB/Duple EWH 647 was withdrawn, presumably for mechanical reasons as it was immediately replaced by an identical 1952 machine (MPT 411) from Riddiford of Thornbury.

By 1966 Mrs Flint was above state retirement age and wanted to reduce her working hours. The Glapwell Colliery service had long gone, but the Monday-Saturday stage service from Carr Vale to Bolsover continued and (with falling revenue) had started to seem like a lot of work for very little in the way of financial gain. Private-hire work was much less labour intensive and far more profitable. A decision was made, the relevant authorities were informed, and the licence for the stage service was surrendered to the Traffic Commissioners in November 1966. An interim replacement service was provided by Clarence

Briggs, a Glapwell coach operator, but the route was soon incorporated into the local network of East Midland Motor Services. Mrs Flint continued in the private-hire business for several years, operating second-hand Bedford SB variants on visits to an assortment of tourist attractions.

Heeley of New Tupton

The village of Tupton lies astride the main road from Chesterfield to Clay Cross, Alfreton, and Derby, an important thoroughfare since Roman times. The original village (later known as Old Tupton) was situated on the western edge of the Roman road, but in the industrial age a second village centre was developed to the east of the highway. With inescapable logic this became known as New Tupton. When Chesterfield Corporation began a motor bus service to Clay Cross in 1914 it followed the main road, convenient for Old Tupton but not for New Tupton which extended almost a mile to the east from the new bus route.

Arthur Heeley was born in New Tupton in 1897 and gained skills as a driver and motor mechanic during his military service in the First World War. In October 1921 he bought a brand-new Ford Model T, R 7638, which could be used as a van or as a primitive 14-seat bus. The vehicle was used to start a regular (evenings and Saturday daytime) operation to Chesterfield. In March 1923 the Ford was joined by another new vehicle, 20-seat Albion bus NU 199, and this was put to work on an extended Clay Cross-New Tupton-Chesterfield service which ran throughout the day on Monday-Saturday and after lunch on Sundays. The extension to Clay Cross was useful to New Tupton residents but upsetting to Chesterfield Corporation which was now dealing with a competitor for end to end traffic. Chesterfield's self-serving unwillingness to give Heeley a licence meant that no fares could be collected within the municipal boundaries, and Heeley's service took a longer route and was less frequent, but Heeley was slightly cheaper and for some Clay Cross residents this was tempting – especially if Heeley's bus was in sight and Chesterfield's was not.

A new 14-seat Fiat bus, NU 6230, replaced the Model T in May 1925. The next arrival was the first of a long sequence of Albion products. RA 2908, new in June 1927 was an Albion

Bedford OB/Duple Vista C29F coach HOU 863 was new to Basil Williams' Hants & Sussex group in 1949, but came to Flint from Taylor of Long Buckby in April 1957. Two years later it was replaced by a Churchill-bodied Commer Avenger and passed to Stringer of Pontefract. *(Omnibus Society - Roy Marshall)*

A nine-penny ticket from Flint of Carr Vale (3.75 pence in decimal money), which might seem like a bargain, but at the time this ticket was issued the same investment could have bought you a pint of bitter. As Flint's only stage carriage service was just a mile and a half long it was quite expensive by contemporary standards. Flint's contract service to Glapwell Colliery used orange tokens, an example of which can be found on the oldminer web-site. *(Mark Smith Collection via oldminer.co.uk)*

1	2	3	4	5	6	7	8	9	10	11	12	13	14	15

Williamson, Printer, Ashton

FLINT'S SERVICE

This ticket must be punched in the Section to which the passenger is entitled to travel, and must be shown on demand.

To be used on day of issue only.

1243

16	17	18	19	20	21	22	23	24	25	26	27	28	29	30

Albion Valkyrie BNU 962 carried a Burlingham C32R body and was new to Heeley in April 1935. When fleet numbers were introduced in 1947 it became number 5 as shown here, and survived for long enough to pass to East Midland in March 1953 as fleet number AC19. Three months later they sold it to a dealer and it found no further use. *(Omnibus Society - Roy Marshall)*

Heeley's fleet number 19 was NNU 771, a Denis Lancet III with a Burlingham C33F body. New in April 1949, it also passed to East Midland in March 1953, becoming fleet number DC28. It was renumbered as C13 in 1954, and after withdrawal in 1958 ran for two small operators in South Wales until 1962. *(Omnibus Society - Roy Marshall)*

PJ26 with a 26-seat bus body by an unidentified manufacturer. It was followed in May 1928 by RA 6007, a PNA26 Viking coach with a 26-seat Massey body, and in May 1929 by RA 8464, a PJ26 bus with Reeve & Kenning bodywork. Next came another coach, RB 6337, a PW65 Valkyrie with a Massey C31F body delivered in May 1932. The 20-seat Albion of 1923 and the Fiat had been withdrawn by then, and Heeley's modern fleet of Albions presented a very attractive face to the new Traffic Commissioners who granted a licence for the Clay Cross to Chesterfield service despite the objections of the corporation's representatives. A licence was also granted for Heeley's new seasonal express service from Staveley, New Tupton, and Clay Cross to Blackpool.

With stability guaranteed the chain of new Albions continued. BNU 962 arrived in April 1935 and was a PW69 Valkyrie coach with a Burlingham C32R body, while CRA 787 was a PH115 Victor with Burlingham C26F bodywork, delivered in May 1936. The final pre-war Albion, ERB 988, arrived in July 1938 and was a CX9 Valkyrie with a Plaxton 35-seat coach body. It was not quite the last pre-war delivery. In May 1939 Mr Heeley decided to have a change and bought a new Bedford WTB with a Plaxton C26F coach body, FRB 793. Four months later war was declared against Germany and the most immediate effect at New Tupton was the loss of the newest Albion, ERB 988, requisitioned by the Air Ministry. It never returned and after the war it ended up with Morecambe Motors carrying the new registration HTD 195.

A second Bedford (OWB/Roe utility bus HRA 742) was delivered in November 1942, but its basic bodywork did nothing for its popularity and it was decided that second-hand vehicles were a better option. Mr Heeley managed to obtain three more Albion Valkyries during the war, with the first two arriving in 1944. CP 9836 was a PW65 with a Brush B32F body, new to Hebble in 1932, and TJ 5081 was a ten year old PW67 with a Plaxton C32F body which came from Mills of Radcliffe. The last of the second-hand Albions, PW67/Plaxton C32R, YG 7524, arrived in 1945. New to Advance of Maltby in 1934, it passed with that company to East Midland before moving down the road to New Tupton.

The first new vehicle of the post-war era was Albion CX13 Valkyrie/Plaxton C33F coach

JRB 124, delivered in June 1946. A bigger surprise was the arrival of two brand-new Commer Commando/Plaxton C30F coaches in October 1947 (LRA 31) and January 1948 (LRA 944). They replaced the two Bedfords and became the first Heeley vehicles to wear fleet numbers. LRA 31 was number 10 and LRA 944 number 11, while fleet number 12 was reserved for a third of the type which eventually arrived in November 1948 as MRA 812 – a happy numerical coincidence. Other deliveries during 1948, all brand-new, included Dennis Lancet III/Burlingham C33F coach MNU 359 (delivered in May as fleet number 16), two Albion CX13 Valkyries with similar bodywork which arrived in June (LRB 984/985, fleet numbers 14/15), a Daimler CVD6 with a Plaxton C33F body (MNU 358, fleet number 17, another June arrival), and an Austin CXB with Plaxton C29F bodywork (MRB 190, fleet number 18) which arrived in November alongside the third Commer Commando. The first two Commandos were then sold. Two other departures during the year, made redundant by the sudden influx of 'C33F' coaches, were pre-war Albions CRA 787 and YG 7524.

Earlier members of the fleet still in service in October 1947 also received fleet numbers. RB 6337, the 1932 Albion coach, became fleet number 1 although its remaining time in the fleet would be brief. The same was true of the two Bedfords which only had a month to go but nevertheless became fleet numbers 7 (the WTB) and 8 (the OWB). Fleet numbers 2-4 went to the three second-hand Valkyries (CP 9836/TJ 5081/YG 7524 respectively) while BNU 962 became number 5 and CRA 787 number 6. Fleet number 9 went to the first post-war Albion, JRB 124.

The first arrival during 1949 was another new Dennis Lancet III. NNU 771 (fleet number 19) arrived in April and carried a fully-fronted Burlingham C33F body. It replaced Daimler CVD6 number 17 which was less than a year old. The next new coach had fully fronted bodywork. NRA 760 (fleet number 20) was a Foden PVSC6 with a Plaxton FC33F body and arrived in July. It replaced Heeley's final service bus, Albion CP 9836. In October the remaining Commer Commando and the Austin CXB were sold and replaced by a single new vehicle, Albion FT3AB Victor/Plaxton C31F coach NRB 444 (fleet number 21).

The fleet expanded again in 1950 with the delivery of three new vehicles and the withdrawal of just one older machine. The new coaches were a third Dennis Lancet III with a half-cab Duple C33F body (NRB 557, fleet number 22, delivered in April) and a pair of Albion CX39N Valiants with fully-fronted Burlingham Sunsaloon FC33F bodies (ORA 350/1, fleet numbers 23/4, both delivered in May). The withdrawal was of Albion coach TJ 5081, the last of the pre-war examples. The company was left with one of the most up-to-date fleets in the entire county of Derbyshire, and all journeys on the stage service were operated by modern luxury coaches.

Tragedy struck the thriving business on the 23rd of November 1950 when founder Arthur Heeley died at the age of 53. The firm had become incorporated in August 1935 as Arthur Heeley Ltd, and control passed to his widow and children. Arthur Jr, who was already involved with a haulage business, found time to look after the coaches as well, but lorries were his first love and no further coaches were bought after the founder's death.

Circumstances had made the Heeley business a more tempting target than most. For many years the managers at East Midland, Midland General, and Trent had dreamed of operating a through service between Chesterfield and Derby via the direct route. These ambitions had been thwarted by Chesterfield Corporation which held the only stage carriage licence for the section of the main road between Chesterfield and Clay Cross. East Midland had an infrequent service, inherited from an independent in the 1930s, which left Chesterfield on the correct road but then deviated to the west through narrow lanes to Wingerworth, regaining the main road just to the north of Tupton before heading more irrevocably to the west towards the Ashover area. It never reached Clay Cross and could not be used as a segment of a longer service. Chesterfield was perfectly willing to provide the missing link, but at the price of participation as an equal partner all the way through to Derby. This was not acceptable to the three area agreement companies and so the stalemate persisted for many years. Arthur Heeley's death and his inheritors' willingness to sell (at the right price) presented a new possibility.

On the 29th of March 1953 the price on offer finally reached an irresistible figure of £20,000 and Arthur Heeley Ltd was sold to East Midland Motor Services. Midland General and Trent made a contribution to East Midland's outlay, and Heeley's Chesterfield-New Tupton-Clay Cross service was joined with Midland General's D2 from Clay Cross to Alfreton and Trent's route 1 from Alfreton to Derby to create the long dreamed of through route. It received service number 44 which was acceptable to all three of the joint operators. Double-deck buses became a frequent sight in New Tupton in place of Heeley's coaches.

While the route mileage was now operated by three companies, Heeley's vehicles all went to East Midland. Those transferred were fleet numbers 5, 9, 14-6, and 19-24 and most entered service with their new owners. The fully-fronted coaches and the half-cab Lancet were the final survivors, lasting with EMMS until 1957. A direct route from Chesterfield to Derby is still operated, but since deregulation the dog-leg through New Tupton has been forsaken in favour of the main road, as the reason for the 'kink' in the straight line has been removed. Few residents will now remember the days when Arthur Heeley's coaches ran on the Chesterfield route, or even that later time when there was a direct bus service from New Tupton to Derby as a legacy of the Heeley company.

Naylor of South Normanton

Thomas William Naylor (usually known as William) was born in 1861 in the mining village of South Normanton, half way between the important towns of Alfreton in Derbyshire and Mansfield in Nottinghamshire. His father was a miner and young William followed him into the pit, but by 1888 he was living with his wife Eliza at 24 Queen Street in South Normanton and describing himself as a farmer. This was a slight exaggeration – the piece of land behind the house amounted to just 180 square yards which was more of a large garden than a small farm. Most of William's income at that time was actually derived from his horse and cart, which was available for everything from colliery work to household removals. He also carried passengers and established a regular Thursday service from South Normanton to Mansfield.

William and Eliza would produce 11 children, seven sons and four daughters, and all would become involved in the family business from

CNU 690 was a Leyland LT7 Lion with a Burlingham C32R coach body, new to Hallam of Somercotes in 1935. Within a year of its delivery it had been sold to Naylor of South Normanton who kept it in service until 1955. *(Omnibus Society - Roy Marshall)*

JNU 796, new to Naylor in 1945, was a Guy Arab 5LW with a Strachans L27/28R body and shows the operator's original maroon, red, and pale cream livery (later simplified to a slightly darker red and pale cream). The vehicle was included in the Trent take-over and became their fleet number 1216 in July 1956. *(Omnibus Society - RN Hannay)*

VO 8566, an AEC Regent with a Weymann H30/24R body, was delivered to Mansfield District Traction in September 1932. Naylor bought it in 1946 and in November 1949 replaced its original body with the new Burlingham H30/26R unit depicted here. It became Trent's fleet number 1218. *(Omnibus Society Roy Marshall)*

AEC Regal III/Burlingham C33F coach NNU 648 was new to Naylor in March 1949. It passed to Trent as fleet number 643 in July 1956, blending in comfortably with native vehicles bodied by Willowbrook and Windover. *(Omnibus Society Roy Marshall)*

the time they could walk. William was fined on several occasions for persistently keeping his children out of school, and later progressed to keeping other people's children out of school to provide yet more cheap labour. As one local teacher put it, the Naylors were 'a rough lot'.

William Naylor died in 1903 at the age of 42. His widow Eliza took control of the family firm, by then known as TW Naylor & Sons, and gained a reputation for ruling the clan with an iron hand despite her diminutive stature. One son had died in infancy, but the other six all become employees as did the daughters and their husbands. There were a lot of mouths to feed and the firm's haulage business grew to match the need for income.

Another of Eliza's sons, William Jr, was killed during the First World War. The remaining sons (Albert, Ernest, Walter, Joseph, and John) became their mother's trusted lieutenants, out to prove that they could perform work more quickly and more cheaply than any of their rivals. The colliery owners admired their single-mindedness and gave them a steady supply of light haulage contracts. A slight diversification came in 1923 with the acquisition of a six-seat Ford Model T taxi, R 4441, from a Mansfield dealer. Horses and carts had already been abandoned for motorised goods vehicles but the earliest examples have remained unidentified. The Thursday passenger outings to Mansfield were maintained by mounting removable seats in one of the lorries, but in April 1924 a more dignified alternative was acquired in the form of 20-seat Lancia Tetraiota bus NU 3204. It was the family's first real PSV, and in April 1925 was joined by a similar Lancia Pentaiota registered NU 6708. Both were used on the Mansfield runs (now increased to operate on Thursdays, Fridays, and Saturdays) and on private-hire work and excursions.

E Naylor & Sons

In June 1925 Ernest Naylor was working a haulage contract at the Winning Colliery when his lorry stalled on an internal railway crossing. A locomotive demolished the vehicle and the impact was so severe that Ernest was decapitated. In the wake of this grisly incident Eliza decided that the family would withdraw from the haulage trade (except for home coal deliveries) and concentrate upon carrying passengers. A separate partnership,

E Naylor & Sons, was established for this purpose, leaving no doubt that Eliza was still the person in charge despite her loss of first a husband and then three of her sons.

Eliza's first move as a dedicated bus operator was to open a daily through service from Alfreton to Mansfield via South Normanton and Sutton-in-Ashfield. It was a major commitment and attracted fierce competition from Wright Bros of South Normanton which operated an identical route. By 1927 the two original Lancias had been joined by couple of small (14-seat) 'chaser' vehicles in the shape of Ford Model-T NN 1742 and Fiat RR 120. Competition continued to be intense and the Naylors decided to invest in a fleet of new Albions. RR 5569 arrived in 1927 and was followed by two more in 1929 (RA 8706 and WE 6778), another in 1930 (RB 1844), and a further pair in 1931 (RB 4127 and RB 4676). This large outlay was made necessary by the intrusion of Trent Motor Traction (which had bought the Wrights' business) and was more likely to complain about 'irregular' behaviour by Naylor's drivers and by the need to impress the new Traffic Commissioners that this was a respectable business which had eschewed the cut-throat tactics of yesteryear.

This expenditure on new vehicles helped to sway the Traffic Commissioners as Naylor's competitors attempted to portray the family as unfit to receive Road Service Licences. A licence was granted for the key stage carriage route from Alfreton to Mansfield (operating daily, roughly hourly until mid-day and then half-hourly), and another for a fortnightly (during the football season) express run to Derby County's inappropriately named Baseball Ground. Excursions and tours from South Normanton were also authorised. Eliza (by this point in a wheelchair and thus incapable of dancing a jig) celebrated by ordering a seventh new Albion, a PW65 Valkyrie with a Northern Counties C32F body, and this was delivered in May 1932 as RB 6359.

Another new Albion, PV70 Valiant/Duple C32F coach ARA 85, was delivered in the summer of 1934 and replaced the last of the Lancias. It was followed by three more new Albions before the outbreak of the Second World War. CRA 622 and DRA 901 were 30-seat PK115 Victor coaches, delivered in 1936 and 1937 respectively, while FNU 404 was a CX9 Valkyrie with a C32R coach body delivered in 1939. A further CX9, GNU 184, was delivered in April 1939 with a high capacity Willowbrook 39-seat body.

Two of the Albions were requisitioned during the war, RB 6359 (which was 'redistributed' to Robin Hood Coaches in Nottingham) and virtually new FNU 404 (which went to the War Department). It soon became obvious that this was a mistake given Naylor's importance to local coal-miners working round-the-clock shifts, and the gaps in the fleet were filled by two second-hand Leylands. LT7 Lion/Burlingham C32R coach CNU 690 came from Hallam of Somercotes, while SKP2 Cub/Willowbrook C20F coach EAL 7 had previously been owned by Sir Julian Cahn who had used it to transport his privately funded cricket team.

Eliza Naylor died in 1940 at the age of 78, having out-lived her husband by 37 years. Her daughter and son-in-law, Ann and Frederick West, assumed day-to-day responsibility for the administration of the business and moved its registered office from Queen Street to their house at 66 Market Street, closer to the garage. The house and yard at Queen Street continued as the premises for the coal delivery business, then being run by John Naylor, but Market Street had become the new focal point for the clan in 1926 when Eliza had purchased three adjacent terraced houses to be occupied by Walter Naylor and his married sisters Olive (Mrs Bill Clifford) and Ada (Mrs John Harrison). Brothers Albert and Joseph also lived nearby.

Double-deckers and Seagulls

By 1944 the passenger loads on some of Naylors' colliery shift-change timings were requiring one or more duplicates, and the company applied for a double-decker to help ease the situation. This finally materialised just after the end of the war as JNU 796, a Guy Arab Mk II with a lowbridge utility body by Strachan. A second double-decker arrived from Mansfield & District during 1946. VO 8566 had been new in 1932 and was a petrol-engined AEC Regent with a Weymann H30/24R body. The Naylors fitted it with an AEC diesel engine before putting it into service and it replaced 1931 Albion RB 4127 (which had been fitted with a new Duple C32F body in February 1937).

Two more double-deckers were acquired during 1948 so that the stage service could be worked exclusively by such vehicles. MNU 777, a brand-new Guy Arab III with Northern Coachbuilders H30/26R bodywork, arrived in August 1948 and was joined in December by MRB 709, an AEC Regent O961 with a Brush H30/26R body. The latter had been ordered by the Ebor Bus Co of Mansfield (which competed with Naylor on the Alfreton-Mansfield route), but that operator's financial difficulties had resulted in the machine being diverted to South Normanton. It might be imagined that some ghostly cackling could be heard on Market Street after its delivery.

For the rest of the company's existence all bodywork was provided by HV Burlingham of Blackpool, and all new vehicles were on AEC chassis. An AEC Regal III coach with a half-cab Burlingham C33F body was delivered in March 1949 as NNU 648, and in November of the same year the pre-war Regent VO 8566 received a new Burlingham H30/26R body to replace its 17 year old Weymann unit. Another new Regal III coach, ORA 151, was delivered in October 1950 and carried a fully-fronted Burlingham Sunsaloon FC33F body.

In 1951 the 1934 Albion coach ARA 85 was finally withdrawn and replaced by Naylors' first underfloor-engined vehicle. PRB 709 was an AEC Regal IV with a classic Burlingham Seagull C37C body. By this time there were already disagreements within the Naylor family about the future of the business, with some members anxious to cash in on their inheritance. Joseph Naylor managed to resist this pressure in the short term, but for four years no replacement vehicles were acquired and the age profile of the fleet crept upwards. By 1955 private-hire business was being lost and it was agreed that two new coaches should be acquired. These materialised in May 1955 as XRB 50/51, a pair of AEC Reliances with Burlingham Seagull Mk III C37C bodywork very similar to that on PRB 709. They would be the operator's final acquisitions.

On the 7th of July 1956 Trent Motor Traction acquired the issued share capital of E Naylor & Sons Ltd for £37,500. The deal included the 'goodwill' of the company's Road Service Licences, the garage and yard on Market Street, and nine vehicles which became Trent fleet numbers 643 (NNU 648), 644 (ORA 181), 645 (PRB 709), 646 (XRB 50), 647 (XRB 51), 1216 (JNU 796), 1217 (MNU 777), 1218 (VO 8566),

Naylor's next Regal III coach was also bodied by Burlingham, but carried that manufacturer's fully-fronted Sunsaloon design. ORA 181 was delivered in June 1950, later passing to Trent as fleet number 644. *(Omnibus Society - Roy Marshall)*

A second appearance by JNU 796, this time in Trent livery as their fleet number 1216. *(Dennis Johnson Collection)*

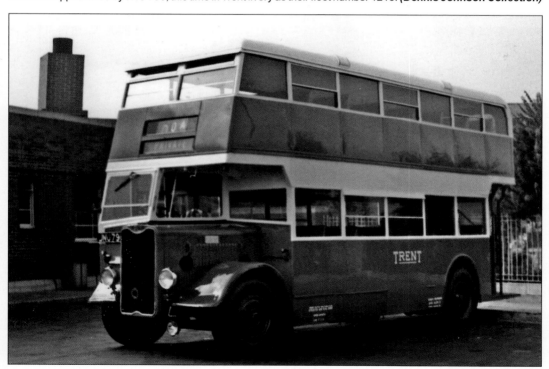

MNU 777 was a Guy Arab III with an NCB H30/26R body, new to Naylor in August 1948. It became Trent's fleet number 1217 in July 1956, as seen here at Morledge bus station, Derby. *(Dennis Johnson Collection)*

In 1951 Naylor bought an underfloor-engined Regal IV coach with a Burlingham Seagull body, and when the lighter weight Reliance chassis became available decided to take a pair with similar Seagull Mk IV bodywork. They arrived in May 1955 as XRB 50/51, and the earlier of the two is seen here in Trent livery as their fleet number 10. *(Chris Rischer)*

and 1219 (MRB 709). The garage became a Trent out-station but was closed in 1961. It still survives as a carpet showroom.

Many communities forget their local bus companies within a few years of their demise, but memories of Naylors' remain to this day in South Normanton. My thanks are due to Dennis Johnson for allowing me access to an unpublished manuscript covering the company's early years and compiled by members of the South Normanton & Pinxton Historical Society.

Truman of Shirebrook

Shirebrook is a large mining village to the north of Mansfield. Despite its strong ties with that Nottinghamshire town the village lies on the Derbyshire side of the border. The coal-field ignores this man-made boundary and there are numerous collieries, some of which have their pit-heads in one county and a part of their mine-workings beneath the other. Extensive mining operations had left their mark on the landscape but also presented opportunities to young men who had recently returned from the war with mechanical skills. One such was William Truman of Shirebrook and in 1919 he acquired a second-hand Ford Model T drop-side with a removable canvas roof. The unidentified vehicle was mainly used for goods work, but was also available for passenger hire after the temporary addition of inward-facing bench seats. After the purchase of another second-hand Ford in early 1923 (also unidentified although the registration E 7006 has been suggested) a regular service to Mansfield was started, initially on three days per week to dovetail with existing coal delivery schedules.

The service was an instant success and in July 1923 Truman took delivery of a 'real' bus, brand-new Vulcan 20-seater NU 1187. May 1925 saw the addition of another new 20-seater, Guy NU 6267, and in November 1926 the bus fleet grew to three with the purchase of a Guy 26-seater, RA 617. At around this time Truman began a second bus route from Warsop Vale and Shirebrook to Worksop.

A fourth new vehicle, Dennis G/Reeve & Kenning B20F bus RA 6212, was delivered in July 1928 and allowed the frequency on the Worksop route to be increased, while heavy loads on the Mansfield service demanded something larger for the busiest timings. This requirement was met in November 1928 by the purchase of a 1926 Leyland PLSC1 Lion with an unidentified 32-seat bus body, RA 368, from Hatton of Selston.

July 1929 brought another new Guy 26-seater, RA 9316, into the fleet and this replaced the Vulcan. Truman's first new Leyland, LT2 Lion 32-seater RB 2253, followed in July 1930 to replace the 1928 Dennis. The purchase of another new Guy, 32-seater RB 4999, in September 1931 further bolstered Truman's case for Road Service Licences from the Traffic Commissioners, and both stage carriage services were duly authorised along with seasonal (period return) express routes to coastal resorts such as Blackpool and Skegness. Competition from other local operators with similar holiday routes brought a need for more luxurious equipment and Truman's first coach, a new Morris Dictator with Reeve & Kenning C32F bodywork registered RB 6093, was delivered in May 1932. A second new coach, Dennis Lancet/Reeve & Kenning 31-seater RB 6773, arrived two months later.

Three more new coaches were delivered during 1934. Dennis Lancet/Willowbrook 36-seater ANU 12 arrived in January, while Lancet/Reeve & Kenning 32-seater ARA 652 and Guy Wolf/Burlingham 20-seater ARA 791 were both delivered in August. The coach fleet was further swollen by the addition of two more new Lancets in 1935, Burlingham-bodied 32-seater BRA 665 in July and Willowbrook-bodied 38-seater (!) BRB 33 in August. By the end of the year Truman was operating seven modern coaches and four buses (26-seat Guys RA 617 and RA 9316, 32-seat Guy RB 4999, and LT2 Lion 32-seater RB 2253).

The First Double-deckers

The Mansfield route continued to do well and Mr Truman began to consider alternatives to the frequent duplication which was necessary to meet demand. Money was tight after the large expenditure on new coaches, but a cut-price solution was found in July 1936 when two Guy Conquest double-deckers were acquired from Northampton Corporation. The pair both carried Wolverhampton registrations, having served as Guy Motors demonstrators before their sale to Northampton. UK 8074 had been new in December 1929 and UK 8922 in June 1930, and both carried Hall Lewis H24/24R bodywork.

The proprietor's focus then returned to

coaching and two new Bedford WTBs with Duple C26F bodywork were acquired in August 1937 (ENU 497) and July 1938 (FNU 683). It would seem that Mr Truman became inclined toward a pessimistic assessment of the political situation as no further vehicles were ordered for 1939 or 1940 delivery. His viewpoint was, of course, vindicated when Germany invaded Poland. Bedford FNU 683 was requisitioned shortly afterwards for use by the RAF and did not return until 1947.

The company's first acquisition during the war was undoubtedly the most unusual. OV 1194 had been built in 1931 as a Guy BT trolleybus with a Park Royal L24/24R body. After a short period on loan to Birmingham City Transport in full BCT livery it was returned to its place of birth, had all of its electrical running gear removed and a petrol engine fitted. The motor bus thus created served as a Guy Motors staff vehicle for several years before finding somebody desperate enough to make an offer. Another slightly odd machine followed in early 1941. JO 2392 had an AEC Regent chassis and had been delivered to City of Oxford as a double-decker in 1931. It came to Truman from Bunty of Coventry who had fitted it with a Burlingham DP32F body from an unrecorded donor vehicle before selling it on.

In early 1943 Mr Truman managed to secure an important contract for colliery works services, resulting in the arrival of a new Bedford OWB/Roe utility bus (HRA 931) in February and an invasion of second-hand vehicles one month later. The acquisitions included AEC Regal 4/Burlingham B34R bus FS 8557 (new to SMT in 1934), Leyland PLSC3 Lion/Leyland B35F bus VO 309 (new to Baker Bros of Warsop in 1929), PLSC3 Lion/Lawton B32F bus VT 1686 (new to Bloor of Hartshill in 1928 and later with Stoke Motors), and Bedford WTB/Watson C25F coach CRB 557 (new to Hallam of Somercotes in 1936). Further additions later in the year were 31-seat AEC Regal/Burlingham coach VS 2097 (which had been new to Gourock Pullman Coaches in July 1931, passing to Western SMT just four months later) and Leyland TD1 Titan/Leyland L27/24R double-decker HE 4974 (which had been new to Yorkshire Traction in 1930). As the inventory grew larger fleet numbers were introduced, but these were allocated in a somewhat erratic fashion. To give just a few examples, fleet number 5 was JO 2392, number 6 was VS 2097, and number 27 was HE 4974. Many

other vehicles contemporary to these wore no fleet numbers at all and this haphazard practice continued for the rest of the company's existence. These fleet numbers will, therefore, be ignored in the present narrative and readers wanting more details are referred to Part Two of the PSV Circle's excellent fleet history of East Midland Motor Services which includes Truman's vehicles.

There were four more arrivals during 1944, all of them Leyland products. A seven year old TS7 Tiger/Burlingham C32F coach, BTJ 358, was acquired in April and had previously served with Warburton of Bury. It was followed by another TS7 which was actually a year older but wore a 1943 registration mark. This Harrington-bodied coach had been new to Lawrenson of Bootle in 1936 as EM 3147. In 1940 it was requisitioned by the War Department and upon demobilisation in 1943 its original identity was apparently mislaid. It then went to Hartle of Manchester and was given the new registration GNE 73 which is the mark it wore while with Truman. The Tigers were pursued by a pair of Cheetahs. XS 5082/3 were LZ2A bus models with Pickering bodies and had been new to Graham of Paisley in 1939.

Two new Guy Arab Mk II utility buses with Massey H30/26R bodywork were delivered in January 1945 as JNU 242/3, but their arrival was somewhat overshadowed in October of that year by the purchase of a rare 'twin steer' Leyland Gnu. WG 6676 was a 1937 TEP1 with Alexander C40F bodywork, one of a pair built for W Alexander's operational side to test the concept in everyday use. The only other Gnus built were six Duple-bodied vehicles with central entrances for the City Coach Co of Brentwood in Essex, famous for their use on that company's high frequency express service from Wood Green to Southend-on-Sea. Truman's example rarely strayed from the coal-field, being considered too 'experimental' for the coastal express routes.

The first two arrivals of 1946 were quite mundane by comparison to the Gnu. April saw the purchase of another ex-SMT AEC Regal 4/Burlingham bus, FS 8581, and in May a 1933 Leyland TS6 Tiger/MCCW bus, RB 9311, was acquired from Chesterfield Corporation. In June, however, the Gnu itself was placed into the shade by the arrival of WG 9519, the only Leyland Panda ever built. Like the Gnu it had three axles (two at the front), but while the Gnu had

In October 1945 Trumans bought this rare Leyland Gnu, WG 6676, previously operated by W Alexander and carrying their 'in-house' bodywork. Trumans modified the front end so that the radiator could be moved to a central position allowing a slightly less cramped front entrance than in the original design. In October 1952 it was sold to Stanhope Motor Services, Co Durham as fleet number L8 but was withdrawn in July 1954 following an accident. *(Omnibus Society - Roy Marshall)*

The one and only Leyland Panda, WG 9519, carried an Alexander B45C body and came to Truman of Shirebrook in June 1946 as their fleet number 24. It was technically part of the deal when East Midland took over, but was never operated. It soon passed to Aston of Marton and was later scrapped after several years of increasing dereliction. *(Chris Rischer Collection)*

LNU 214 was one of a pair of Daimler CVD6 double-deckers with NCB H30/26R bodies bought new by Truman in June 1947. It carried fleet number 31 and passed to East Midland after the take-over in December 1956. *(Omnibus Society - Roy Marshall)*

There were also Daimler CVD6 single-deckers. LRA 588 was fitted with an Allsop C33F coach body (made in Sheffield) and was delivered to Truman in January 1948 as fleet number 33. It later became fleet number 1 and passed to East Midland. *(John Hellewell Collection)*

Like many other operators, Truman would take anything it could get to meet the demand of the post-war coaching boom. MNU 601 was a Tilling-Stevens K6LA7 Express with a Dutfield C33F coach body, new in April 1948 as fleet number 35. It later became fleet number 2 and was one of the many vehicles which passed into EMMS ownership but did not operate for them. *(RHG Simpson)*

Truman also tried Crossleys and found them acceptable at the price on offer. NRA 248 was an SD42/7 with a Strachans C33F coach body and was new to Truman in August 1949. No fleet number has been recorded. It stayed until the end. *(RHG Simpson)*

Truman quickly became a magnet for second-hand Crossleys. KAL 740, an SD42/7 with a Burlingham C33F coach body, had been new to Clark of Epperstone (near Nottingham) in March 1949, passing to Truman in May 1950 as fleet number 15. It too remained in the fleet until the East Midland take-over. *(Omnibus Society - Roy Marshall)*

The 'buy anything cheap with wheels' philosophy brought an astonishing variety of vehicles to Shirebrook, including the inevitable Bedford OB with Duple Vista C29F bodywork. DFR 987 was new to Batty-Holt of Blackpool in April 1949 and was one of three OBs acquired by Truman in March 1951. *(RHG Simpson)*

its engine at the front end the Panda's was under the floor. By this means the seating capacity in its Alexander centre-entrance body was increased to 45. The Panda had been built in 1941 as a 'proof of concept' prototype and had quickly passed to W Alexander to join their brace of Gnus.

For reasons which have not been ascertained Truman's rented five ageing Tilling-Stevens single-deckers from the Frank Cowley dealership in Salford from October to December 1946. They had been new to North Western in 1928-30, but all five had received new ECOC DP31R bodies in 1935. The machines involved were DB 5205/22/38/40/9396, and three of them donated their ECOC bodies to new Daimler CVD6 chassis for Hartness of Penrith after being returned to Cowley.

In January 1947 Truman acquired a brand-new Guy Arab III chassis and registered it KRA 668. As an economy measure it received the 1931 Park Royal L24/24R body from petrol-driven Guy (and former trolleybus) OV 1194, suitably modified to comply with safety regulations. The modifications included the elimination of the front row of seats (and adjacent sunken gangway), leaving what looked like a fenced-off dance floor for toddlers at the front end of the top deck. It also had a rather woeful external appearance, but the Arab suffered the shame with stoic Gardner-engined dignity until April 1949 when it received a new (Barnsley Co-op) Unity C32F body.

The next arrivals could hardly have provided a greater contrast. LNU 213-5 were brand-new Daimler CVD6s with Northern Coachbuilders H30/26R bodywork which were delivered in June 1947 and became the mainstay of the Shirebrook-Mansfield service. They were followed in January 1948 by LRB 588/9, also CVD6s but with uncommon Allsop C33F coach bodies. The other two deliveries during 1948 were also unusual. MNU 601 was a brand-new Tilling-Stevens K6LA7 Express with a Dutfield C33F coach body and arrived in April, while ACN 794 was a not quite new Guy Arab III with a Meadows 6DC engine and a Guy B35R bus body. Built as a Guy demonstrator (running on trade plates) it had then been loaned to Northern General, who had obtained a local registration mark and used it in service for a brief period before returning it to Guy. It was sold to Truman in December 1948.

The Crossley Era

Colliery contract work had become even more attractive in the new era of the state-owned National Coal Board, and as a result the competition to secure such contracts had become intense. The Truman family (the founder's sons Thomas and Douglas had become involved in the business along with their sister Mrs Winifred Silver) took a look at the state of their ageing contract fleet and decided that something must be done very quickly. The coaching fleet was also in need of further renewal, so the perfect solution was to acquire a large fleet of new (or virtually new) coaches which could be used in both areas of the market. Leylands and AECs were out of the question as their popularity demanded premium prices. Daimlers and Guys were difficult to find in sufficient numbers. The Trumans turned to the Crossley SD42, already noted for its unreliable engine and thus widely available at a discount from both its manufacturer and from later vendors.

The first five turned up in January 1949 and all had C33F bodies. Santus-bodied specimen BHL 835 came from the Comberhill Motors dealership in Wakefield, Plaxton-bodied FAY 524 and FRY 595 from dealers in Leicestershire, Burlingham-bodied EF 8661 had been ordered by Bee-Line Roadways in West Hartlepool but never operated, and MRB 889 was a factory-fresh example with a Strachan body. Three more new Strachan-bodied Crossleys arrived in May (NRA 519), July (NRA 247), and August (NRA 248).

The Crossley floodgates opened to their maximum width in May 1950 when no fewer than 13 second-hand examples with C33F bodywork were acquired in a single month, taking the Crossley fleet to 21. One (KAL 740) came from Clark of Epperstone and another (DRJ 337) from Fieldsend of Salford. The other 11 (EUJ 193, EUX 137/357/456/607/787, FAW 65/873/4/947, and FNT 147) all came from Whittle of Highley who had decided that they really didn't like Crossleys and were busily purging them from their fleet. Of the 13 vehicles acquired two (EUX 357/787) had Plaxton bodies and all the rest carried Burlingham bodywork. The massive intake of Crossleys replaced all of the pre-war rolling stock except for Dennis Lancet coaches ANU 12, BRA 665, and BRB 33 and Bedford WTB coaches FNU 683 and CRB 557. The Lancets would be retired in May 1951, replaced by a trio of second-hand Bedford OB/Duple Vista C29F coaches. SMY 294 (built in 1948) came from Fountain of Cowes, JTJ 903 (another 1948 example) from Kia Ora of Morecambe, and DFR 987 (a 1949 machine) from Batty Holt of Blackpool.

For contracts which needed more capacity than the Crossleys could offer Trumans relied on the two 1945 Arab/Massey double-deckers, the Gnu, and the Panda. One of the Arabs was withdrawn in late 1951 (the other would follow in 1953) and the Gnu was de-licensed in October 1952. To buttress this element of the fleet two 1939 vintage Leyland TD5s with Leyland L26/26R bodywork (GNU 457/9) were acquired from Chesterfield Corporation in March 1952. It was entirely coincidental that the Gnu was being replaced by a GNU. The only other purchases during 1952 were a pair of Leyland PS1/1 Tigers with fully-fronted Plaxton Envoy FC39F bodywork. MTE 323/4 had been new to Bracewell of Colne in 1951 and looked more up-to-date than the half-cab Crossleys. They arrived at Shirebrook in July and became the vehicles of choice for the coastal express runs.

No vehicles were acquired during 1953, but towards the end of that year an important new contract was gained and in January 1954 nine Daimler utility double-deckers dating from 1944-46, with a mixture of Brush and Duple H30/26R bodies, were bought from Sheffield. Seven of them (HWB 309/84/509/823/5/6/37) entered service while HWA 877 and HWB 834 were used for spares. All were AEC-engined CWA6s except for HWB 509 which was a Daimler powered CWD6.

The coach fleet was further modernised in 1954 by the addition of three more second-hand vehicles without the increasingly outmoded half-cab front. The first to arrive (in June) was GAW 671, a 1950 Daimler CVD6 with Burlingham Sunsaloon FC35F bodywork which became the twelfth coach acquired from Whittle of Highley. Later in the same

month a rare Tilling-Stevens L4MA8 Express II with Duple 'Vega lookalike' C37F bodywork, UNO 880, arrived at Shirebrook. It had been new in 1952 to Edwards of Rainham and Truman was its fourth owner in two years. The last of the three used coaches (and the last vehicle ever bought by Trumans) was JTD 107, a Maudslay Marathon III with a Santus FC33F body acquired in July. It had been new to Fairclough of Lostock in 1948 but came to Truman from its second owner, Kershaw of Rochdale.

More than two years went by without any further renewal of the fleet, and the reason became clear on the 26th of October 1956 when Commercial Motor magazine announced that East Midland Motor Services had acquired the Truman business. The take-over officially took place in early December, and EMMS found itself in possession of 11 double-deckers (the three CVD6s new in 1947, one of the ex-Chesterfield TD5s, and seven ex-Sheffield utilities) and 37 assorted single-deckers (21 Crossley SD42s, three Daimler CVD6s, three Bedford OBs, two Bedford WTBs, two Guy Arabs, two Leyland PS1/1 Tigers, two Tilling-Stevens, one Maudslay Marathon, and one Leyland Panda). It was predictable that many of these would never enter service with East Midland – the attractions to the purchaser were the stage services, the coastal expresses, and the industrial contracts, not the company's quirky collection of vehicles.

The Truman siblings had already opened a car dealership next door to their old garage and they expanded this business considerably with the proceeds from selling the bus company. From 1957 onwards they would be competing with other bus companies by trying to sell private cars to their upwardly mobile passengers. The Panda, spurned by EMMS, ended up with Aston of Marton in Warwickshire but was tragically scrapped after sitting in their yard for several years. Of all the highly unusual vehicles operated by Truman over the years not one survives.

GNU 459 was an all-Leyland TD5c with lowbridge bodywork, new to Chesterfield in July 1939. Along with sister bus GNU 457 it passed to Trumans in March 1952, so for 7 month in that year the company was operating one Gnu and two Chesterfield GNUs. *(Omnibus Society - Roy Marshall)*

One of many Daimler double-deckers acquired from Sheffield Corporation, HWB 826 was an AEC powered CWA6 with a Brush H30/26R 'relaxed utility' body which had been new in February 1946. Truman bought it in January 1954. *(RHG Simpson)*

Rare Tilling-Stevens L4MA8 Express Mk II/Duple C37F coach UNO 880 was new to Rainham Luxury Coaches in Essex in June 1952. The type's attractiveness to operators might be gauged from the fact that Truman bought the vehicle only two years later but was its fourth owner. It became fleet number 40 and passed to East Midland who rapidly deported it to a dealer. *(RHG Simpson)*

The Express Mk II was followed by Truman's very last acquisition, a Maudslay Marathon III coach with a fully-fronted Santus FC33F body. JTD 107 had been new to Fairclough Brothers of Lostock (near Bolton) in May 1948. Eleven months later it was sold to Kershaw of Rochdale, and in July 1954 it passed to Truman. This was another one which found no home in the East Midland fleet after the take-over. *(RHG Simpson)*

Goods vehicles are not your author's strongpoint, but the front end of this vehicle appears to embody features of both BMC group and Seddon designs from the mid-1950s. A more knowledgeable friend suggests that it might be based on a forward control Land Rover chassis. Truman used KRR 513 (first registered in 1950) as a mobile booking office for its coaching activities, although in this view the words 'Ice Cream' are written in the dirt on the offside windscreen. *(RHG Simpson)*

Truman's recovery vehicle was this Fordson V8, GXX 171. The vehicle was first registered in London in 1944, but further details remain as much a mystery as those of the mobile booking office shown above. *(RHG Simpson)*

A magnificent panorama of Truman vehicles lined up beneath the railway embankment at the edge of their Shirebrook depot. From left to right we see Daimler CVD6/Allsop coach LRA 588, Guy Arab/Unity C32F coach KRA 668 (which had carried a pre-war double-deck body when new in 1947), Guy Arab III/Guy B35R bus ACN 794, Leyland Panda WG 9519, Tilling-Stevens/Dutfield coach MNU 601, and Maudslay/Duple coach JTD 107. *(Chris Rischer Collection)*

PART THREE
SOUTHERN
DERBYSHIRE

The southern part of the county is less mountainous than the north-west but has far more agricultural land than the north-east, although the Derbyshire coal-field extends southwards into the area around Ripley, Heanor, and Ilkeston and there are other pockets of coal-mining elsewhere along with sites where iron and clay are extracted, so one should not consider the region to be a rural idyll. The region is dominated by four major rivers with associated flood plains, the Trent (which enters the county just to the east of Burton and then heads north-eastwards towards Nottingham and the Humber estuary), the Dove (which begins to the north of Ashbourne and forms the boundary between Derbyshire and Staffordshire before joining the Trent at Newton Solney), the Derwent (which rises in the far north-west of the county before flowing through Baslow, Matlock, and Derby to merge into the Trent at Shardlow), and the Erewash (which starts off in Nottinghamshire and then forms Derbyshire's eastern boundary before turning through Ilkeston to meet the Trent near Long Eaton).

Derby was one of the largest towns in England until it finally became a city as part of the Queen's Silver Jubilee celebrations in 1977. Nearly two thousand years before that there was a Roman fort known as Derventio (taking its name from the River Derwent) in the area, and the town which grew up beside the fort later became a Viking stronghold as Deoraby, one of the 'Five Boroughs' of the Danelaw. The Anglo-Saxon Kingdom of Mercia evicted the Vikings in 917 and precisely 800 years after that the first water-powered silk mill in Britain was built in the town. A generation later, in 1745, Bonnie Prince Charlie's army of rebellious Highlanders reached Derby before turning back northwards with some haste.

In 1840 a predecessor of the Midland Railway opened a locomotive and engineering works in Derby, and in 1907 Rolls-Royce opened an engine factory in the town – originally to produce motors for their famous cars but subsequently for use in aircraft. By 1960 the population of Derby had reached 134,000, but the absorption of surrounding districts over the next three decades took that figure to more than 248,000. It was the undisputed capital of Derbyshire long before it officially gained city status.

To the east of Derby, on the road to Nottingham, was the town of Long Eaton. Traditionally a local market community it became known for its lace mills in the early 19th century and then for its railway wagon works in Victorian times. Despite these new sources of employment its population in 1900 was still only 10,000. In 1921 it absorbed the adjacent municipalities of Sandiacre and Sawley, and by 1980 its population had soared to more than 40,000, making it the third largest town in the entire county.

North of Long Eaton was the town of Ilkeston at the southern edge of the main Derbyshire coal-field. There were also iron ore deposits in the area, leading to the establishment of the enormous Stanton Ironworks complex two miles south of the town centre on the Long Eaton road. With just over 36,000 inhabitants in 1980 it was an important town, and in transport history terms it was known as the place where Barton met Midland General in pre-war skirmishes.

Beyond Ilkeston were the three towns of Belper, Heanor, and Ripley, each with around 20,000 inhabitants. Belper, on the River Derwent to the north of Derby, was a traditional market town but in the industrial age became something of a company town dominated by the enterprises of the Strutt family. The Strutts made their fortune in cotton spinning, and one of their offspring was notable as an early investor in George Crosland Taylor's Chester based Crosville Motor Co. He lost interest when Taylor switched from car manufacture to bus operation. Heanor was a coal town, but there were also major employers in the iron, silk, and cotton trades. Ripley was another town dominated by a single employer, in this case the Butterley Company. Butterley had made its name in construction, having been a major contractor on the Cromford Canal. It went on to develop coal and iron mines and to make high quality rails for the emerging railway network as well as taking a hand in that network's construction. Ripley was also the birthplace of Barnes Wallis, inventor of the 'bouncing bomb'.

To the south of Derby the largest town was Swadlincote which had more than 30,000 inhabitants by 1980. There were coal mines in the area, but the main source of income was provided by another natural resource. The clay around the town was of particularly high quality and was used to produce bricks, pipes, and earthenware goods. Although in Derbyshire Swadlincote lay astride the main road from Burton (in Staffordshire) to Leicester, and economic links with these 'foreign' destinations were probably stronger than with Derby. Midland Red certainly thought so, considering this most southerly of Derbyshire towns as part of their territory rather than that of Trent Motor Traction. Barton Transport paid no heed to these territorial claims and developed a trunk service from Nottingham to Swadlincote, but that (as they say) is a story for another day.

Allen of Roston

James Allen was a tenant farmer at Yoxall in Staffordshire in the mid-1920s when an opportunity arose to move to Lower House Farm in Roston, Derbyshire, which was owned by his older brother. In 1927 he bought his own piece of land at West View in Roston, erected a house and a garage, and bought a taxi which was mainly used by villagers wishing to attend the markets in Ashbourne and Uttoxeter. Demand was high and in November 1927 the taxi was joined by a 14-seat Overland bus, RA 4367. A fixed timetable was established with the arrival of the 14-seater. On Tuesdays and Fridays it ran to Derby, on Wednesday to Uttoxeter, and on Thursdays and Saturdays to Ashbourne. A Saturday evening trip was also made to Uttoxeter for the benefit of cinema-goers. This pattern would prevail for most of the firm's existence. Allen used the trading names 'Dove Valley Bus Service' (for his stage carriage endeavours) or 'Dove Valley Coaches', but only a minority of vehicles would receive these fleet-names – especially in later years when the concept of a standardised fleet livery seemed to be limited to the legal lettering.

The next vehicle recorded by the PSV Circle was RF 8422, a 1931 Bean 14-seater acquired from Whieldon of Uttoxeter in April 1933. By 1935 this had proven too small for the levels of demand and was returned to Whieldon, being replaced by Dennis G 20-seater RF 5799. This vehicle had been new in 1929 and came to Roston from Gee of Leek. In March 1939 the fleet doubled in size with the purchase of a brand-new Bedford WTB coach

with a Thurgood 26-seat body, FRB 944. Another WTB joined the fleet during the war to replace the ageing Dennis. NV 8777 had been new to Kerr of Kettering in 1937 and carried a Grose C25F body. It came to Allen from its second owner, Buckby of Rothwell.

Mr Allen's wife Elizabeth was also active in the business, and in due course their son Charles (born in 1925) became involved. The fleet grew to three in 1948 with the purchase of ANU 833, a 1934 Dennis Ace with a Willowbrook DP26F body from Taylor of Crich (see Part One). A fourth vehicle materialised in June 1949 when a brand-new Guy Vixen with Barnard DP29F bodywork, NRA 172, was delivered. Fleet strength fell back to three in May 1950 when the Grose-bodied WTB was withdrawn. The other WTB lasted until June 1953, being retired at around the same time as the Dennis Ace, and these two vehicles were replaced by just one, 1943 Bedford OWB/Mulliner utility bus HRB 75. This came from Webster of Hognaston but was only a temporary solution. In June 1954 it was replaced by EBU 710, an Austin CXB with Mann Egerton C29F bodywork which had been new to Robinson of Oldham in 1948.

At the end of 1954 there were just two vehicles in the inventory, the Guy Vixen and the Austin, but in January 1955 they were joined by TRE 95, a 1949 Bedford OB with Mulliner DP26F bodywork which came from Bassett of Tittensor. The next change in rolling stock took place in January 1958 when the Vixen was replaced by a second Bedford OB, ECX 82. This had a standard Duple Vista coach body and had been new to Hanson of Huddersfield in 1949. It arrived at Roston from later owner Foster & Webster of Wednesbury. Five months later the fleet strength went back to four with the acquisition of another 1949 vehicle, fully-fronted Crossley SD42/Duple FC33F coach KTD 254, which came from Cutler of Radcliffe-on-Trent. Further fleet expansion took place in September 1958 when 1951 Bedford SB/Duple Vega coach OMA 584 was acquired from Croker of Salford, taking the fleet back to five vehicles.

There were external reasons for the ebbing and flowing of the fleet. The immediate post-war growth was due to the acquisition of a contract to provide works services to the Tatton company's textile mills at Mayfield, and when this contract was lost the fleet shrank accordingly. The resurgence of 1958 reflected the award of

This Dennis Ace with Willowbrook DP26F bodywork, ANU 833, was new to Gervase Taylor of Crich (see Part One) in May 1934. In 1948 he sold it to Allen of Roston, the owner when this photograph was taken outside Whieldon's Green Bus garage in Uttoxeter. In 1953 the machine passed to a showman based in Smallwood, Cheshire, and was last licensed to an owner in Wigan in December 1956. *(Colin White via Tim Jeffcoat)*

Guy Vixen/Barnard 29-seater NRA 172 was new to Allen of Roston in June 1949. The type was briefly popular with some operators as a readily available alternative to the Bedford OB, but most purchasers sold them on as soon as they could afford something more durable and reliable. This one was withdrawn in April 1958 and no further use of it as a PSV has been recorded. *(Colin White via Tim Jeffcoat)*

Allen bought this 1949 Crossley SD42/9 coach with a fully-fronted Duple FC33F body, KTD 254, from Cutler of Radcliffe (near Manchester) in June 1958. It remained in the fleet until 1962. *(Anthony Moyes)*

This vehicle, 1947 Bedford OB/Mulliner bus ORE 359, appeared in Part One while in the service of Steeples of Parwich. Steeples sold it to Allen of Roston in April 1962 to replace the Crossley shown above, and Allen kept it until September 1964. *(Eric Wain)*

another contract, in this case from Staffordshire County Council, to operate schools journeys from Mayfield to both Rocester and Uttoxeter. These new timings were often driven by Charles Allen, who had gained his PSV licence in 1953. A sixth vehicle, fully-fronted Bedford OB/Plaxton FC30F coach GNP 704, arrived in February 1959. It had been new to Ward of Sidemoor in Worcestershire in 1948, but came to Roston from Warwickshire operator Rouse of Blockley. Its stay with Allen was brief as it was replaced in June 1960 by Bedford SBG/Duple Super Vega C36F coach 493 FRE, a 1955 machine which came from Churchbridge of Cannock.

The schools contracts had the added advantage of bringing in extra private-hire work from the Staffordshire side of the border as the sight of Allen vehicles became more familiar to potential hirers. Such work helped to soften the blow when the schools contracts themselves were lost to another operator in July 1962. Three vehicles were withdrawn in that year (the Austin, the Crossley, and Bedford TRE 95) while only one acquisition was made. Bedford OB/Mulliner B28F bus ORE 359 came from Steeples of Parwich (see Part One) and had been new in 1947. Its arrival left the remaining coaches free to concentrate on private-hire work. Bedford OB/Duple ECX 82 was withdrawn towards the end of 1963, taking the fleet back to three vehicles.

The Steeples OB was quite old when it arrived, and in September 1964 it was replaced by 1950 Bedford OB/Duple Vista C29F coach VMK 568, previously operated by Beach of Staines. It was Allen's very last Bedford OB purchase as all subsequent acquisitions would be Bedford SB variants. The first of these, 1958 Bedford SB3/Duple Super Vega C41F coach YUP 472, arrived in February 1966 and replaced the ex-Churchbridge SBG.

Charles Allen and his wife Maureen were running the business by this time, but ownership remained with the founder. When James Allen died in the summer of 1966 the business passed to his widow, Elizabeth. The first purchase by the new proprietor was KFX 506, a 1956 Bedford SBG/Duple Super Vega coach which came from Elgar of Inkpen in September 1967. It replaced Allen's final Bedford OB, VMK 568. A similar 1955 SBG/Duple, UJH 18, arrived from Gilbert of Bovington in February 1968 and replaced

the 1951 SB/Duple OMA 584. The fleet then stabilised until January 1970 when Allen's first ever diesel powered Bedford arrived. A Bedford SB1 coach with Plaxton Embassy C41F bodywork, NBF 908, had been new in 1961 and previously operated by the famous Staffordshire independent Turner of Brown Edge. It replaced UJH 18 which had proven to be rather labour intensive from a maintenance viewpoint.

The fuel economy figures produced by the SB1 were difficult to ignore, and the two remaining petrol-engined Bedfords were sold in January 1972. Their replacements were two more SB1s, both of them 1960 examples with Duple Super Vega C41F bodywork. XCG 712 came from Worrell of West Croydon and 4949 NA from Mills & Seddon of Radcliffe, Lancashire. The very last addition to the Allen fleet was a Bedford SB5 with a Plaxton C41F body, EJU 444C, which arrived in March 1974 from Stoddard of Cheadle in Staffordshire. For seven months the fleet was back to four vehicles until the withdrawal of XCG 712 at the end of the summer season.

In the mid-1970s Mrs Elizabeth Allen expressed her willingness to sell the business to her son Charles, but she was only willing to sell the vehicles and the 'goodwill', not the garage at West View. Acquisition of new premises would have made the business unviable in Charles's opinion, and so the impasse continued until the firm's closure and the sale of its vehicles in October 1976. The surviving stage carriage routes were transferred to Glover of Ashbourne (qv) who had already acquired the neighbouring business of Carter of Hales Green (qv) and various other local services. Charles Allen became a driver for Glover, later moving to Stevenson of Spath. At the time of writing he is 91 years old but still in good health.

Blue Bus of Willington

By the early 1920s Trent Motor Traction was already operating a daily service between Derby and Burton-upon-Trent in Staffordshire, running via the main road (now the A38), Willington, Repton, and Newton Solney. Among the drivers who worked for Trent were Jack Dean and Arthur Allen and in late 1922 the two men decided to go into business for themselves, operating a similar route between Derby and Burton but also serving the village of Findern and offering lower fares. Although there is some confusion on this point it is believed that their first vehicle was Ford Model T 14-seater R 4848, a 1921 machine acquired from Bayliss of Ashbourne. Burton Council gave the new route a licence and allocated it a stand in Horninglow Street, but Derby Corporation was less welcoming and the service operated from private land next to a pub in Cheapside. Without a licence in Derby the alternative was to operate on a 'return ticket' principle, collecting no fares within the municipal boundary.

Their endeavour was a success and in March 1923 a brand-new 14-seat Model T, NU 126, was acquired along with a second-hand Fiat, AY 5524. The Fiat had been new as an Italian Army lorry in 1917 and received a 14-seat Wilkinson body after Messrs Dean and Allen bought it from a London dealership. With fleet strength up to three the frequency of the service was increased to six times daily. The vehicles were initially housed at the premises of the Derby Asphalt Co, although the contact address given for the partnership was a house in Littleover. Both Ford Ts were in the overall black 'colour scheme' preferred by Henry Ford while the Fiat was painted dark green.

Dean & Tailby

As the business grew additional employees were hired, including the firm's first conductress, and in 1924 Percy Tailby joined the company as General Manager. He was inadvertently a source of friction between the two founders, with Jack Dean arguing that Tailby should be made a full partner while Arthur Allen was equally determined to preserve the existing two-way arrangement. As a result Arthur Allen left the business, founding a new partnership on the Derby-Repton sector of the route with Cecil Culliver. This did not last for very long and Allen ended up as a driver with Derby Corporation.

Allen's departure left Dean and Tailby strapped for cash and in June 1924 the two Ford Model Ts were sold, leaving only the Fiat to maintain a reduced schedule over the summer. Things returned to normal with the delivery of two brand-new Chevrolet 14-seaters, NU 4445 in September and NU 4651 in October. These were partly financed by the inclusion of a third partner, Harold George. The new member of the partnership worked on the night shift at Rolls-Royce's plant in Derby, and for the first two years after investing in the bus company he kept his job there while Dean and Tailby ran the business. The second Chevrolet was not the only addition to the fleet in October 1924. EH 4023 was a 1923 Oldsmobile 14-seater and was acquired from Bayliss of Ashbourne to replace the Fiat which was kept in open storage. The operating base had moved from the Derby Asphalt yard to the appropriately named Wheel Inn in Findern, and would shortly move again to the Boot Inn in Repton. The other change in October 1924 was the introduction of an increased frequency on Fridays and Saturdays when up to 12 round-trips would be made between Derby and Burton.

Despite the increase in the total number of journeys, demand was still out-stripping supply. In July 1925 the company's first larger capacity vehicle arrived to solve this problem. NU 6959 was a brand-new Hulley with a B28F bus body built by Smith of Castle Bromwich. On the down side Chevrolet NU 4651 was withdrawn in August 1925, but this was only a temporary reduction in fleet size as a brand-new Chevrolet 14-seater, NU 7739, was delivered in October.

More growth took place during 1926 as four vehicles were delivered and only two withdrawn. The first to arrive was another new Chevrolet 14-seater (NU 8357) in February, followed by Morris Commercial NU 8443 in March. The latter was a new chassis but was fitted with the 14-seat Wilkinson body from the stored Fiat. Another new Morris Commercial (NU 9407) was delivered in May and carried a 20-seat bus body by an unidentified manufacturer, while RA 176 (delivered in July) was another Hulley with a Smith body – on this occasion with 32 seats. All of these vehicles were painted in a new livery of Argyll Blue and cream with 'Blue Bus Services' fleet-names. The two withdrawals during the year were of Oldsmobile EH 4023 in February and Chevrolet NU 7739 in December.

Tailby & George

In June 1927 Jack Dean decided to leave the partnership, taking Morris Commercial NU 4907 with him in lieu of his equity. He started operating in his own right between Findern and Derby, but this venture was not a success and soon ended. Both of the founding partners had left the original business to compete with it, and both had failed.

Maudslay ML3E/Willowbrook B32F bus RB 4504 was new to Tailby & George (Blue Bus Services) of Willington in June 1931, and was retired in October 1946. Here it is seen at Willington shortly before withdrawal. *(Blue Bus Services)*

The Daimler COG5/40 offered a Gardner 5LW diesel engine with a maximum seating capacity of 40, making it a best-seller of its day. BRB 645 had a Willowbrook DP39F body and was new to Blue Bus in November 1935. In this shot it is seen in Derby bus station operating a 'Burton via Repton' departure and appears to retain the khaki painted roof of the wartime years. It was sold to Stevenson of Spath in April 1959 for further service. *(David Stanier Collection)*

Blue Bus took delivery of Daimler CWA6/Brush L27/28R utility bus, HRB 686, in May 1944, having previously received a pair with Duple bodywork. Just over 16 years later the vehicle was sold at auction to a new owner in Walsall before ending up in the scrapyard. *(David Stanier Collection)*

JRA 983 was also a Daimler CWA6 but arrived after the end of the war and carried a Duple L27/28R body of a more curvaceous outline than its utility bus predecessors. The bodywork had been further modernised by the time this photograph was taken in Derby bus station, and the vehicle remained in service until October 1966. Sold at auction in the following February it was then scrapped. *(David Stanier Collection)*

The surviving partners, Percy Tailby and Harold George, would be the names that would be remembered for their decades of service to the local community.

The Morris Commercial which had left with Mr Dean was replaced by a brand-new Reo Speedwagon 20-seater, RA 3613, delivered in July 1927. The other Morris Commercial, NU 8443, was withdrawn in September and not immediately replaced, but in June 1928 the fleet came back up to strength with the addition of a brand-new Leyland PLSC3 Lion carrying a Smith B29F body and registered RA 6262. It was followed in August 1928 by a new 20-seat Reo Sprinter, RA 6584, which replaced Chevrolet NU 4445.

The company's very last new Chevrolet 14-seater, RA 7822, was delivered in March 1929 and replaced earlier example NU 8357. A more significant vehicle arrived in August when RA 9538, a new Maudslay ML3B with Wilkinson B32F bodywork, was delivered to replace Halley NU 6959. It was the first of seven Maudslays to be operated by Tailby & George, and would soon be put to work on a second major stage carriage service. This was introduced in the following year and operated from Derby to Burton via Mickleover, Etwall, and Egginton. Two more Maudslay buses arrived during 1930 to cope with this expansion, ML3BC/Sanderson & Holmes 32-seater RB 1253 in April and similar (but Wilkinson-bodied) RB 2341 in August. The third new vehicle of 1930 was RB 2996, a GMC T20 with a B20F body delivered in November.

The operating base was moved again during 1930, this time from Repton to a new purpose-built garage in Willington alongside Harold George's bungalow. The site was cheap for a reason – it was flooded regularly by an over-exuberant River Trent. Fortunately, buses are mobile assets so this was more of a recurring nuisance than an all-out disaster. To give one example of the scale of the problem, the garage found itself under two feet of water in May 1932 during its initial baptism by the river. Whenever the river flooded large sections of Blue Bus route mileage were also left unusable, and this caused far more disruption over the years than any localised flooding at Willington.

With the reign of the Traffic Commissioners on the horizon more new vehicles were acquired to make the company appear respectable again after countless unseemly tussles with Trent

Motor Traction. A fourth Maudslay for the Etwall route, ML3E/Willowbrook B32F bus RB 4504, was delivered in June 1931 and was followed in March 1932 by a fifth example of the marque, ML4B/Willowbrook B26F bus RB 5783. A second Leyland, LT5 Lion/Leyland B30F bus RB 6419, was delivered in June 1932 (replacing Halley RA 176) and a sixth Maudslay, ML3F/Brush B32F bus RB 8299, arrived in May 1933 to further expand the fleet. Licences were duly awarded for both Derby-Burton routes despite the usual persistent objections by Trent and their railway company allies. Derby Corporation was also forced to accept Blue Bus's legalisation and the company's services were allocated a stand in the new municipal bus station.

In 1934 the two partners decided to incorporate the business as Tailby & George Ltd, and this would remain the legal name of the enterprise to the end of its independent existence although the trading name of Blue Bus Services would always be more visible on both vehicles and timetables. The only delivery during the year was another Leyland Lion, an LT5A model with a Burlingham B32F body, which arrived in June and was registered ARA 172. Two more Leylands were delivered in May 1935 as BRA 52/53. Both were TS7 Tigers with Willowbrook dual-purpose bodies (DP39F on BRA 52, DP38F on BRA 53), but BRA 52 had an ordinary gearbox while BRA 53 was equipped with a torque converter automatic box which made it a TS7c. The pair replaced a single Maudslay (RB 1253), further increasing the fleet strength.

A seventh new Maudslay was delivered to Willington in full Blue Bus livery in November 1935 but never entered revenue earning service. BRB 644 was an ML5 with Willowbrook DP39F bodywork and after sitting in the garage for a month it was resold to Hylton & Dawson of Leicester who re-registered the vehicle as JU 7452. The reason for its rejection became clear when a Daimler COG5/40 with Willowbrook DP39F bodywork, BRB 645, arrived on the 22nd of November 1935 – just in time to wave goodbye to the unused Maudslay. The new COG5/40 design was superior in every way to Maudslay's offerings of the era and more of them were ordered but no more Maudslays. The first of the Daimlers replaced Lion RA 6262, while identical COG5/40s CNU 872 (delivered in March 1936) and DRA 735 (new in March 1937) supplanted Maudslays RA 9538 and RB 2341 respectively.

Willowbrook had evidently started to take Blue Bus's patronage somewhat for granted, as in September 1937 they fitted a Bedford WTB with a C26F body, painted it in full Blue Bus livery, and then drove it to Willington to see if Messrs Tailby and George wanted to buy it! This is how the story goes, but at the back of my cynical author's mind there is at least a suspicion that it might be a myth. The purchase of the Bedford coincided with Blue Bus's need for a smaller vehicle to operate a new service from Repton to the small village of Foremark, acting as a feeder to the main Derby-Repton-Burton route. One suspects that somebody at Willowbrook had noticed the licence award in 'Notices & Proceedings' and had enough local knowledge to predict the imminent need for a new bus. The service to Foremark was never a money-spinner and would be withdrawn in 1951.

Two more Daimler COG5/40s were delivered in February 1938 (ERB 92) and May 1939 (GNU 750). The 1938 delivery was another Willowbrook dual-purpose vehicle and replaced five year old Maudslay RB 8299, but the 1939 example carried a Willowbrook C35F coach body and replaced bus-seated Lion RB 6419. GNU 750 was the company's first ever full-size coach and would later be preserved as a fine example of Blue Bus's pre-war fleet. It survives to this day.

Wartime and Double-deckers

The Daimler coach was taken out of service as soon as war was declared, after only four months of use, and placed into storage off-site for the next two years. According to some witnesses it was concealed beneath a haystack, not from fear of the Luftwaffe but out of concern that it might be requisitioned for use elsewhere. There are several known examples of independent operators employing this kind of mildly treasonous subterfuge to preserve their cherished flagship vehicles, so it may well have happened.

Wartime restrictions resulted in a reduced timetable with many late evening services suspended for the duration of hostilities. The remaining journeys were often severely over-crowded as production (and staff numbers) were increased at many of the strategic industrial sites in the area. Double-deckers were an obvious solution, but the railway bridge at Willington

had a restricted clearance (13ft 8ins) which meant that lowbridge examples were essential. The manufacture of low height utility buses lagged behind that of highbridge examples and as a result the requirement for extra capacity remained a problem until 1943. Initially two Guy Arab chassis were allocated to Blue Bus, but negotiation resulted in the substitution of three Daimler CWA6s. The first two, HRB 243/4, arrived in August 1943 and carried Duple L27/28R bodywork. Given Blue Bus's aversion to the Guy Arabs originally offered it was rather ironic that the Daimler chassis were actually built at Guy's Wolverhampton works after Daimler suffered bomb damage to their main works in Coventry. The bodywork on the buses was also non-standard, having been assembled from Duple components by aircraft manufacturer AV Roe.

The third utility CWA6, HRB 686, was delivered in July 1944 and carried a Brush L27/28R body. A fourth example was then allocated, but this arrived long after the end of the war in September 1946. Registered JRA 983 it carried a Duple L27/28R body to the 'relaxed utility' design which featured more curves on the outside and a more comfortable interior. A major bodywork refurbishment programme took place in 1946/7 which involved sending TS7 Tiger BRA 52 and Daimlers BRB 645/CNU 872/ DRA 735 to Willowbrook for restoration to 'as new' condition. The wartime double-deckers also received attention and were fitted with upholstered seating in lieu of their original wooden slatted benches.

Untimely Deaths and More Daimlers

Percy Tailby's wife Maude died in 1948 after a long illness. She had been involved in the business since her husband had become a partner and had specialised in looking after the needs of its drivers and conductors. More unexpected was the death of Harold George in the same year. His wife Katherine ('Kitty') inherited his share of the company.

In May 1948 the original Willowbrook DP39F body was removed from Daimler ERB 92 and sold to Stevenson of Spath for use on another vehicle. The chassis of the Daimler was then sent to Willowbrook and fitted with a new DP35F

Daimler CVD6 MRB 530 was new to Blue Bus in November 1946 and carried a Strachans L27/28R body of a design supplied to a dozen or so independent operators in 1946/7. Unfortunately, Strachans had used inferior quality timber in the production of this model and all of its customers were forced to undertake expensive remedial work. By the time of this late 1950s shot in Derby bus station (in front of a company CD650) the bodywork had been rebuilt and platform doors had been added. After being mended it lasted until October 1962. *(David Stanier Collection)*

Daimler CD650/Willowbrook 53-seater PRA 388 was the second of four of the type delivered to Blue Bus and arrived in April 1951. Most historians would date this photograph to 'after 1966' due to the presence of the Derby Corporation Fleetline in the background, but David Stanier is such an expert on this operator that he can narrow it down to 'after May 1967' due to the presence of flashing indicators on the CD650! The bus was sold for preservation in July 1970 but had been scrapped by 1974. *(David Stanier Collection)*

The second pair of CD650s arrived in 1953 and in this mid-1950s shot SRB 425 is awaiting departure from Derby to Burton via Repton. Behind it (and acting as a duplicate) is ERB 92, a 1938 Daimler COG5/40 which had received a new Willowbrook body in 1948. The CD650 passed into the ownership of Derby Corporation in December 1973 and has been in preservation since March 1975. *(RHG Simpson)*

Few CD650s were sold and the model had been deleted from the catalogue well before Blue Bus needed another double-decker. Undeterred they decided to try a Gardner-engined Daimler CVG6 with similar Willowbrook bodywork, and this arrived in September 1955 as YRB 483. It passed to Derby and was later transferred to Ascot Drive depot. This saved it from the inferno at Willington, but not from the scrapman who bought it in February 1977. *(David Stanier Collection)*

body to their post-war saloon bus design. Two new double-deckers arrived in November 1948 as MRB 529/0. They were Daimler CVD6s (with Daimler's own new 8.4 litre engine) and carried Strachan L27/28R bodywork. Like many Strachan bodies of this period they were made from poor quality timber and after only five years in use the two vehicles were despatched to Willowbrook for remedial work. This included new windows, a new rear platform, and platform doors, which radically altered their appearance.

By 1950 Daimler coach GNU 750 was already 11 years old and Mr Tailby and Mrs George decided that it was time for a new addition. The choice was a Daimler CVD6 with a Duple 'FS1' C33F body which arrived in July as ORB 277. This was a fairly conventional option for a small independent operator, but the same could never be said of Blue Bus's next four purchases. PRA 387/8 (delivered in March 1951) and SRB 424/5 (new in February 1953) were Daimler CD650 double-deckers with Daimler's new 10.6 litre engines. They were immediately distinguishable from other Daimler double-deckers because of their wide radiator grilles, necessary to cool the relatively enormous engines. They were also equipped with 'state of the art' hydraulic brakes and other innovative features which deterred most potential customers and fewer than 20 were built for the British market. Blue Bus's four carried Willowbrook L27/28RD bodies and all remained in service for 19/20 years despite the type's reputation for unreliability and expensive maintenance. This uncharacteristic longevity was a remarkable tribute to Tailby & George's engineering prowess as far larger operators (Halifax for example) had withdrawn their CD650s in despair at relatively early ages.

The next delivery took place in September 1955 after the ill-fated CD650 had been deleted from Daimler's catalogue. As a result the new double-decker, YRB 483, was a CVG6 (with a Gardner 6LW engine). It carried a Willowbrook L27/28RD body which was virtually identical to those on the CD650s, but its external appearance was radically altered by the choice of a 'concealed radiator' disguised by a Birmingham-style vertically slatted cowling. In pre-war days Blue Bus had been enthusiastic about the Gardner 5LW engine fitted to the COG5/40 single-deckers, and they belatedly took a shine to the engine's six

cylinder big brother. The next two double-deckers would also employ the 6LW power plant, but they would not be Daimlers.

Highbridge but Low Height

The lowbridge layout for double-deckers had never been ideal as the four-across bench seats and sunken gangway upstairs made both passenger movements and fare collection difficult. The state-owned Bristol company had solved this problem with their Lodekka design which went into mass production in 1954, but the Lodekka was only available to state-controlled bus operators. Similar designs for the private sector did not appear until the 1956 Commercial Motor Show when AEC introduced their Bridgemaster and Dennis their Loline. The Dennis contender was basically a licence-built Lodekka with some Dennis-designed components and Blue Bus decided to try a couple with Willowbrook H37/33RD bodies. They were the first 'non-Daimler' purchases in 20 years and the company's first 30ft long double-deckers.

The first of the pair, 465 FRB, arrived in November 1957 and the second, 303 GRB, in May 1958. Percy Tailby, who had championed the purchase of the Lolines after seeing the prototype at the Motor Show, failed to see them arrive. He died during 1957 and his share of the business passed to his daughter Bunty and her husband Douglas Marshall.

Blue Bus had always concentrated on its stage carriage business with coaching work forming a relatively small proportion of total revenues. With only two half-cab Daimler coaches in the fleet (and one of those a pre-war specimen) this source of income had dwindled even further during the 1950s as competing firms re-equipped with sleek underfloor-engined machines. To halt this decline the company acquired a brand-new Daimler D650H Freeline coach in June 1959. This vehicle, 120 JRB, employed a horizontally mounted version of the engine used in the CD650 double-deckers and carried a Burlingham Seagull Mk VII C37F body. The Mk VII was a desperate attempt to modify the original (elegant) Seagull design to compete with Plaxton's up and coming Panorama coach and it looked dreadful when compared to the classic 1950-55 Seagull. It was also one of the last two Daimler-engined Freelines to be built (the other went to Burwell & District), so it may have been acquired at a knock-down price. The only other possible explanation for this curious choice was that Blue Bus would buy anything with a Daimler badge on the front.

After buying the two Dennis Lolines in 1957/58 the company returned to Daimler for its next double-decker and to the lowbridge internal configuration. 702 PRA, delivered in August 1960, was a 27ft CVG6 with a Willowbrook L27/28RD body. An expansion of the coaching fleet came next with the delivery of two petrol-engined Bedford SB3s with Duple Super Vega C41F bodywork, 33 SRB in April 1961 and 230 WNU in March 1962. They replaced the two half-cab Daimlers on coaching duties, but GNU 750 and ORB 277 were retained and demoted to stage carriage and/or contract work.

The Fleetline Era

As the purchase of 702 PRA indicated, Blue Bus had been unimpressed by the Lolines and when Daimler finally came out with their own low-height double-deck design at the 1960 Commercial Motor Show the company was among the first to sign the order book. Production of the new rear-engined Fleetline model began in earnest in 1962 and the first pair for Blue Bus arrived in October as 324/5 YNU. They had Gardner 6LX engines and carried Northern Counties H40/33F bodywork. Two more Northern Counties-bodied Fleetlines arrived in August 1964 (ARA 762B) and February 1966 (JRB 481D). Between the Fleetlines two diesel-powered Bedford SB5 coaches with Duple Bella Vega C41F bodies were delivered, 8609 NU in April 1964 and CRA 882B in December of the same year.

The company lost its last link with its pioneering days in March 1965 when Mrs Kitty George passed away. Percy Tailby's daughter and son-in-law, Bunty and Douglas Marshall, were left in control of the business. Two more Bedford coaches were acquired during 1966. KRB 426D was Blue Bus's first 36ft long vehicle, a Bedford VAL14 with Duple Vega Major C52F bodywork which arrived in April, while NRA 680D was a shorter VAM14 with a Duple (Northern) Viscount C45F body and was delivered in October. The final delivery of 1966 was an old friend. Fleetline 7000 HP had started life as a Daimler demonstrator and carried Weymann H44/33F bodywork. During its time with Daimler it had already visited Willington twice while on loan from the manufacturer and

was sold to Blue Bus in November 1966. This was the company's first second-hand purchase since 1924 and further rarity value was added by the Fleetline's non-standard Cummins engine. The latter feature proved troublesome (earning the vehicle the nicknames 'Tick-Tock' and 'The Threshing Machine') but not before Blue Bus had committed itself to another Cummins-engined Daimler product.

The theory that Blue Bus had only bought the Freeline coach because it had a Daimler badge was given fresh momentum in September 1967 when the company took delivery of Daimler Roadliner/Plaxton Panorama C51F coach TNU 687F. By then the foibles of the Cummins-engined Roadliner were well publicised and orders had fallen away to a trickle. Perhaps the engineers at Willington thought that they could perform miracles where others had failed (as they had with the CD650 double-deckers) but on this occasion the beast was irredeemable and spent most of its time with Blue Bus in the garage surrounded by cursing fitters.

Mostly Bedfords

With passenger numbers in decline the directors of Tailby & George decided that they needed something cheaper than Fleetlines to make ends meet. Sadly they opted for another type with a dreadful reputation, the bus version of the Bedford VAL70. The VAL had been designed as a low-cost 36ft coach for operators with modest vehicle utilisation figures. In this role it was fine (apart from its 'iffy' brakes and high internal noise levels!) but as a service bus on high frequency schedules it was a bit of a disaster. A few bus operators (notably Wigmore of Dinnington) stuck with the type but most customers had disposed of their solitary examples at the earliest opportunity. The track record of the VAL bus was already widely known by the time that Blue Bus acquired two in October 1968 (YRB 203G) and March 1969 (BRB 674G). Both had Willowbrook bodies loosely described as 'dual-purpose', a description which hardly matched their sardine tin seating capacities of 56 (YRB 203G) or 54 (BRB 674G). No more were purchased.

After the VAL bus experiment the company reverted to more conservative choices, Another Bedford SB5/Duple Bella Vega C41F coach arrived in January 1970 as FRA 631H, and a final

Blue Bus was an early purchaser of the Dennis Loline, a licence-built version of the Bristol Lodekka available for general sale. The design allowed a central aisle on the upper deck, eliminating the sunken offside gangway of lowbridge types, but maintaining a low overall height. Willowbrook provided the 70-seat bodywork for Blue Bus's pair and 303 GRB was delivered in May 1958. In November of 1975 it was sold to a dealer in Bolton and then vanished, presumed scrapped. *(Omnibus Society - Roy Marshall)*

The final two examples of the Daimler-engined version of the Daimler Freeline were delivered in 1959. One went to Burwell & District, the other to Blue Bus as 120 JRB. The vehicle was equipped with a Burlingham Seagull Mk VII body with panoramic side windows, a rather ugly descendant of the classic Mk I Seagull design of 1950. Compared to its contemporaries the D650HS Freeline was a thirsty beast and Blue Bus's example was sold into preservation as early as 1972. *(Simon Harper Collection)*

After the two Lolines, Blue Bus decided to go back to the lowbridge layout for its next double-decker. Daimler CVG6/ Willowbrook 702 PRA arrived in August 1960 and is seen here at Willington garage in January 1968 alongside a CD650. The CVG6 passed to Derby and was destroyed in the Willington fire in January 1976. *(David Stanier)*

The rather 'retro' CVG6 was followed by a growing fleet of rear-engined Daimler Fleetlines. ARA 762B, the third to arrive, was delivered in August 1964 and like its predecessors carried attractive Northern Counties bodywork. Seen here in Horninglow Street in Burton in around 1973, the vehicle passed to Derby at the end of that year and was then destroyed in the Willington fire. *(Omnibus Society - Roy Marshall)*

The fourth of the Fleetline/Northern Counties double-deckers, JRB 481D, was delivered in February 1966. Flooding was a frequent problem in the villages alongside the River Trent, and in this view (from July 1973) the Fleetline is passing very slowly through Egginton in the capable hands of driver John Peacock. The vehicle burned out in the Willington fire. *(David Stanier)*

Bedford VAM 14/Duple (Northern) Viscount C45F coach NRA 680D was delivered in October 1966 and replaced a four year old Bedford SB3/Duple Super Vega. The VAM passed to Derby at the end of 1973 and was destroyed in the Willington inferno just over two years later. *(Simon Harper Collection)*

Daimler introduced their new Fleetline double-decker to the bus industry at the 1960 Commercial Motor Show at Earls Court. Weymann-bodied prototype 7000 HP was the vehicle on display and remained in use as a Daimler demonstrator until November 1966, latterly with a Cummins V6 engine. It was sold to Blue Bus who had operated it on loan several times before. This historically important vehicle was sadly lost in the Willington fire. *(Omnibus Society - Roy Marshall)*

Blue Bus's sixth and final Fleetline received an Alexander lowheight-body and was delivered in May 1971 as NRA 49J. At the end of 1973 it passed to Derby was another victim of the Willington fire in January 1976. *(Omnibus Society - Roy Marshall)*

Fleetline (with a Gardner engine and an Alexander AD type H44/31F body) in May 1971 as NRA 49J. The next vehicle to arrive was another Bedford SB5/Duple C41F coach, ORB 883K. This was delivered in August 1971 and carried Duple's new Vega 31 body style.

Having experienced the Bedford VAL bus the company decided to try a Bedford type with a better reputation as a stage carriage work-horse, the YRQ with 45-seat Willowbrook 001 bodywork. Some caution was exercised, however, and the two new acquisitions were both former Vauxhall Motors demonstrators albeit with low mileages. DXE 137J arrived at Willington in December 1971 and EXE 276J in June 1972. They were followed in September 1973 by two Bedford YRTs with Duple Dominant C53F 'grant coach' bodies (suitable for driver-only operation on bus work as required) registered ORA 818/9M. These vehicles were Blue Bus's last ever purchases as an independent bus operator.

Several Terrible Endings

Given some of the types operated it is perhaps surprising to discover that the Fleetlines killed Blue Bus. At the beginning of February 1973 both of the 1962 machines (324/5 YNU) were out of service with gear-box problems. Two days after 325 YNU was returned to traffic the gear-box on ARA 762B seized up. At around the same time the Cummins engine in 7000 HP failed, leaving three of the six Fleetlines off the road at the same time. Added to the now routine problems with the VAL buses (not to mention the Roadliner) these difficulties caused serious service disruptions.

On the 30th of June 1973 the directors of Tailby & George Ltd announced that they had been involved in negotiations to sell their company to the corporations of Burton-upon-Trent and Derby. The deal was scheduled to be concluded on the 1st of September, but in the intervening period Burton dropped out of the transaction after Trent Motor Traction indicated that it would object to any transfer of Blue Bus's licences. After some deliberation Derby Corporation decided to go it alone and Tailby & George Ltd became a wholly owned subsidiary of the municipal operator on the 1st of December 1973.

The deal included 23 buses and coaches (the last surviving CD650, two CVG6s, two Lolines, six Fleetlines, two VAL70 buses, two YRQ buses,

two YRT grant coaches, three SB5 coaches, a VAL14 coach, a VAM14 coach, and the accursed Roadliner), a Humber recovery vehicle, the premises at Willington, and the 'goodwill' of Blue Bus's Road Service Licences. The Traffic Commissioners approved the transfer of the licences to Derby Corporation in March 1974 and in the following month the first Blue Bus vehicle was repainted into Derby livery. Surprisingly, this first repaint was of Loline 465 FRB which was already 16 years old. Vehicles older than the Loline were soon replaced by Derby vehicles sent to Willington. The two stage carriage routes from Derby to Burton remained largely unchanged save for the colour schemes of the vehicles operating them and the allocation of Derby route numbers – the Repton service became the 45 and the Etwall service the 46. Both routes were still worked from the depot at Willington.

At around 2330 hours on the 5th of January 1976 a fire broke out at the Willington garage, less than 15 minutes after the premises had been locked up for the night. The alarm was raised by local residents, but by the time the first fire appliance arrived at 2355 the garage was well ablaze. A total of 19 vehicles were destroyed, all but four of them former Blue Bus vehicles including all six Fleetlines, CVG6 double-decker 702 PRA, the Roadliner, and seven Bedfords. CVG6 double-decker YRB 483 and Loline 465 FRB survived the blaze (the other Loline was away on maintenance at the time), but the final chapter of the Blue Bus story had clearly ended. Operations on the two Derby-Burton routes were transferred to Derby's Ascot Drive depot and operated by vehicles new to Derby rather than Blue Bus alumni. For some curious reason Derby decided to use the Blue Bus name for its small coaching fleet, but this too disappeared before very long. One of the most widely respected names in the independent bus industry had been obliterated except for a few (thankfully) preserved survivors.

Further Reading

In a book like this which covers an entire county one can never do justice to an operator of Blue Bus's magnitude. Those who want more details should read David Stanier's masterly work on the company 'Blue Bus Services'. The first (duplicated and comb-bound) edition of this volume came out in 1979, but the second edition (professionally printed in 1985 by JM Pearson & Son) is even better. My thanks are extended to David for permission to use the information contained in his book which is a classic of its genre.

Carter of Hales Green

In 1925 Mr Ernest Frost of Hales Green bought an unidentified Ford Model T equipped with rudimentary passenger seating and began regular market day bus services from his home village of Hales Green to Uttoxeter (on Wednesdays) and Ashbourne (on Thursdays and Saturdays) along with a regular outing on Fridays to Derby. Things went well and in July 1928 the makeshift Ford was replaced by a brand-new Bean with an 18-seat Willowbrook body registered RA 6382. Mr Frost's success was a fleeting triumph as he died in April 1930.

The Bean and the services passed to his widow, Frances Frost, who added a second vehicle in August 1931. This was RB 4674, a new Morris Viceroy with a 24-seat bus body by an unidentified concern, and Mrs Frost's two buses continued to provide shopping trips from the local villages for the remainder of the decade. In 1932 licences were granted by the new Traffic Commissioners for services from Hales Green to Uttoxeter via Yeaveley, Alkmonton, Great Cubley, and Marston Montgomery, from Alkmonton to Ashbourne via Yeaveley, Rodsley, Edlaston, and Clifton, and from Wyaston to Derby via Rodsley, Yeaveley, Alkmonton, and Longford. It is believed that the routes to Uttoxeter and Derby were suspended for the duration of the Second World War, but this has been impossible to confirm from official records.

The Bean and the Viceroy were still in service in June 1942 when the proprietor remarried. Her new husband was Ernest Carter and he assumed all legal responsibilities for the business including its Road Service Licences. The Bean was on its way out by this time and had vanished by August 1942. A belated replacement arrived in February 1944 in the shape of a second Morris Viceroy, RB 7913. This was a 1933 machine with a Willowbrook B20F body and came from Machin of Ashby.

The second-hand Viceroy was withdrawn from use in April 1947, reducing the 'fleet' to one vehicle again until November 1948 when a brand-new Bedford OB with a Duple Vista C29F body, MNU 336, was acquired. The other

ageing Viceroy was retired in December 1949. Its replacement, in March 1950, was another OB/Duple Vista registered EUN 318. This vehicle had been new to Jones of Ruabon in January 1948.

The fleet then stabilised at two OB coaches for the next 16 years. During this period a local boy, David Glover, began to hang around at the garage and offered to do odd jobs for the Carters in exchange for the privilege of close contact with the Bedfords. He would later find work as a farm labourer, use his income to obtain an HGV licence, and then use his new skills in the service of several Ashbourne area businesses. He also bought a taxi, finding a relief driver for the periods when he was too busy driving lorries to take care of his own vehicle.

In January 1964 the Carters acquired their first 'Big Bedford', a fourth-hand 1956 SBG with Duple 'Butterfly Front' Super Vega C41F bodywork registered 143 CLG. This came from Neave of Catfield and replaced Bedford OB/Vista EUN 318. Another SBG, DDJ 309, was acquired from Ellison of St Helens in the summer of 1965 and was a slightly earlier (1954) model with a Duple 'Fish Mouth' Super Vega C36F body. For the first and only time there were three vehicles in the Carter fleet, a state of affairs that lasted until October 1968 when Bedford OB/Vista MNU 336 was retired after more than 20 years of service.

By this time the Carters were both in their late sixties and starting to think about retirement. Their old helper David Glover had expressed his desire to buy the business, but lacked the capital to make an outright purchase. A deal was agreed whereby Glover would take one coach (DDJ 309) on approval and use it on private-hire work to raise the rest of the capital required. Ownership of the SBG was transferred in October 1968, money was made, and in December 1969 Glover came back for 143 CLG and the stage carriage licences. The garage at Hales Green remained in the Carters' hands but was rented to the new proprietor at a very reasonable rate. Glover's registered office was at his home in Ashbourne, so the remainder of this story will be found under the heading 'Glover of Ashbourne' (qv).

Dove Valley

See Allen of Roston

Bedford YRQ/Willowbrook 001 DP45F saloon EXE 276J was one of a pair of former YRQ demonstrators acquired from Vauxhall Motors. It arrived at Willington in June 1972 and is seen here at Wetmore Bus Park in Burton. After passing to Derby it was destroyed in the Willington garage fire. *(David Stanier Collection)*

Blue Bus turned to grant coaches in 1973 in the form of a pair of Bedford YRTs with Duple Dominant C53F bodywork. The second of the pair, ORA 819M, was the very last vehicle to be registered by Blue Bus when it was delivered in September 1973. Three months later it passed with the company to Derby Corporation and two years after that it was incinerated at Willington. *(J Walker via David Stanier)*

This 1930s shot outside the garage at Hales Green shows Mrs Frances Frost (then the local bus operator) with 18 seat Bean 30cwt/Willowbrook bus RA 6382. The vehicle was new to her late husband in July 1928 and lasted long enough to pass into the ownership of her second husband, Ernest Carter, in June 1942. Two months later it was withdrawn from use. Note the dog on the bonnet of the Bean. *(Eric Wain Collection)*

Bedford OB/Duple Vista C29F coach MNU 336 was new to Carter of Hales Green in November 1948 and is seen here with Mr Carter and a later family pet. The OB gave almost 20 years of service, being withdrawn in October 1968. *(Tim Jeffcoat)*

Felix of Stanley

Stanley is a medium sized village with around 800 residents to the west of the town of Ilkeston and to the north of Derby. Traditionally an agricultural community, it became a coal-mining village in the late 19th century. Samuel Frost was a miner at the local pit when his son Norman was born in 1899 and, knowing the hardships endured by his profession, became determined that Norman would not follow in his footsteps. When Norman Frost was 14 his father secured for him an apprenticeship as a motor mechanic, a trade he continued to pursue after being called up for service in the First World War in 1917.

Returning from the military he found work as a mechanic and in 1921 took the enormous step of borrowing £500 from his father to assist in the purchase of a war-surplus Crossley lorry which was registered R 7831. Having borrowed what was then a small fortune from Samuel he could not afford to fail and the Crossley achieved a very high utilisation. From Monday to Friday the vehicle would carry miners to work at local collieries at shift-change times and between those duties would revert to goods configuration and deliver coal to customers in Stanley and the surrounding villages. On Saturdays the wooden benches and canvas roof stayed on all day to ferry Stanley residents to and from Ilkeston Market Place, and on Sundays was (usually) available for private-hire work.

Norman Frost recognised that the lorry was far from ideal as a conveyance for passengers and in 1922 he invested in a second (unidentified) war surplus Crossley and had it fitted with a 14-seat char-a-banc body. Further commitment to the passenger side of the business came in 1924 when R 7831 had its lorry body removed and replaced by a 14-seat Dickens bus body. This was needed as Frost had decided to extend his bus service to Derby on Tuesdays, Fridays, and Saturdays, terminating on private property in a pub yard. This was necessary due to the refusal of Derby Corporation to grant a licence.

With R 7831 proving a reliable performer on the Ilkeston-Stanley-Kings Corner-Chaddesden-Derby service, the Crossley char-a-banc was liberated to roam more freely. By the summer of 1924 Frost was offering day excursions to Skegness and other coastal resorts. Larger vehicles followed in the shape of three 30cwt Dennis buses (RA 575/1780/5361, delivered in 1926-8) and Dennis G (RA 7068), new in 1929. This influx of vehicles was occasioned by Derby Corporation's decision to award a licence and the development of a daily, hourly, schedule between Ilkeston and Derby. Vehicles operated under the 'Felix Bus Service' name, as Felix the Cat was a well known character from an American (silent) cartoon series and Mr Frost was rather fond of the character's signature tune.

With a fleet of four relatively new vehicles and existing municipal licences in his pocket there was never any real doubt that Norman Frost would receive approval from the new Traffic Commissioners in 1931/2. Having been impressed by his fleet of Dennis Gs he moved on to the new Dennis Lancet. The first was ordered for delivery in early 1933, but was delayed for six months at the manufacturers. It eventually turned up as RB 7906 and carried a Willowbrook C32F body. All future deliveries until 1963 (except for two wartime utility buses) would be coaches, affording an unusual level of comfort for a route which took less than 45 minutes from end to end.

In 1934 Felix opted for some smaller Dennises. ANU 821 and ARB 472 were Dennis Aces with Willowbrook C20F bodies and were ideal for excursion and private-hire work, although they also appeared on the Derby route. A second Lancet/Willowbrook C32F coach, BRA 86, followed in 1935, pursued by two of the improved Lancet II version with similar bodywork in 1937 (DRB 861) and 1938 (ERB 398). Since the early days of the firm its vehicles had been based at premises in New Street in Stanley, but in July 1937 the growing fleet moved into a new garage on Station Road which would remain in use for many decades.

Before the outbreak of the Second World War an order had been placed for yet another Dennis, this time a lighter weight Falcon with a C32F body by Dennis themselves, but this vehicle (GRB 739) was finally delivered in early 1940 and almost immediately requisitioned by the War Department. Lancets BRA 86 and ERB 398 were also requisitioned and the three vehicles were belatedly returned to Felix in 1947.

During their absence Mr Frost managed to acquire another other Lancet on the second-hand market. VJ 6437 was a 1934 machine and came from Wye Valley of Hereford. It carried a

Another of Carter's OB/Vista coaches, EUN 318, is seen here in Derby alongside Allen of Roston's OB/Mulliner TRE95.The Carter machine had been new to Jones of Ruabon in January 1948 and migrated to Hales Green in March 1950. It gave 14 years of service to the firm before its eventual withdrawal. *(Omnibus Society - Roy Marshall)*

This 1956 Bedford SB3 with Duple Super Vega C41F bodywork came to Carter from Neave of Catfield (in Norfolk) in January 1964 and was never repainted into Carter's green livery. In December 1969 it was sold along with the stage licences to David Glover but continued to be based at the Hales Green premises. *(Tim Jeffcoat)*

Willowbrook C32F body very similar to Felix's 'native' examples. The only other vehicles obtained during the war were a pair of Bedford OWB utility buses. HRB 5 arrived in March 1943 and was equipped with a Mulliner body, and HRB 814 was delivered in June 1944 and was a Duple-bodied example. The two OWBs replaced the 1934 Dennis Aces.

The first delivery after the end of the conflict was very close in appearance to the OWBs. JRA 476 was, however, an early post-war example of a Bedford OB with Duple Mk II bus bodywork and entered service in February 1946. It arrived with 32 seats but was later (along with the two OWBs) down-seated to 28 to comply with peace-time regulations. While the three Bedfords were dedicated to the stage carriage service, along with several pre-war machines, the profits from the route were invested in a renewal of the coaching stock. LNU 36 was a brand-new Lancet III with a Yeates C35F body and arrived in January 1947. The next coach to be delivered was not quite what it seemed. Its pre-war Dennis Lancet chassis had originally been used in a goods vehicle registered in Cheshire as AMB 596. Felix bought the chassis in 1947 sent it to Yeates to receive a C32F coach body, and upon its return in early 1948 it received the new registration mark MRA 279. The other addition to the fleet during 1948 was MRA 903, a Crossley SD42/5 with a Yeates C35F body, which was to remain the only Crossley bought by Felix apart from the original two war surplus machines. In February 1950 the firm's preference reverted to Dennis with the acquisition of a second Lancet III with Yeates C35F bodywork, ONU 706. Pre-war Lancet BRA 86 received a similar body to replace its original 1935 Willowbrook structure, a move which extended its life beyond that of its slightly younger sisters.

The villagers of West Hallam, situated around half a mile to the south of Felix's bus route, half-way from Ilkeston to Stanley, had been campaigning for a regular service for some time and the village was added to certain departures from early 1950. The journeys chosen for diversion were those which already needed a duplicate vehicle (Felix never operated double-deckers) and so this extra mileage was achieved by means of diverting the duplicate. This low-cost solution brought in extra revenue without requiring any additional vehicles, making everybody happy.

The down-turn in excursion and private-hire work from 1951 onwards resulted in a change of purchasing policy at Felix. For several years second-hand coaches were bought in place of the usual brand-new specimens, starting with a pair of post-war Bedford OBs which allowed the retirement of the two OWB utility buses. EX 5777, a 1947 OB with a Duple C27F body, came from Calver of Great Yarmouth in 1952 and KWA 279 (with an SMT 'Vista lookalike' C29F body) was acquired from Sims of Sheffield in 1953. The next addition, in 1954, was Felix's very last purchase of a Dennis vehicle. LDD 507 was a Falcon L6 with a Duple 'Vega style' C33F body and had been new to Say of Gloucester in 1952. Two more second-hand Bedford OB coaches joined the fleet in the second half of the 1950s. Both carried Duple Vista C29F bodywork. LTO 715 was a 1949 example and was acquired from Makemson of Bulwell in 1955. Four years later it was replaced by 1950 machine BSN 259 which arrived from McAteer in distant Dumbarton. Meanwhile, an attempt had been made to modernise the existing coach fleet by removing the original Yeates half-cab body from Lancet III LNU 36 and replacing it with a new (1956) Yeates Riviera body with a full front. The old body was sold to a local farmer for use as a storage shed and could still be found on his property as late as 1968.

After a nine year absence new vehicles returned to the fleet in May 1959 with the delivery of 618 KRA, a Bedford SB1 with a Yeates Europa C41F body. Identical sister 47 UNU joined the fleet in July 1961 and was followed by SB5/ Yeates Europa 3 XRA in July 1962. As a regular Yeates customer Felix was an obvious target for the company's front entrance Pegasus design as fitted to modified Bedford SB chassis. Mr Frost agreed to try one, and this materialised in June 1963 as 6881 R, an SB5 with a 45-seat dual-purpose body. The front entrance was rather wasted on Felix as conductors were still carried on all stage carriage work, but it undoubtedly made the conductors' lives more comfortable as the entrance door on the Pegasus was operated by the driver. The sliding doors on the Europas, which were also used on the Ilkeston-Derby route, were much more labour intensive – especially on journeys when one conductor was working two vehicles in convoy.

Norman Frost had intended to buy at least one more Pegasus, but this possibility was eliminated when WS Yeates decided to withdraw from bodywork production at the end of 1963. As a result Plaxton would become the company's new supplier of PSV bodies from 1964 until 1976. With the Pegasus out of the running Felix returned to conventional forward entrance Bedford SB5s, beginning with ANU 158B in July 1964. This carried a Plaxton Embassy III C41F body and was followed in July 1965 by a broadly similar Embassy IV example, FRB 114C. They replaced Crossley MRA 903 and Lancet ONU 706, the last two half-cab vehicles in the fleet.

The proprietor had always been active both as a driver and as a mechanic, leaving administration in the hands of his trusted employee Miss Ida Bacon. In 1966 he gave up driving, partly due to his advancing years but also because he found the newer vehicles less pleasurable to command. The garage then became his full-time place of work. New coaches continued to arrive at regular intervals to replace older stock. Bedford SB5s with Plaxton Panorama C41F bodywork were delivered in March 1966 (KNU 452D), January 1968 (URA 414F), and July 1969 (DRA 35G). They replaced the Falcon L6, the Lancet III with a Yeates Riviera body, and the oldest of the three Yeates Europa-bodied Bedfords.

Tempted by the bus grant scheme Felix acquired two Bedfords with Plaxton Derwent II DP45F bodies in 1970/1. GNU 699H arrived in March 1970 and was a VAM70, while ORB 554K followed in August 1971 and used Bedford's new YRQ chassis which had replaced the VAM70 in their catalogue. Their arrival occasioned the departure of the solitary Pegasus and of another Yeates Europa. Mr Frost then turned to 'grant coaches' which featured full luxury interiors but were adapted to make them suitable for driver-only operation. The first four were built on Bedford YRQ chassis and all had Plaxton C45F bodywork. VNU 484K arrived in May 1972, BRA 191L in February 1973, PRA 836M in November 1973, and HNU 731N in February 1975.

Norman Frost died in March 1975 and control of the bus company passed to his nephew Mr Geoffrey Middup, then living in Grantham in Lincolnshire. The new owner's first move was to incorporate the business as Felix Bus Services Ltd, registered in July 1975 with Miss Ida Bacon as its company secretary. Fleet acquisitions were put on pause until November 1976 when a fifth grant coach, Bedford YMT/Plaxton C51F, RCH 76R, arrived in Stanley. A change of purchasing policy in 1978 saw the delivery of two YMTs with Duple Dominant C53F bodywork, WRC 826S in February and BRR 684T in December. A shorter YLQ model with a 45-seat Dominant body took the consecutive registration BRR 685T but was delivered in February 1979.

The theme of brand-new Bedford grant coaches with either Plaxton or Duple bodywork continued until 1986 when the second (and more drastic) Deregulation Act took effect. Felix's immediate response was to buy two second-hand Leyland PSU3 Leopards with Plaxton C53F bodywork, DTN 958W from Holmes of Clay Cross in October 1986 and BES 270V from Earnside of Glenfarg in March 1987. A further surprise came in April 1987 with the delivery of D694 WNU, a brand-new Bedford YMT with a Plaxton Derwent III B55F service bus body.

Felix continued to thrive during the quarter century after deregulation. The main service was extended at the Ilkeston end to serve Shipley View Estate in 1986, and further extended to the local hospital in 1987. The 'Felix the Cat' cartoon logo was eliminated from the sides of the vehicles in 2009 after threatening letters from a California company which claimed to own the copyright of the image. By then Felix's original service was using 'Black Cat' route-branding and this remained in place minus the cartoon cat. A second service from Ilkeston to Derby, running on a limited-stop basis via Kirk Hallam and Spondon, was already operating by then and had been route-branded as 'The Ilkeston Flyer'. Both of the 'branded' Derby services were jointly operated with Trent which had initially tried to compete with Felix on the Stanley routing but had swiftly concluded that compromise was a better solution. Felix customers were fiercely loyal.

In December 2011 the Middup family decided to sell Felix's stage carriage services to the revived Midland General, a low-cost unit within Trent's Wellglade holding company. Felix's coaching activities were sold separately to Swiftsure Coaches of Burton-on-Trent, and Felix Bus Services Ltd surrendered its operating licence in April 2012. It was an unexpected ending for a company which had proved beyond all doubt that it could survive in the deregulated world.

Crossley R 7831 was first registered in 1921 but came from military surplus stock. Originally mounted with a fairly primitive 'lorry bus' body, in 1924 it received this more respectable 14-seat bus body made by Dickens. The gentleman at centre left in this shot is Norman Frost, the founder of Felix of Stanley. This vehicle was later sold to Parrish of Hatfield (near Doncaster) who kept the livery and Felix fleet-name, becoming the 'other' Felix for the next 53 years. *(Felix Bus Services)*

Felix of Stanley's second vehicle was this unidentified Crossley char-a-banc. The registration begins with the letters 'NU' but the following numbers are concealed. According to PSV Circle records this was a 14-seater, but in this photograph there are 19 on board including one passenger on Norman Frost's knee. Those were the days. *(Felix Bus Services)*

Dennis Lancet BRA 86 was delivered to Felix in 1935 and originally carried a Willowbrook C32F body. It was requisitioned by the War Department in 1940 but returned in 1947. The petrol engine was replaced by a diesel unit in 1947 and at the same time the machine received a new Yeates C35F body as shown here in Derby bus station. Felix kept it for nine more years and it then gave further service to Scutt of Owston Ferry. *(Omnibus Society - Roy Marshall)*

In 1933 Dennis AMB 596 was registered in Cheshire as a flat-bed lorry. Felix bought the machine in 1948, replaced its petrol engine with a diesel, and converted it into a PSV with a Yeates C32F body. It then received the new registration MRA 279, as seen here in Derby bus station in company with Trent PD2 LRC 435 and Felix's 1947 Lancet III with a 1956 Yeates Riviera body, LNU 36. *(Omnibus Society - Peter Yeomans)*

Delays in obtaining further Dennis Lancets during 1948 led to the purchase of this brand-new Crossley SD42/5 coach with a Yeates C35F body, MRA 903, which was the first of its marque to enter the fleet since the early 1920s. Seen in Ilkeston Market Place alongside one of Barton's home-made BTS1 single-deckers, it gave 15 years of service to Felix. *(Omnibus Society - Roy Marshall)*

After its third and final Crossley the company turned back to Dennis, taking delivery of brand-new Lancet III/ Yeates C35F coach ONU 706 in January 1950. The vehicle, seen in Derby bus station, was withdrawn from use in November 1964. *(RF Mack)*

Felix really didn't fancy the underfloor-engined version of the Lancet and turned to Bedford as its main chassis supplier. Bedford SB1/Yeates Europa C41F coach 618 KRA was new in May 1959 and is shown at the Derby end of the stage service. In June 1969 it passed to Parkin of Borrowash, trading as Luxicoaches. *(John Holmes)*

Almost identical vehicle 47 UNU was delivered in July 1961 and is also seen in Derby bus station. In 1970 it was replaced by a new Bedford VAM70 with a Plaxton Derwent II body. *(John Holmes)*

Further Reading

'Felix Bus Services Ltd of Stanley, Derbyshire', by Paul D Chambers was self-published by the author in 2006. Despite scouring second-hand stalls at bus rallies, combing second-hand book-shops, and asking all of my regular contacts if they have a copy I could borrow, I have still never seen this book 'in the flesh'. I suspect that the author may have seriously under-estimated the interest in Felix when deciding upon the print-run. You may be luckier than I have been!

Glover of Ashbourne

David Glover was born in 1935 and in his teenage years became fascinated with the Bedford coaches in use with his local operator, Carter of Hales Green (qv). After leaving school he was forced to seek a living elsewhere, becoming a farm labourer. The income from this job was used to obtain an HGV licence, and the income earned from driving lorries was used to buy a taxi to further boost his finances.

The amount accumulated was still not enough to buy his beloved coach firm when the Carters decided to sell out in 1968. Fortunately, they admired Glover's enthusiasm and agreed to a deal in which he bought the business in instalments. The purchaser's first instalment saw the transfer of 1954 Bedford SBG/Duple C36F coach DDJ 309 to Glover's ownership along with Carter's private-hire business. This was somewhat limited in nature given the small populations of the neighbouring villages, but the new owner was aggressive in seeking additional private-hire work in Ashbourne and beyond.

The stage services remained in Carter ownership until December 1969 when they too were transferred to Glover along with 1956 Bedford SB3/Duple coach 143 CLG. The two SBs were still kept in Carter's garage in Hales Green which was rented to the new operator. At this stage DDJ 309 was still painted in Carter's traditional two-tone green livery, while 143 CLG had never been repainted by them and wore a maroon and white colour scheme from a previous owner. The fleet grew to three in January 1971 with the arrival of 1965 Bedford SB5/Duple (Northern) Firefly coach CVD 852C from Park of Hamilton.

David Glover's first new coach was acquired in August 1972 and introduced a standard colour scheme of blue and cream. XNU 656L was a Bedford YRQ with Duple Viceroy C45F bodywork and replaced DDJ 309. The next change came in March 1975 when CVD 852C was replaced by a 1972 Bedford SB5/Plaxton C41F coach, ATY 929K, acquired from Rowell of Prudhoe. An eight year old Ford Transit minibus, KVM 428F, was acquired in March 1976 and was joined in July by NRA 550J, a 1971 SB5/Plaxton C41F coach previously operated by Bowers of Chapel-en-le-Frith. The latter vehicle took the 'full size' fleet to four, but NRA 550J was a short-lived resident, being replaced in April 1977 by a two year old Ford R1114/Plaxton C53F coach, HAT 754N, acquired from Xanthine of Hull.

In October 1976 the neighbouring business of Allen of Roston (qv) ceased to trade and its stage carriage licences passed to Glover along with 1961 Bedford SB1/Plaxton Embassy C41F coach NBF 908, although this did not enter service with its new owner until June of the following year and had been sold by November 1977. The growing portfolio of stage carriage routes demanded something more appropriate than the ageing Bedford 143 CLG, and in July 1977 this was sent for scrap and replaced by a 1966 Bristol MW6G coach with an ECW C39F, FEL 751D. The Bristol came from Hants & Dorset which had adapted it for driver-only operation. It was an uncommon vehicle to find with a small Derbyshire independent, but it did the job for more than three years.

Bedford YRQ coach XNU 656L was sold in February 1978 and replaced by a second-hand Ford R1114/Duple Dominant C53F coach, KVP 944P, acquired from Arnold of Tamworth. The other purchase of the year was considerably older. NFM 685E was a 1967 Bedford VAM5 coach with a Duple Viscount C45F body and arrived from Walker of Anderton (Cheshire) in May 1978. It was the last second-hand (full size) vehicle to join the fleet for several years as the proprietor had decided to concentrate on brand-new coaches.

Two Bedford YMTs with Duple Dominant C53F 'grant coach' bodywork were acquired in January 1979 (CAL 584T) and February 1980 (HRB 932V), followed by a Leyland PSU3E/4R

Leopard with similar bodywork (NNU 71W) in January 1981. This trio of Dominants became the regular performers on Glover's stage carriage network which by then also included villages to the north of Ashbourne, such as Parwich and Tissington, served on routes subsidised by Derbyshire County Council.

Bedford YMP/Duple Dominant C45F grant coach URA 481X joined the fleet in July 1982, and Leyland TRCT Tiger/Plaxton C53F coach YNN 396Y in March 1983. The original Transit minibus (and its second-hand successor of the same breed) had given way to brand-new Mercedes 12-seaters by then, but Glover's first full-size vehicle of foreign manufacture was Volvo B10M-61/Plaxton C53F coach B252 KTO, delivered in May 1985.

After deregulation Glover's Coaches continued to be active in the tendered services sector of the market, covering much of the company's traditional (ex Carter and Allen) mileage as well as other routes in the Ashbourne area. Interesting vehicles of this more recent era included a Leyland National acquired from Trent (PRR 446R) and an unusual Dennis Lancet with an Alexander P type B53F bus body which had been new to Northern Scottish (A506 FSS).

In 2003 David Glover, by then 68 years old, decided to retire and sold the business to Mason Travel of Roston Common. Mason had started operations in 1977 with a single Ford Transit minibus and had specialised in smaller vehicles for most of its existence. The Glovers trading name was retained for local bus services and full-size coaching activity along with the blue and cream fleet livery. David Glover died in February 2014, aged 78.

North of Derby

Messrs Hall & North of Horsley Woodhouse, near Heanor, bought a brand-new 14-seat Chevrolet, NU 1506, in August 1923 and put it to work on a bus service from Heanor to Belper via their home village. Mr Hall vanished from the story at an early stage, but Harold North continued with the endeavour and bought a second brand-new vehicle, Austin 14-seater NU 4537, in September 1924. In the following month the original Chevrolet was sold for use as a lorry and replaced by a new Lancia bus with a 20-seat Hartshorn body, NU 4622.

During 1926 the Austin and the Lancia were part-exchanged for two new Dennis 30cwt buses with 14-seat bodies. NU 9384 arrived in May to replace the Austin and RA 1061 in November to replace the Lancia which was sold to Barton. Three more Dennis 30cwt buses (with 18 seats) were added to the fleet in September 1927 (RA 3989), and June 1928 (RA 6137/51), and this increase in fleet strength from two to five allowed Mr North to open a second stage carriage route, from Heanor to Derby via Horsley Woodhouse.

By the autumn of 1929 a larger vehicle was required, prompting the delivery of a new Dennis E with a Reeve & Kenning B32F body, RB 277, in December of that year. This was immediately before the effects of the Wall Street financial crash began to be felt in terms of pit and factory closures and drastically reduced local employment. Mr North persisted in his optimism and bought two new Morris Dictators with 32-seat Reeve & Kenning bodies in May 1931 (RB 4341) and December 1932 (RB 7174). The Dennis E and the two Dictators had all been acquired on hire-purchase agreements from the Kenning Group, clearly an unwise move by Mr North in the face of plummeting revenues, but the modern fleet had helped to ensure that his stage carriage routes were authorised by the new Traffic Commissioners. A third Morris Dictator, HA 6987, joined the North fleet in early 1933. It was a 1930 vehicle with United B32F bodywork and had been a Morris Commercial Motors demonstrator.

A limited company, HS North Ltd, had been formed in October 1931 with a registered office at 16 St James Street in Derby. This address was the headquarters of another independent operator, Kingfisher Services Ltd, which operated stage carriage services from Derby to Allestree, Darley Abbey, and Quarndon. The majority of shares in HS North Ltd were owned by Kingfisher's founder, Mr EJ Knight, although Harold North remained in charge at the Horsley Woodhouse premises.

Despite the new ownership HS North Ltd continued to make irregular payments to the Kenning Group and by late 1933 Kingfisher was also in trouble. Sir George Kenning sent his trouble-shooter, Mr SO Stevenson of Eagle Services (see Introduction) into 16 St James Street to see what could be salvaged – Kingfisher had also bought vehicles on hire-purchase from

Given the company's liking for Bedfords with Yeates bodywork, it came as no great surprise when Norman Frost decided to try a Yeates Pegasus dual-purpose vehicle. Built on a modified Bedford SB5 chassis, 6881 R was new in June 1963 and is seen at Derby bus station. Note the 'Felix the Cat' image in the dash panel moulding where one would normally find an image of Pegasus the flying horse! *(RHG Simpson)*

The Pegasus was replaced by this brand-new Bedford YRQ with Plaxton Derwent II DP45F bodywork, ORB 554K, in August 1971. This machine, seen in Derby bus station, was replaced in its turn by a later Bedford with a Duple Dominant grant coach body. *(Colin Anderson Collection)*

Dennis Lancet BTO 389 was new to Dutton's Unity of Nottingham in 1935 and quickly passed with that business to Trent as their fleet number 1233. North of Derby bought it in 1945, replaced its original Willowbrook C32F body with an ECOC B34F bus body previously fitted to a West Yorkshire Lancet, and installed an AEC 7.7 litre diesel engine. In 1949 it received a brand-new Burlingham C33F body as seen here and was finally withdrawn from use at the end of 1962. *(Les Dickinson Collection)*

Dennis Lancet YG 5730 had been new to West Yorkshire in 1933 and was originally fitted with an ECOC B34F body. In May 1949 North's equiped it with the new Burlingham C33F body seen here, and transferred its ECOC bus body to a former North Western machine. YG 5730 remained in service until December 1963. *(Omnibus Society - Robin Hannay)*

Kenning. To deter other creditors who might have thoughts of jumping the queue, North's vehicles were transferred into the ownership of Eagle Services and received Eagle fleet-names on their running boards.

At an early stage in the local hire-purchase crisis Sir George Kenning had considered the possibility of using Eagle Services (a mixed bag of routes acquired from bankrupt customers) as the nucleus for a new regional bus company, but Trent Motor Traction soon persuaded him that this would be a very rocky road to travel. Instead they offered to buy his various bus operating assets at a high-end valuation and the opportunity to become the leading minority shareholder in Trent itself. Kenning agreed to this plan and gradually transferred his operations to Trent, the piecemeal approach reflecting the various final settlement dates on outstanding hire-purchase arrangements. As part of this process Kingfisher and HS North Ltd were sold to Trent in the Spring of 1935 along with all of their stage carriage routes.

A Second Chance

At the time of the Trent take-over the HS North Ltd fleet had included three Morris Dictators (Trent took RB 4341/7174 while HA 6987 was sold to Foster of Dinnington), the Dennis E 32-seater RB 277(which passed to the Kenning Group's Heanor & District operation), and Dennis 30cwt 18-seaters RA 6137/51 (which also passed to the Kenning Group for resale). RA 6151 became a lorry, but RA 6137 was given back to Mr North in early 1936 along with nearly £1,000 in cash – the surplus from the sale to Trent minus the money owed on the hire-purchase agreements. Harold North renewed his optimistic outlook, acquired a new garage at Holbrook Moor, and in May of 1936 went back into the local bus business.

P & JW Poundall of Belper (trading as Poundall Brothers) had built up a small network of stage carriage services radiating from their home town. In January 1932 they sold their Belper-Ripley route to Trent but continued to operate services to Heanor and to the small village of Shottle to the west of Belper. In May 1936 the brothers decided to dispose of the rest of the business. The Heanor route then lapsed but the daily service to Shottle was sold to Harold North along with RA 9026, a 1929 Crossley Eagle with Economy B32F bodywork. A third

vehicle, 1932 Albion PH49 Victor/Taylor B20F bus VO 7858, joined the reborn HS North fleet in the same month.

The Crossley Eagle was retired at the end of 1937 and not immediately replaced. The fleet remained at two vehicles through the outbreak of the Second World War but returned to three in late 1940 when Albion PH115 Victor/Cadogan C26F coach CSP 111 arrived. This machine had been new to W Alexander in 1938 and had been requisitioned by the War Department before reallocation to North. It came just in time as 1928 Dennis RA 6137 finally expired a few months later. The next additions arrived in September 1943 and carried brand-new Derbyshire registrations HRB 370/1. The first was actually a 1935 Leyland Tiger with a pre-war Burlingham C32F coach body from another vehicle. Originally registered ARU 72 with Hants & Dorset, it came to North via the War Department. The second 'new' machine had started life in 1937 as ABU 277 with Shaw of Oldham and was an AEC Regal with a Duple C32F body. This too had passed to the War Department and lost its original identity.

Albion Victor CSP 111 was sold in December 1944 and replaced by two older vehicles more suited to a newly awarded works contract. The additions were EK 8771, a 1932 Leyland TS2 Tiger which had acquired an Alexander C32F body, and TF 8476, a 1932 Leyland KP3 Cub with a Santus C20R body. A second 1932 vintage KP3 Cub arrived in early 1945 in the shape of UG 163 which carried a C26F body by an unidentified builder.

Fleet numbers made an unexpected appearance in the summer of 1945 when 1943 Bedford OWB utility bus EAC 79 was acquired from Haunchwood Collieries Ltd and received No 21. It will be noted that Mr North had previously operated a total of 20 vehicles and so had been meticulously keeping count! The next arrival, 1932 Dennis Lancet coach RB 6738, logically became No 22. Fleet numbers 23-25 and 27 went to some of North's most famous vehicles, a quartet of AEC Qs acquired from the Red & White group of South Wales in August 1945. Nos 23/25/27 (TG 8499/9953/9001) carried Berw DP39F bodywork and dated from 1934/5, while No 24 (ATG 835) had been new in 1936 and had a DP39F body by J Norman. Missing fleet number 26 went to ATV 4, a 1935 Dennis Lancet with a Willowbrook C32F coach body acquired at around the same time and quickly followed by identical vehicle RB 8452 as fleet number 28.

The fleet numbering system then went to hell on a handcart as two more AEC Qs were acquired from Red & White (ATX 338/937) and both were given the number 29! Fleet number 30 was awarded to 1936 Dennis Lancet/Willowbrook C32F coach JE 2510 and then the concept was abandoned. Other second-hand acquisitions during 1945 included 1929 TS2 Tiger coach KD 6462, 1930 Gilford 168OT/Metcalfe C30F coach VX 4560, 1932 KP3 Cub/Alexander B20F bus WG 1181, 1934 Lancet/Willowbrook C32F coach ANU 412, 1935 Albion PK 115 Victor/Mumford C26F coach JY 6032, and 1936 Lancet/Willowbrook C32F coach BTO 389. Most of these ageing vehicles were allocated to contract works journeys which serviced local coal-mines, engineering factories, chemical plants, and construction sites.

A further influx of vehicles in 1946 was of a bewilderingly complex nature and will only be dealt with briefly as few (if any) of the vehicles involved were operated on the stage service from Belper to Shottle. First of all a batch of eight Dennis Lancets with ECOC B31R bodywork, JA 2231/3/7/8/40/5/9/50 (new to North Western in 1934), were acquired from a dealer. Another four complete Dennis Lancets with ECOC B34F bodies, YG 5730 of 1933 along with YG 8962/4/75 of 1934, came from West Yorkshire along with at least half a dozen ECOC B34F bodies removed from other West Yorkshire veterans. Next came a batch of six 1930 AEC Regals from Timpson of Catford, five with their original Harrington C31R bodies (GC 4817/26/7/31/8) and one which had received a Burlingham UB36F utility bus body (GN 7281). The full story of what happened next could fill a book, but the abridged version is that some of the North Western Lancets received West Yorkshire bodies as did most of the Timpson Regals. Other Lancets (including the now bare chassis of three WYRCC machines) received new Burlingham C33F bodies. Bodies were also swapped between vehicles, with several of the Willowbrook C32F-bodied Lancets first receiving ECOC bus bodies and then new Burlingham C33F units. Let's move on.

Purchases during 1946 which did not involve complicated body-swaps included 1931 LGOC B29F single-deckers GT 7446/7, 1935 all-Dennis

Lancet coach TJ 9083, and rare 1937 Dennis Pike coach ELC 319. A surprise at the end of the year was brand-new Bedford OB/Duple Vista C29F coach KRA 504. Even more surprisingly, it carried fleet number 36, leaving us to guess which of the vehicles above had been designated as fleet numbers 31-5. Further new OB/Vista coaches took the fleet numbers 37 (LRA 443 in October 1947), 38 (LRB 191 in December 1947), 39 (MRA 610 in August 1948), and 40 (MRB 934 in March 1949), and then the practice was abandoned once again. Between the numbered OBs were several other vehicles which received no fleet numbers, including identical brand-new OB/Vista MNU 939 which was delivered in July 1948.

Also un-numbered was MNU 766, first registered in June 1948. Beneath the new identity was the chassis of 1934 West Yorkshire Lancet YG 8962 which had donated its ECOC body to JA 2250 and then received a new Yeates C33F body and a new registration mark. Another Duple Vista C29F coach was acquired in May 1949, but on this occasion the (1947) body was mounted on a 1943 Bedford OWB chassis which had previously carried a Roe utility bus unit. The vehicle retained its original identity of HWA 653 and came from Jeffcock of Sheffield who had been responsible for its rebodying.

Many of the industrial contracts had gone by 1950 and the North fleet began to dwindle as the unreconstructed vehicles went for scrap. The new OBs and the pre-war Lancets with post-war coach bodies catered for private hire and excursion work along with the stage service to Shottle. The only acquisition during 1950 was ALJ 786, a Leyland LT5A Lion with Brush B34F bodywork new to Hants & Dorset in 1935. It briefly replaced a deceased Lancet/ECOC bus in the much reduced contract fleet. There were then no additions until 1953 when two last pre-war Lancets were acquired. DCA 282 carried a wartime Burlingham UB34F body and came from Davies of Wrexham to join the contract fleet. The other Lancet had started life back in 1932 as VV 1164 and arrived with North as a bare chassis. They sent it to Yeates of Loughborough where the chassis was refurbished, extended in length, fitted with a fully-fronted FC37F body, and then returned to North with the new identity TNU 584. In this new incarnation it lasted for another nine years, with the chassis having given 30 years of service.

It should perhaps be mentioned that although North liked pre-war Dennis Lancet chassis, it didn't much like Dennis engines. All of the Lancets fitted with post-war coach bodies were also fitted with AEC 7.7 engines before returning to use, as were several of the buses devoted to contract duties. It would appear that the principal appeal of the Lancet chassis lay in its sturdy chassis frame and low second-hand purchase price. By 1954 the supply of bargain Lancets had dried up and North's was faced with a change in its purchasing policy. During this re-think it was concluded that the company should continue as a low cost coach operator using second-hand equipment, and that the stage service should be sold. It had made little or no profit for several years, involved the operation of much 'dead mileage' between the garage and Belper, and occupied a vehicle which might be more usefully deployed.

On the 31st of July 1955 the Belper to Shottle route was sold to Trent for £2,500. North then turned to second-hand Bedford SB coach variants, buying more than a dozen with a mixture of Yeates, Duple, Burlingham, and Plaxton bodywork before turning to VALs and VAMs in the latter half of the 1960s. A new limited company was established in July 1962 as North's Transport (Derby) Ltd and this was superseded by another corporate entity, North's Coachways Ltd in October 1971. In the following year the business ceased to trade.

Tailby & George

See Blue Bus of Willington

Victoria Motorways of Woodville

After the First World War Mr Ernest Marcus ('Mark') Sales opened a garage in the south Derbyshire village of Netherseal (population 923), eight miles to the south of Burton-upon-Trent in Staffordshire, and in April 1921 expanded his motor business by purchasing a six-seat Renault taxi, R 3205. This vehicle was soon in high demand for trips into Burton, to Swadlincote (the nearest town in Derbyshire) and to the railway stations in the area. At some stage in the early 1920s the taxi was joined by a 1921 Ford Model T 14-seater, FA 727, and this vehicle launched a bus service linking Netherseal to Measham, Overseal,

and Donisthorpe. It would appear that this initial foray into stage carriage work was not a success as the Ford was sold in June 1925.

Public transport connections to Burton-upon-Trent from this part of southern Derbyshire were provided by the trams of the Burton & Ashby Light Railways, a subsidiary of the Midland (later LMS) Railway, which ran every ten minutes on a Burton-Winshill-Swadlincote-Woodville-Ashby route and less frequently on a branch line from Woodville and Swadlincote to Church Gresley and Castle Gresley. Regent Motor Services of Church Gresley had run a competing service to Burton via Swadlincote since 1919. Regent would soon find itself in competition with Midland Red, which had started working into the Burton/Swadlincote area from its Tamworth depot and then established another garage at Coalville in late 1925 to further develop its presence in the Burton-Leicester corridor.

By the end of 1926 Midland Red's buses had taken so much traffic from the tramway that closure became inevitable, and the last Burton & Ashby tram ran in February 1927. Despite the looming presence of Midland Red, Mark Sales decided to have another go at becoming a bus proprietor in June 1927. Two new fourteen-seater buses were acquired from local dealerships, Overland RA 3155 and Reo UT 1173, and a service from Measham to Burton via Netherseal, Overseal, Linton, and Castle Gresley commenced under the fleet-name of Victoria Motorways. The name came from the proprietor's wife, Mrs Minnie Victoria Sales. In February 1928 Burton-upon-Trent Corporation granted Mr Sales a licence and the service moved from a terminus on private ground to the council's official bus stands on Horninglow Street.

Money Troubles

Things did not go as well as had been hoped despite an increase in fleet size to three in February 1928 when the Overland was replaced by a Chevrolet X of similar age and size (UT 33) and a brand-new Reo Pullman coach with a 26-seat Bracebridge body, UE 5643. This came on hire-purchase from the Arlington Motor Co (whose Midlands regional office was in Warwickshire, hence the registration), and was followed by an identical example in March registered UE 5951. The next Arlington sourced vehicle to arrive was a two year old Reo Sprinter with a 20-seat bus body, UE 1003, but by June 1928 Regent Motor Services had sold out to Midland Red, Victoria Motorways was facing ruin at the same hands, and Sales was forced to seek a bridging loan to keep his company going. This came from William Lloyd who had been a director of Regent Motor Services until late 1926 before joining with Donald Leitch to found Viking Motors, a Burton based coaching operation. Two of Victoria Motorways vehicles (UT 1173 and UE 5951) were temporarily re-registered in the joint names of Messrs Sales and Lloyd as security for the loan.

Arlington were apparently happy with this rather desperate transaction as they went on to supply another 20-seat Reo Sprinter in July 1928 (UE 6904) and a brand-new Maudslay ML3 with a 32-seat coach body in August 1928 (UE 6961). These two machines replaced Reos UE 1003 and UE 5951. Two more Arlington vehicles arrived in March 1929 in the shape of new Gilford 166OT coaches UE 7865/6, and in the same month an unidentified Maudslay ML4 was rented from the manufacturer for a one year term. The new vehicles replaced UT 33 and UE 5643.

The Gilfords had a very short stay in Netherseal. In July 1929 they went to Barton in exchange for RA 5547, a 1928 Thornycroft A2 with a 20-seat Challand Ross body, and an unidentified 14-seat Reo. By this point hire-purchase payments were being missed, Arlington had become disturbed, and no more vehicles were available. Mark Sales was in desperate straits once again and welcomed a proposal from Midland Red to help him out. They drafted a five-year agreement which would leave Sales with his existing stage service but prohibit him from beginning any new ones within an 80 mile radius of Swadlincote during the period of the contract. He would also need their consent to change fares, routings, or timings. Why they were willing to offer this agreement rather than just wait for the business to die is unrecorded –they were seldom as altruistic elsewhere in their vast empire.

Sales only received a payment of £285 for agreeing to this voluntary restraint of trade, but the stability it gave changed the mood of his creditors. Talk of receivers changed to talk of a reasonable outcome. By the end of the year they had agreed to convert the remainder of Sales' debts into shares in a new company, Victoria

Motorways Ltd, incorporated in March 1930 with Arlington and various other creditors as shareholders alongside Mr and Mrs Sales. The new company took baby steps. In July 1930 Maudslay coach UE 6961 was sold to Maun of Whitwick and 1926 Guy BA/Northern Counties bus NR 8262 was taken in part-exchange. Two new vehicles were acquired from dealers in April 1931, a Ford AA 20-seat bus (UT 8190) and a 20-seat Commer Invader coach (VT 6172), and the same month saw the purchase of a 1929 AEC Reliance with Dixon B32F bodywork (VT 2901) from Caswell of Tunstall.

One advantage of the agreement with Midland Red was that Victoria Motorways had no fear of objections from that source to its application for route licences. The Burton service was duly authorised by the Traffic Commissioners in early 1932. The following year saw the addition of garage premises in Burton-upon-Trent as a 'dormy shed' to avoid unprofitable early morning workings from Netherseal. In June 1933 another high capacity service bus joined the company when a 1928 Bristol B/Bristol B30D, EK 6409, arrived from Wigan Corporation. This addition helped to cover a new service from Netherseal and Overseal to Donisthorpe and Measham, virtually a revival of the route attempted in the early 1920s. This second attempt was more successful as Victoria could now offer onwards connections to Burton. Because of the 1929 agreement Midland Red was technically a joint operator, but provided no vehicles and took no revenue. The other major event of the year was the acquisition of a local coach operator, Clamp & Bailey of Church Gresley, with excursions and tours licences, a seasonal express service to Blackpool, and a 1931 Albion PKA26/Rushton & Wilson C26F coach (RB 3764).

By 1934 Victoria was starting to attract new investors. In May Mr Ernest Manners of Netherseal Hall became a director, which was the local equivalent of endorsement by the Rockefellers. The Manners family controlled three of Burton-upon-Trent's largest breweries, Worthington, Burton, and Bass. The agreement with Midland Red ended in July, giving the company more freedom in the matter of licence applications, and in November an old friend returned to the fleet in the shape of 1928 Maudslay UE 6961, bought back from Maun of Whitwick.

Victoria Motorways bought three Daimler CVD6s with Willowbrook B35F bus bodywork in 1947 and then in May 1950 added a fourth, FA 9847 (fleet number 7), which had slightly more comfortable seating and was officially classified as DP35F. Seen at the company's Woodville depot (shared with Viking Motors), the vehicle is in Victoria/ Viking's traditional livery of 'Antique Red and Dark Tan' which meant red and brown. Note the Staffordshire Knot logo. Number 7 outlasted its sisters and was finally withdrawn in December 1964. *(Tim Jeffcoat)*

FA 9847 again, this time at Burton's Wetmore Bus Park alongside AEC Reliance/Willowbrook Express Stage Coach C41F DFA 550. The Reliance had been new to sister company Viking in 1955, primarily for use on the seasonal holiday routes, and had been transferred to Victoria in 1961 as fleet number 10. *(Tim Jeffcoat)*

Another view of Reliance/Willowbrook coach DFA 550, this time at the end of its career and shoved into a corner at the company's Woodville depot next to a farm cart. The vehicle was withdrawn from use in June 1966, replaced by a brand-new Bedford VAM/Strachans bus. *(Tim Jeffcoat)*

Leyland Tiger Cub/Willowbrook Viking C41F coach HFA 3 was another refugee from the Viking fleet which ended up with Victoria on stage carriage work. New to Viking in 1958, it was one of the very first coaches with this body design, and it is possible that Willowbrook may have chosen the name 'Viking' to reflect this early enthusiasm. It is seen here at Wetmore Bus Park on a winter's day. Officially transferred to Victoria in May 1962, in this view it is still wearing Viking livery and its Viking name 'Viceroy II'. It was withdrawn in 1972. *(Tim Jeffcoat)*

It gave Victoria another four years of service. In December another new investor joined the board. Mr J Hawthorne had started his first bus company in Stoke-on-Trent in 1919 and had recently sold that operation to Potteries. He paid for his share in Victoria by bringing a factory-fresh vehicle to the company, Leyland LT5A Lion/Burlingham C34F coach BEH 401, which had been ordered for his company in Stoke and not included in the sale to Potteries.

The highlight of 1935 was the delivery of a brand-new coach to act as the flagship of the Victoria Motorways fleet. FA 5840 arrived in June and was a Leyland TS6 Tiger with a stylish fully-fronted Burlingham FC31F body. The vehicle was painted in a distinctive overall black livery with the image of a diving hawk on both sides and was given the name 'The Black Hawk'. Two more modest acquisitions turned up towards the end of the year. GX 2743 was a 32-seat TSM C60A7 coach which had been new to a London operator in 1932, and MV 2669, a 32-seat Leyland TS4 Tiger coach which came from Valliant Direct of Ealing. Two more second-hand vehicles arrived during 1936, both of them 20-seat buses. JD 4828 was a Bedford WHB and had reportedly been new as a lorry in 1934, while UT 7601 was a Chevrolet U and had been new in 1930.

In May 1937 two brand-new Bedford WTB coaches with Duple C25F bodywork joined the fleet as FA 6627/56. In contrast the two acquisitions in 1938 were both second-hand buses. FS 1762 was an Albion PV70 Valiant with Alexander B32F bodywork and had been new to SMT in 1931, and was joined by VT 8132, a TSM B39A7 with a Lawton B36F body. This vehicle had been new to Wilshaw of Cheadle in 1932, passing with that operator to Potteries before being sold to one of Victoria's neighbouring independents, Brooks Brothers of Castle Gresley, in early 1938. Brooks rapidly decided that the TSM was not for them and passed it on to Victoria.

War and a Change of Ownership

There were no vehicle acquisitions during 1939 and at the end of 1940 'The Black Hawk' was requisitioned and reallocated to Mann of Smethwick. It never returned although Mann (known for the longevity of its vehicles) kept it in service until 1956. By way of compensation Victoria received a 1931 TSM C60A6 coach with Lawton C32F bodywork, VT 7065 (another former Wilshaw/PMT machine), and a 1931 Leyland TS2 Tiger coach with Harrington C32F bodywork, FV 1689. The Tiger had been new to Wood of Blackpool with a Burlingham body, later passing to Standerwick and then being rebodied in 1938 by a dealer, possibly after an accident.

William Lloyd, alumnus of Regent Motor Services and co-founder of Viking Motors, had been appointed as wartime co-ordinator of transport for the area around Burton-upon Trent (including the southernmost part of Derbyshire), and he quickly authorised the extension of certain journeys on Victoria's Burton service to Branston Ordnance Factory. He also permitted Victoria to obtain four Leyland Lion buses 'on hire' from Darwen Corporation in Lancashire. These arrived in the summer of 1941 and operated in full Darwen livery complete with Darwen fleet numbers. No 9 (TF 3172 of 1930) was an LT2 with a Leyland B32F body while Nos 11-3 (ATE 77-9) were LT7s with English Electric B32R bodies and had been new in 1936. A 1930 Guy C with a Guy B26F body, FA 3889, was acquired from Burton Corporation in December 1941 but not operated. Identical sister FA 3893 would be purchased in July 1942 and placed into service, staying with Victoria until 1947.

A Leyland TS2 Tiger coach with a Spicer C32F body, CK 4336, also joined the fleet in July 1942. It had been new to Scout of Preston in 1930. The same month saw the arrival of three more 26-seat Guys from Burton, but none of them made it into service with Victoria. The first acquisition of 1943 was ARA 172, a Leyland LT5A Lion with a Burlingham B36F body which had been new to Blue Bus of Willington (qv) in 1934. Victoria gave it fleet number 10 to fill in the gap amid the Darwen machines. The only other addition to the fleet during the year was GG 4946, an Albion PMB28 Viking Six with a 29-seat Cowieson coach body. This had been new to a Dumbarton independent but came to Victoria from Central SMT. It received no fleet number and lasted for less than a year before being sold to Viking Motors of Burton.

In July 1943 the directors of Viking Motors, Messrs William Lloyd, Donald Leitch, and Horace Atkins, acquired 2,490 of the 2,500 shares issued in Victoria Motorways Ltd, with Lloyd and Leitch holding 40% each and Atkins 20% – the same ratio as their shareholdings in Viking. All three were elected as directors of Victoria at an EGM held on the 26th of July, while Mark Sales was re-elected to the board for a further two year term. Minnie Sales stepped down as a director, thus breaking her connection to the firm which bore her middle name. Three months later Mark Sales resigned from the Victoria board, although he retained a token 10 shares in the company until November 1946.

It should be noted that Viking Motors did not acquire Victoria Motorways as stated by some historians, but rather they became sister companies under the same ownership. Mr and Mrs Sales retained ownership of the garage at Netherseal and Victoria's vehicles were moved to Viking's main premises in Burton or to their out-station at Woodville near Swadlincote. No more vehicles joined the fleet before the end of the war, but in 1944 the quartet of rented Darwen Lions were officially purchased and gave particularly long service. The 1930 example lasted until 1949 while the 1936 machines survived until 1957.

Post-War Triumphs

In May 1945 neighbouring operator Brooks Brothers of Castle Gresley decided to pull out of the stage carriage business and sold their service from Swadlincote to Linton via Church Gresley and Castle Gresley to Victoria Motorways. Midland Red's local managers were not very happy about this development as they ran an almost identical service and had always presumed that Brooks would give them first refusal. William Lloyd proposed a compromise. Victoria would sell the 'goodwill' of the former Brooks route to Midland Red if the larger operator would withdraw its own Donisthorpe-Overseal-Burton route and make no objection to an application by Victoria to cover the mileage by a combination of its two existing services. The BET affiliate reluctantly agreed, which might be seen as a belated revenge for the 'peace treaty' imposed on Victoria back in 1929.

Brooks Brothers continued as a coach operator until 1961 and a year after selling their stage service to Victoria sold them a 1932 Maudslay ML3E with a Rushton & Wilson C32F coach body, OV 9147. This became fleet number 14 but the other second-hand acquisition of 1946, ten year old Albion PK115 Victor coach ADG 742, received no fleet number. Two brand-new AEC

Regal I buses with Burlingham B34F bodywork were delivered in April/June 1946 as FA 8167/224 and became fleet numbers 16/7. It seems that fleet number 15 had been reserved for 1935 Tiger coach 'The Black Hawk' in the expectation that it would be returned after the war, but in the event it stayed with Mann of Smethwick. The new Regals were followed by four brand-new Daimler CVD6 buses with Burlingham 35-seat bodywork. Fleet numbers 18/9 (FA 8791/2) arrived in September 1947, 20 (FA 8822) in October 1947, and FA 9847 (inexplicably given fleet number 7) in May 1950. This represented a considerable investment and there were no more additions to the fleet for ten years.

In 1954 ownership of part of Viking's premises in Woodville was transferred to Victoria Motorways, but this seems to have been for tax purposes as the Woodville garage was sold in the following year and Viking's out-station (along with Victoria's headquarters) were transferred to a larger site a short distance away in High Street. This was to be Victoria's main base for the rest of its existence.

The Regal I and Daimler CVD6 buses were withdrawn from use in 1959-61 with the exception of FA 9847 which had slightly more luxurious seating and remained in use as a 'back-up' vehicle until 1964. Their replacements were coaches transferred from the Viking Motors fleet. In 1960 fleet numbers 14 and 15 were reallocated to Leyland PSUC1/2 Tiger Cub coaches BJP 387 and BJP 271. These had Alexander C41F bodywork and had been new in 1955 to Smiths Tours of Wigan. Next to arrive, during 1961, was a pair of AEC Reliances with Willowbrook 'Express Stage Coach' DP41F bodywork which had been new to Viking in 1955. DFA 548 became Victoria's fleet number 8 while DFA 550 became number 10. Another pair of Viking cast-offs followed, both with Willowbrook Viking C41F bodywork. HFA 3 was a PSUC1/2 Tiger Cub of 1958 vintage and became Victoria's No 2 in May 1962 while AEC Reliance JFA 519 dated from 1959 and became fleet number 12 during 1963.

There was then another long pause until the surprise arrival of four brand-new Bedford VAM5s with Strachan Pacemaker II B45F bodies, EFA 497-500D (fleet numbers 7-10) in May 1966. Even more surprisingly, they were replaced only 13 months later by four more examples of the

After operating brand-new front-engined half-cab buses and then second-hand underfloor-engined coaches, Victoria went back to brand-new front-engined buses in May 1966 with the delivery of four Bedford VAM5s with Strachans Pacemaker II B45F bodywork. EFA 499D (fleet number 9) wears the dreary two-tone grey livery introduced in the early 1960s. Three of the four (including this one) were sold to Monty Moreton of Nuneaton in June 1967. *(David Penlington Collection)*

Victoria renewed its fleet at very short intervals after 1966. The 1967 VAM5s which replaced the first batch were in turn replaced in March 1970 by a trio of Ford R192s with Willowbrook 001 bodywork. OFA 919H is seen here in Burton's Wetmore Bus Park alongside a Blue Bus Fleetline. Replaced by yet more new vehicles in January 1973, two of the three R192s (including OFA 919H) went to Weetabix as staff buses. *(Colin Anderson Collection)*

same combination, HFA 207-10E (which confused many bus enthusiasts by also carrying fleet numbers 7-10). The new number 8 (HFA 208E) was sold to General of Chester-le-Street in July 1968, but the other three remained in service until March 1970 when they were replaced by three new Ford R192s with Willowbrook 001 B45F bodywork, OFA 917-9H (fleet numbers 7-9).

A 1966 Bedford VAL14/Duple Vega Major coach, EFA 494D, was transferred from the Viking fleet in December 1972 and received Victoria fleet number 4. It appears to have been needed for a schools contract (an increasingly important source of revenue for Viking and Victoria) as it left the company in July 1973. The next arrivals were another trio of new Ford R192/Willowbrook 001 service buses, DFA 125-7L (fleet numbers 8-10) which arrived in January 1973 to replace the 1970 vehicles. It should be mentioned that OFA 917/9H were subsequently used by Weetabix as staff buses. Presumably they couldn't manage all three.

Another Viking coach, 1971 Ford R226/ Duple 53-seater UFA 517J, was transferred to the Victoria fleet in December 1973 as fleet number 17 – did they pick these numbers out of a hat? It was followed in June 1974 by SFA 196M (fleet number 16), a brand-new Bedford YRT with a Plaxton Panorama Elite II C53F coach body. There was then another hiatus in new additions until the summer of 1977 when two new Fords were acquired from a well-known Leicestershire dealership. TFP 25R (fleet number 2) was an R1014 with 45 seats and TRY 3S an R1114 with 53 seats, but both carried Plaxton Elite Express 'grant coach' bodies and in 1978 they replaced DFA 125/127L as the front-line equipment on the stage carriage services. DFA 126L would be retained as a back-up vehicle for another nine years.

In 1985 Victoria took advantage of the first deregulation act by introducing new express services in the Swadlincote-Burton corridor, alongside its traditional route. The company also became more involved in schools journeys, and on occasion hired Viking's pair of double-deckers (ex-West Riding Northern Counties-bodied Fleetlines BHL 621/5K) for use both on these and on busy Saturday timings. A pair of 1982 Leyland PSU3F/4R Leopards with Willowbrook 003 C47F bodies were acquired for the local express services in July 1987. DDM 35X (fleet number 9) came from Crosville and LOA 834X (no number allocated) from Midland Red. They would be the very last Victoria vehicles. In October 1987 the Lloyd family sold Viking Motors and the stage services of Victoria Motorways to Stevenson of Spath for an undisclosed sum. Back in the financially shaky days of 1928-34 few would have predicted that Mark Sales' enterprise would last that long.

Further Reading

The 'bible' for those interested in William Lloyd's various bus and coach companies is 'Regent, Viking, and Victoria' by Harold Nelson Twells, self-published in 2005 but still fairly widely available on the second-hand market. I recommend it to anyone interested in Derbyshire independents.

Fodens were quite rare in BET group fleets, but this one ran with East Midland for several years. Foden PVSC6/Plaxton FC33F coach NRA 760 was new to Heeley as fleet number 20 in July 1949. After the East Midland take-over in March 1953 it became their fleet number FC26. Renumbered C14 in 1954, it was sold in 1958 and was last licensed in 1967 in the service of its third subsequent operator. *(Philip Stone Collection)*

Most Burlingham Sunsaloon bodies were built on AEC, Daimler, or Leyland chassis, but this one is mounted on an Albion CX39N Valkyrie. ORA 350 was new to Heeley in May 1950 as fleet number 23, passing to East Midland as fleet number AC24 (later C18). They kept it until July 1959 when it was sold to Falcon Coaches of Sutton Coldfield. It was last licensed in 1963. *(Philip Stone Collection)*

PART FOUR
DERBYSHIRE IN
COLOUR

The Derbyshire bus industry came in every colour of the rainbow although both of the municipal operators in the county used green and cream, Chesterfield's deep and dignified, Derby's less so in both regards and more of an acquired taste. Of the area agreement companies Midland General held on to its non-standard blue and cream livery from Balfour Beatty days, Trent used red and off-white, North Western red and pale cream (which was immediately distinguishable from Trent's rather colder relief shade), and Midland Red lived up to its name with an all-over red livery for service buses. East Midland's chocolate, yellow, and cream livery was one of the most distinctive liveries in the country until replaced by a drab dark red with pale cream relief in the mid-1950s. Barton at least retained their classic mixture of red, maroon, and cream.

It was left to the independents to provide the missing colours. In Ashbourne bus station one could find North Western and Trent vehicles side by side with yellow and black buses from Stevenson's of Spath (often double-deckers on market days), a green Bedford OB from Carter of Hales Green next to a red and cream one from Allen of Roston, a two-tone green OB owned by Webster of Hognaston in front of an elderly red and cream Bedford SB from Warrington of Ilam (just across the border in Staffordshire), and to top it all an overall blue OB from Steeples of Parwich. Given that some of Stevenson's vehicles looked a bit 'orangey' in the right lighting conditions, only indigo and violet were left unchosen.

Many of the same independents could be found in Derby itself on Fridays when OBs and similar from the fleets of Carter, Allen, Webster, Steeples, and Taylor of Crich (in two tone brown), congregated at the Traffic Street car park to await their shopping laden passengers for the return to the wild. Derby's daily independent menu already included the majestic dark blue and cream double-deckers of Blue Bus and the red and maroon coaches of Felix, as well as many intruders from the Barton fleet based in Nottinghamshire, so the armada of OBs was the icing on the cake.

Bakewell was another place with a pleasing collection of colour schemes. Predominantly red vehicles from North Western and Trent mixed with the blue and very pale cream buses of Sheffield's 'B' and 'C' fleets, providing a backdrop for the rather more adventurous liveries of the two local independents. Hulley of Baslow's vehicles nearly always included red in their colour schemes (one notable exception being a Guy Warrior coach which remained in its original owner's blue and grey for some time), but might use either cream (varying from rich to pale) or light grey as a relief colour, and might or might not also include either maroon or black! The red also varied from one batch of paint to the next, and yet somehow there was no mistaking one of Hulley's vehicles from a distance. The miniscule lettering on the destination displays was one sure give-away. Silver Service's vehicles were presented in a more uniform livery of dark blue and silvery grey with light blue relief, but by the early 1970s some service buses had adopted a simplified livery of dark blue and pale cream.

Changes came to Bakewell's omnibus palette in the second half of the 1970s. North Western had already gone, Trent had adopted NBC poppy red, and Sheffield's successor (SYPTE) had chosen an awful weak coffee and cream colour scheme. Meanwhile, the Woolliscrofts had bought out the Hulleys, and the new 'Silver Service Group' used light blue and beige for Silver Service vehicles and medium red and beige for the Hulley's fleet. The latter looked quite attractive when painted on something less monstrous than an ex-Merseyside PTE Panther.

Across the Staffordshire border in Burton-upon-Trent, Blue Bus's double-deckers from Derby met up with Victoria Motorways single-deckers which also came in from Derbyshire. Victoria's 1950s livery of 'Antique Red and Dark Tan' was not that attractive (being in desperate need of a lighter relief colour), but it was positively beautiful in comparison with the ghost-like two-tone grey livery adopted from 1962 onwards. The contrasting liveries of Blue Bus (at the traditionalist end of the spectrum) and Stevenson's (at the avant-garde bee-impersonating end) both put it to shame.

Hulleys famous Guy Arab II/Windover Huntingdon C33F coach, NEH 155 (fleet number 26), had a powerful (if often temperamental) Meadows 6DC engine and could reputedly 'go like the clappers'. New in June 1949, it had been registered by the dealer before delivery to Baslow. This delightful machine was withdrawn from use in November 1962 and scrapped. *(Chris Rischer Collection)*

And here is Hulleys most famous vehicle of all, Guy Otter/Alexander C29F coach NTB 403 (fleet number 2). New to Monk of Leigh in May 1951, it migrated to Knightsbridge of Burnley and then McFarlane of Balloch before arriving at Baslow in June 1959. It hibernated from June 1965 until November 1969 and then gave two more years of active service. After withdrawal it was sold for preservation but was tragically scrapped in 1984. *(Geoff Lumb)*

Very few BMMO types escaped into the wider world after their retirement, but Hulleys took a grand total of five former Midland Red vehicles between 1963 and 1971. The first to arrive was HHA 697, a 1947 S6 bus which had originally carried a Brush B40F body. This was later lengthened by Roe to increase the seating capacity to 44. It came to Baslow in January 1963 as fleet number 20 and was withdrawn in February 1965 to act as a source of spares for the other three BMMO S type buses. *(Geoff Lumb)*

Bedford SB3/Yeates Europa C41F coach 903 CPT was new to Favourite No 2 in County Durham in May 1959. Hulleys became its fifth owner in January 1968 and gave it fleet number 3. After withdrawal in 1975 it passed in turn to a scout troop in Whaley Bridge and then to a dance troupe in Romiley. *(John Holmes)*

Hulley's fifth and final BMMO type was 795 GHA, new to Midland Red in 1959 as a C5 with a BMMO C37F coach body. Later fitted with a turbocharger to improve its performance (making it a CS5), the vehicle was withdrawn in 1971 and arrived at Baslow 'on hire' in May as fleet number 14. Hulleys bought it in January 1972 and kept it until April 1973. It was then converted into a stock-car transporter. *(Chris Rischer Collection)*

Another well-loved Hulley vehicle, Bedford SB5/Yeates Pegasus B45F bus 2626 UP, is seen at Rutland Square in Bakewell bound for Youlgreave. New to Armstrong of Ebchester in September 1962, Hulley became its fourth owner in April 1972. As fleet number 1 it remained in service until August 1978 and was then sold for preservation. After spending some time in the yard of Webster of Hognaston it deteriorated markedly and had been scrapped by February 1980. *(John Holmes)*

AEC Regal O662/Willowbrook DP35F dual-purpose vehicle FRB 122 was new to Silver Service of Darley Dale in January 1939 as fleet number 6. It is seen here at Friden brick-works in company with Silver Service's rebodied TS7 Tiger WN 7754. The Regal was finally withdrawn in September 1966 after more than 27 years with the company. It was later scrapped on site at Darley Dale. *(Chris Rischer Collection)*

Although built to the pre-war O662 specification, Regal/Willowbrook DP35F saloon KNU 446 was new to Silver Service in October 1946 as fleet number 4. Withdrawn from use in March 1970 after more than 23 years of service, it was sold for preservation five months later. In 2004 it returned to its home territory as a working PSV with Burton Coaches of Alfreton and in 2011 moved on to Exclusive Car Hire of Nottingham who named it 'Walter'. *(John Holmes)*

In December 1947 Silver Service took delivery of two brand-new AEC Regal III coaches with elegant Duple A type C35F bodywork and the larger 9.6 litre engine. They were nicknamed 'The Heavenly Twins'. LRA 907 (fleet number 14) kept its original bodywork until withdrawal in May 1970 and was subsequently preserved. LRB 62 (fleet number 15) was sent to Yeates in 1959 to have a pseudo-Europa front end grafted onto its face. Despite the ill-advised attempt at modernisation it went first, in August 1969, and was then scrapped. *(John Stringer)*

Bedford OB/Duple Vista C29F coach JTG 280 was new to Starkey of Ton Pentre in August 1949. Silver Service bought it in January 1957 as fleet number 1 and kept it until August 1971. Initially preserved, it was later scrapped. Identical Silver Service OB/Vista GVJ 190 is still a survivor although it has not been seen in public for many years. *(John Stringer)*

The 39-seat Strachans Pacesaver bus was developed from a utilitarian design produced for military and industrial customers. This example, like most, was mounted on a Bedford SB5 chassis and was delivered to Silver Service in March 1965 as DRB 10C (fleet number 11). It stayed in the fleet for almost 12 years, five years longer than its identical twin DRB 11C (fleet number 12). After withdrawal in January 1977 it vanished without trace. The vehicle is shown at Rutland Square in Bakewell, operating a short-working to Winster. *(John Holmes Collection)*

An interesting line-up at Darley Dale featuring, from left to right, Regal III/Duple coach LRA 907 (fleet number 14, famous as a 1/50 scale Corgi model), Bedford SBG/Yeates Europa 950 DNU (fleet number 17, still wearing the livery of Strange of Tansley more than three years after the takeover), and ex-Halifax Nimbus/Weymann RJX 252 (fleet number 2). The two coaches were withdrawn in 1970 while the Nimbus stayed until 1974. *(John Stringer)*

Steeples of Parwich abandoned the concept of a fleet livery in the early 1950s and vehicles remained in the colours they arrived in. Bedford OB/Duple Vista ECL 190 was blue and stayed that way from its arrival in May 1959 until the closure of the business at the end of October 1967. It is seen in Ashbourne bus station. *(Nigel Segrott Collection)*

In complete contrast here is Webster of Hognaston's USO 168S, a Ford R1114 with Alexander AYS B53F bodywork, new to Northern Scottish in 1977. It came to Webster in 1988 with two similar (but shorter) Ford R1014s, and this trio remained active until the sale of the business to Patrick Brown in 1991 and its resurrection as Express Motors. *(Colin Anderson Collection)*

AEC Monocoach/Park Royal B45F buses were rare in the fleets of English independent operators, with only Laycock of Barnoldswick and Booth & Fisher taking new examples. Booth & Fisher's WRA 12, delivered in January 1955, is seen at the company's depot wearing the 1950s version of the livery with a brighter red and more cream relief. The vehicle passed into SYPTE ownership and then into preservation, and is currently on display at the South Yorkshire Transport Museum at Aldwarke near Rotherham. *(John Stringer)*

Seen in Booth & Fisher's coach livery of cream with red relief, 518 GRA was an AEC Reliance with a Roe DP41F body, new in May 1958. It passed to the PTE as fleet number 1082 in 1976, but by the autumn of 1978 had been sold to a dealer and was soon scrapped. *(John Stringer)*

Bedford OB/Mulliner B31F bus GEW 58 was new to the St Neots Hotel in November 1948, passing to Chiltonian of Chilton Foliat in February 1953 and then to Booth & Fisher in July 1958. It stayed in the fleet for almost ten years, retaining this dark red 1950s version of the company's livery throughout its tenure. *(Geoff Lumb)*

In 1965 Booth & Fisher acquired a batch of five Albion Nimbus/Willowbrook B31F buses which had been new to Great Yarmouth in 1959. CEX 491 entered service at Halfway in September 1965, passing to SYPTE in February 1976. They later allocated fleet number 1028 to the vehicle, but this was never actually used as it went for scrap in July 1978. *(John Holmes Collection)*

Albion Nimbus/Weymann B31F bus RJX 251 was new to Halifax in June 1963 and exactly three years later was sold to Booth & Fisher. In February 1976 it passed to the PTE, becoming fleet number 1059, but shortly afterwards it was sold to the T&W dealership in Clay Cross (infamous as the source of Hulley's Merseyside Panthers). In the following year it turned up with Chesterfield Cricket Club, but had been scrapped by the end of 1983. *(John Stringer)*

Booth & Fisher bought four second-hand AEC Reliances with Weymann DP40F dual-purpose bodies from a batch new to Maidstone & District in 1961. This one, 336 NKT, arrived at Halfway in July 1973 and then passed to the PTE in February 1976, becoming fleet number 1087. All four of the M&D Reliances were sold to Silver Star in North Wales in 1980, but 336 NKT was used for spares to keep the other three roadworthy. *(Les Dickinson Collection)*

Blue Bus Daimler CVG6 702 PRA was fitted with the very last lowbridge body produced by Willowbrook. New in August 1960, it is seen here in Burton's Wetmore Bus Park in company with a PD3/Roe and a Leopard/Burlingham DP of Stevenson's (both of them new to Sheffield), and a Midland Red Leyland National. In December 1973 the vehicle passed to Derby and was later destroyed in the fire at Willington garage. *(David Stanier)*

Northern Counties-bodied Fleetline JRB 481D was delivered to Blue Bus in February 1966 and is shown shortly after departure from Derby bus station for Burton. Another picture of this vehicle, up to its ankles in flood water, can be found in Part Three. The Fleetline passed with its sisters to Derby Corporation in 1973. All were destroyed in the Willington fire. *(John Stringer)*

This Bedford VAL70 with Willowbrook 'DP54F' bodywork, BRB 674G, was really too much of a sardine tin to merit its 'DP' designation. The second of its breed acquired by Blue Bus, it arrived in March 1969 and is shown here ducking under the railway bridge at Willington which was the reason for the company's low-height double-deckers. The VAL70 passed to Derby in 1973 and then escaped incineration by being sold for use as a mobile home. *(David Stanier Collection)*

Blue Bus bought two 45-seat Bedford YRQ/Willowbrook 001 saloons which had previously served as Vauxhall Motors demonstrators. DXE 137J came first, in December 1971, and is pictured leaving Derby bus station for Burton. It too passed to Derby in December 1973 and was sold for further use by an owner in Cornwall in 1975. The other ex-Vauxhall YRQ, EXE 276J, was less fortunate and perished in the Willington inferno. *(David Stanier)*

Bedford OB/Duple Vista C29F coach MNU 336 was new to Carter of Hales Green in November 1948 and was finally withdrawn from use in October 1968. In this atmospheric shot the vehicle is seen leaving Alkmonton, one of half a dozen villages which depended upon this small rural independent for their only public transport provision. *(Tim Jeffcoat)*

By July 1962 when this Bedford SB5/Yeates Europa C41F coach, 3 XRA, was delivered to Felix of Stanley, most of Yeates' customers had changed over to the new Fiesta design with sloping window pillars. Norman Frost was having none of that and insisted on a Europa to match the other two already in the fleet. The vehicle was sold to Beeley of Allestree in June 1972, quickly passing with Mr Beeley himself to Webster of Hognaston. *(John Holmes Collection)*

And here is the third 'Gnu' to be illustrated in this book, although it lacks the vintage charisma of the two machines belonging to Truman of Shirebrook. Bedford VAM70/Plaxton Derwent II DP45F saloon GNU 699H was new to Felix in March 1970 and remained in service until sold to TRS of Leicester in February 1978. *(Colin Anderson Collection)*

FRR 686V, a Bedford YMT with Plaxton C53F bodywork to grant coach specification (ie suitable for driver-only operation on stage carriage work), was new to Felix in February 1980 and is seen at the Derby end of the route. Note the increased prominence of the cartoon cat motif. *(David Stanier)*

A third appearance by Victoria Motorways' Daimler CVD6/Willowbrook saloon FA 9847, this time in glorious 'Antique Red and Dark Tan'. The vehicle is seen at Burton's Wetmore Bus Park shortly before its withdrawal in December 1964, operating a journey to Donisthorpe. *(Philip Thomas via David Stanier)*

In 1962 Victoria Motorways' boss John Lloyd (son of William) bought a two-tone grey Rover car and liked the colour scheme so much that he started to use it on Victoria (and Viking) vehicles. This almost seems like a waste of good colour, but here is Ford R192/Willowbrook 001 B47F bus DFA 127L, new to Victoria in January 1973. It was sold in October 1978. *(Colin Anderson Collection)*

The closest Andrews of Tideswell came to 'proper' stage carriage services in the years covered by this book were a couple of works contracts and another to ferry holidaymakers from Millers Dale station to some chalets at Great Hucklow. Nevertheless it was impossible to resist this shot of Bedford OB/Duple Vista coach MRB 765, new to Andrews in January 1949 and seen here in its native Tideswell. The exciting news is that the vehicle still survives and has been re-acquired by Andrews who plan to restore it as a heritage vehicle. *(Tim Jeffcoat)*

In 1950 Swain of Somercotes bought a rare Foden PVFE6 coach, ORB 952, and had it fitted with this even rarer Bellhouse-Hartwell Atlantic FC39C body. The combination of the PVFE6's noisy two-stroke engine and the Atlantic's wilfully odd appearance was not to everybody's taste, and only ten Atlantic bodies were built. *(John Holmes Collection)*